Enacting Integral Human Development

Enacting Integral Human Development

CLEMENS SEDMAK

ORBIS BOOKS
Maryknoll, New York 10545

Founded in 1970, Orbis Books endeavors to publish works that enlighten the mind, nourish the spirit, and challenge the conscience. The publishing arm of the Maryknoll Fathers and Brothers, Orbis seeks to explore the global dimensions of the Christian faith and mission, to invite dialogue with diverse cultures and religious traditions, and to serve the cause of reconciliation and peace. The books published reflect the views of their authors and do not represent the official position of the Maryknoll Society. To learn more about Maryknoll and Orbis Books, please visit our website at www.orbisbooks.com.

Library of Congress Cataloging-in-Publication Data

Names: Sedmak, Clemens, 1971– author.
Title: Enacting integral human development / Clemens Sedmak.
Description: Maryknoll, NY : Orbis Books, [2023] | Includes bibliographical
   references and index. | Summary: "Emphasizes integral human development
   of the whole person and of each person through a dignity lens"—
   Provided by publisher.
Identifiers: LCCN 2023022562 (print) | LCCN 2023022563 (ebook) |
   ISBN 9781626985520 (trade paperback) | ISBN 9798888660102 (epub)
Subjects: LCSH: Dignity. | Human ecology—Social aspects. |
   Economic development—Social aspects.
Classification: LCC BJ1533.D45 S43 2023 (print) | LCC BJ1533.D45 (ebook)
   | DDC 179/.9—dc23/eng/20230731
LC record available at https://lccn.loc.gov/2023022562
LC ebook record available at https://lccn.loc.gov/2023022563

To Barbara Lockwood and Scott Appleby,
co-pioneers of Integral Human Development

CONTENTS

viii   *Contents*

7. Doing Justice to a Context 110
    Local Epistemic Justice. 111
    The Necessity and Fragility of Planning. 114

8. The Moral Biography of Projects 118
    The Value Basis 120
    Moral Challenges 125

PART III: COMMON GOOD-ORIENTED POLICIES 131

9. Moral Relevance of Policies and Political Decisions 139
    A Case Study. 141
    Laws, Culture, and Values 144

10. Big Questions: The Point of Policies. 150
    Freedom or Dignity? 152
    Dignity and Inequality. 157

11. Epistemic Justice and Policy Making. 161
    The Ethics of Policy Making 164
    The Enduring Need for Judgment 169

12. Institutionalizing Integral Human Development 173
    Building Dignity-Sensitive Institutions 177
    Three Examples 181
    A Final Note on Accompaniment 187

Epilogue: Beyond Development Ethics. 191

Bibliography 197

Index 225

Preface

Integral Human Development is a concept that expresses an idea and a vision—the vision of a dignity-centered society where all can live in accordance with their dignity. This idea implies a notion of "dignity needs," a sense of rights to a decent life, but also deep responsibilities for the common good.

When the idea was first put into widespread circulation through Pope Paul VI's 1967 social encyclical *Populorum Progressio*, it evoked different responses as John McGreevy observed in March 2021 in a blog post for Notre Dame's Keough School of Global Affairs: "The *Wall Street Journal* dismissed the encyclical as 'warmed over Marxism.' And after an initial burst of enthusiasm, both the idea of integral human development and the phrase went into eclipse."

With the pontificate of Pope Francis the idea of Integral Human Development re-emerged as a key concept to respond to the social and ecological challenges of our times, to "the cry of the earth and the cry of the poor."

The Keough School of Global Affairs at the University of Notre Dame, opened in 2017, reflects crucial priorities of Pope Francis. The Keough School has embraced "integral human development" as its defining slogan. It is a school that has been established to enact a commitment to the development of each person and the whole person.

This book is the fruit of many conversations with my colleagues here at Notre Dame's Keough School of Global Affairs. I am grateful for and to this community of scholars. I also owe a lot to our students who bring many insights and questions from many different countries. I would also like to express my gratitude to Robert Ellsberg, Mari Angelini, and Tom Hermans-Webster from Orbis book for their kind support.

Integral Human Development is too complex to be fully realized and too simple to be ignored. Carolyn Woo who served as president and C.E.O. of Catholic Relief Services for five years, summarizes the challenge succinctly: "*Hunger, for example, results from myriad factors such as degraded soils, disadvantaged bargaining positions for actors such as small farmers, the unequal treatment of women and the inability to access public transportation, roads or other government services. That is why C.R.S. uses the integral human development framework for systemic interventions. It means working with individuals, families and communities to attend not only to material needs but also to long-term economic security, family stability, health services, community building and conflict resolution—and giving stakeholders the skills they need to advocate for their rights."* (America Magazine, March 2017).

Integral Human Development is a response to hunger; at the same time, integral human development expresses the hunger for a better world. It is an open-ended concept that reflects the promise of Matthew 5:6: "Blessed are those who hunger and thirst for righteousness, for they will be filled."

Notre Dame, Summer 2023

"Integral Human Development"

An Introduction

A few years ago, the *Washington Post* featured an article in its September 10, 2018, edition that described Chamseddine Marzoug, a fifty-two-year-old former fisherman who scours the beaches of his Tunisian town for bodies of drowned refugees every morning. "When he finds one, he puts it in a body bag. He delivers the bodies to the hospital for a medical report. Later, he washes the corpses and takes them to the graveyard—marked by a sign displayed in six languages: Cemetery for Unknown—where he has dug the graves with a spade and pickax." The article is entitled *A Tunisian Gravedigger Gives Migrants What They Were Deprived of in Life: Dignity*.[1] Chamseddine Marzoug's engagement reflects a commitment to the dignity of the human person beyond an obvious economic advantage. He has a sense of the human person that motivates expressions of respect and solidarity beyond the lifespan. Terms like "piety" or "a sense of the sacred" could be used to characterize this practice. There seems to be a specific moment at work here, a moment of being in the presence of something bigger than oneself, be it death, be it the dignity of the human person, be it human suffering. Chamseddine Marzoug's service is a sign of a commitment that is nourished by something deeper than sympathy with the living. In short, Marzoug's engagement could be seen as a commitment to Integral Human Development (or IHD).[2]

The concept of "Integral Human Development" seems grand and lofty. It can however be explained quite easily through a short formula: *Integral Human Development is the development of the whole person and the development of each*

---

[1] Sudarsan Raghavan, "A Tunisian Gravedigger Gives Migrants What They Were Deprived of in Life: Dignity," *Washington Post* online, September 10, 2018.

[2] One colleague reflected on this story with the words: "Whose dignity is really at stake in the case of Chamseddine Marzoug? Is Marzoug dignifying the deceased, or is he unable to live with indignity he will incur upon himself were he to let the corpses be? The core practical question then becomes: 'What conduct is most dignifying to the self?' Self-dignifying conduct, when genuine and sincere, confers dignity to others."

person. This deceptively simple characterization dates back to 1967, when Pope Paul VI, in his encyclical *Populorum Progressio*, talked about "authentic human development." Development "cannot be restricted to economic growth alone. To be authentic, it must be well rounded; it must foster the development of each person and of the whole person."[3] The official Latin version uses the word *progressio* for "growth," whereas the Italian and the Spanish translations work with "sviluppo" and "desarrollo" (development), respectively. Growth, progress, and development point to different aspects of organic change that happens in steps whereby one step is based on the previous one.

Origins of the Term

The origin of this idea is indicated in the quoted passage from *Populorum Progressio* with a reference to Louis-Joseph Lebret.[4] Lebret himself used the term *développement authentique* (Lebret 1961, 75). Lebret had been one of the experts the pope had consulted in the making of the encyclical and was explicitly mentioned in the press conference on March 28, 1967, by Monsignor Poupard, when the encyclical *Populorum Progressio* was officially presented. Lebret, a French Dominican priest and economist, was inspired to take a closer look at ethical questions of development on noting that processes of societal advancement that benefit some give rise to the deprivation and suffering of others. In 1929, he came face to face with the dire poverty of French fishermen in his own homeland on the coast of Brittany; he traced the roots of their poverty and found them to stem from global changes and the fact that family fishermen no longer stood a chance of making a decent living against large-scale commercial fishing with its mechanization.[5] The internationalization and the industrialization of

---

    [3] *Populorum Progressio* 14. Lori Keheler subtitles her entry on Integral Human Development (or IHD) in the *Routledge Handbook of Development Ethics* with the defining words "development of every person and of the whole person" (Keleher 2018). The explicit point about the limits of economic growth express a concern with a dignity-centered economy that can also be found in the important document of the Second Vatican Council, the Constitution on the Church in the Modern World, which stated that "in the economic and social realms, too, the dignity and complete vocation of the human person and the welfare of society as a whole are to be respected and promoted. For man is the source, the center, and the purpose of all economic and social life" (*Gaudium et Spes* 63). For good reasons, Lebret can be seen as an important scholar-practitioner who prepared the ground for some discussions of the Second Vatican Council (Garreau 2011).
    [4] Footnote 15 of *Populorum Progressio* contains a reference to Lebret's *Dynamique Concrète du Développement* (Paris: Economie et Humanisme, Les Editions Ouvrierès, 1961) in the context of the discussion of the key notion of "authentic development."
    [5] Cf. Cosmao (1970), Lavigne / Puel (2007), Astroulakis (2013).

fishing found its victims in village fishing communities and family fisheries. "The experience of fishing exploitation by a foreign industry at the expense of local workers gave him concrete knowledge of the injustice of a system that was not limited to the problems of a particular region" (Bossi 2012, 253). There is a value-dimension from the beginning in Lebret's thinking about development.

> In the late 1960s, the concept of "development" had been conceived mainly in terms of economic progress. It included agricultural assistance, water purification plants, installation of new wells, distribution of medicine, and a variety of other measures. Economic planners argued that the greatest poverty in Latin American countries could be alleviated by massive job creation unleashed by substantial infusion of investment capital. (Pope 2019, 126)

Lebret challenged this view. Through participatory research in France and in Latin American communities, he arrived at an understanding of the necessity of human-centered development. Development is not the same as economic growth; this also means that development is not the same as measurable living standards and that ethics and theology are no less important as conversation partners on development than political science and economics. Development is not something that is done to people, but rather done through people, with people. Lebret's first concern was people, not processes, projects, or products. Lebret was deeply interested in and committed to social transformation. In 1941, he founded Économie et Humanisme, a Dominican-supported movement of research and practice. He also helped found IRFED (Institut Internationale de Recherche et Formation en vue du Développement Harmonisé) in Paris in 1958, a training and research center on development, worldwide, thus "pursuing his ambition of developing a practical ethical vision for development globally" (Anaehobi 2021, 129).

Lebret's vision of development is a vision of organic and harmonious growth and change—using "a living image: a plant develops, an animal develops, and a human person develops. It is about an internal balance that continues in growth. It concerns a harmony that is related to the nature of being in the process of development" (Lebret 1961, 38). This idea of organic growth works best with the idea of an order in which the human person is embedded; it is less compatible with a constructivist understanding of reality and the person, and also less compatible with an approach to "top-down planned development." Lebret's image of organic growth expresses his sense of and respect for the human person. He coined the term "human economy," that is, an economy that would be "favourable to human development," to "a fully human life," as he wrote in his 1954 essay "Économie et Humanisme."

A "fully human life" is more than a provision of basic goods. It respects "dignity needs." Dignity needs are a class of personal needs that allow a person to live a dignified life. They include, according to Lebret, *space*—a space to which one can retreat and contemplate, perhaps also a space to entertain friends or to ponder a literary work or other artistic evocations of one's inner life (Bossi 2012). A dignity perspective moves us beyond food and shelter and necessary external conditions. It moves us to an inner sphere, to the inner life, to the space that has been called the soul. Even though psychologists and theologians may talk about different things in their discourses on the soul, the concept of the soul generally points to interiority, an inner "force" or "space" that can be formed and that animates the person. Integral human development expresses an understanding of development that recognizes the importance of (the idea of) the soul.

Immanuel Kant famously made the point that the existence of the soul cannot be proven but that the postulate of its existence plays an important role in moral philosophy. Belief in the soul allows us to tell a different story about human agency and the human person. It allows us to tell a story about the "More" of human existence (there is more to human life than the visible and tangible and material and even the temporal). Development ethicist Denis Goulet, who had studied with Lebret, expressed this point well: "Societies are more human, or more developed, not when men and women '*have* more' but when they are enabled to '*be* more.'" (Goulet 1995, 6–7). Qualitative human enrichment becomes the point of development and a sense of community that recognizes the human need of belonging and the reality of dependence and interconnectedness. The choice between "being" and "having" can be seen as a fundamental choice, an insight developed by Erich Fromm in his influential book, *To Have or to Be?* For good reasons, a key notion in Lebret's work and thinking was the word *compassion*: "It expressed an existential fellowship with every man [person] who strives to unite the world under a common destiny and to collectively create the structures that the realization of this aspiration calls for. To love is to identify oneself with one's neighbour, with all men [persons], and to create with them the conditions for their self-fulfilment" (Cosmao 1970, 68).

This commitment to "More" ("Magis") is an important aspect of the human condition. The understanding of human flourishing is linked to the idea of the growing realization of one's potential. In this sense, Integral Human Development points to a kind of "fullness." The meaning of "integral" in the context of "Integral Human Development" is linked to Jacques Maritain's understanding of integral humanism; *Populorum Progressio* 42 talks about a full-bodied humanism that points the way to God.[6] Integral Human Development has been

---

[6] See also the reference to authentic humanism in Pope Benedict XVI's encyclical *Caritas*

characterized by Anthony Annett as "a eudaimonistic vision. It recognizes that every person, in line with his or her dignity, is called to flourishing and self-actualization, and it presumes a common duty to make this a reality" (Annett 2016, 49).[7] There is a relational aspect at work here (persons as relational beings) and a teleological aspect (persons have a "direction of growth"). Flourishing is an expression of the communal nature of the person and also a moral task for communities to support the flourishing of persons. Development in this thinking has a direction, the direction of an ever-more humanized world. Development is seen by Lebret as a humanizing process of standing in relationships of solidarity, based on the recognition of universal human dignity and a commitment to promoting the common good in all spheres of life. This is what Lebret called "human ascent," the primary goal of Integral Human Development.[8]

By embracing the idea of a human-centered economy and an understanding of development based on human dignity and the common good, Lebret offers a vision of human growth and social change that speaks to people from many different moral and religious traditions. This horizon that transcends the Catholic and Christian context is also noticeable in the sources used by Lebret. Even though his central inspiration remained Catholic, he made use of ideas from various sources, including existentialist philosophy or the writings of Mahatma Gandhi and Rabindranath Tagore (Lebret 1961, 128). "Integral human development" is a term capacious enough to integrate different traditions and inspirations. There can be no doubt that Louis-Joseph Lebret has contributed to a specific and human-centered understanding of development that continues to

---

in Veritate 16, 18, 78 with the explicit message that "man cannot bring about his own progress unaided, because by himself he cannot establish an authentic humanism. Only if we are aware of our calling, as individuals and as a community, to be part of God's family as his sons and daughters, will we be able to generate a new vision and muster new energy in the service of a truly integral humanism" (*Caritas in Veritate*, 78). "The word 'integral' is a reference to French philosopher Jacques Maritain's writings on 'Humanisme Intégral', a humanism open to the transcendental dimension, and for which the realm of human affairs and the spiritual realm are autonomous without being separated, each influencing the other" (Deneulin 2021, 22).

[7] In the Catholic Social Tradition, integral development is connected to the realization of one's potential—for good reasons Pope John Paul II talks about "the integral development of the human person through work" in his encyclical *Centesimus Annus* (4).

[8] "According to Lebret, for the 'human ascent' of 'being more' to be realized in development, it is necessary that the doctrine of development be ethical, having as principles the 'active respect for every human person' and the 'value of common good'" (Anaehobi 2021, 131). In Lebret's own words, "Development is the series, or more precisely the ordered series, of passages, for a given population and for all the fractions of the population that compose it, from a less human phase to a more human phase, at the fastest possible pace, at the lowest possible cost, taking into account the solidarity between the sections of the national population and the solidarity between the nations" (Lebret 1961, 49). Solidarity and a sense of a global common good emerge as key pillars of this understanding of development.

be relevant and influential.[9] The term *"Integral Human Development"* is, at the same time, the end of a journey and the beginning of a journey. There is much work to do for the concept to do its work.

Further Developments

This brings us to the question, what is distinctive about the concept of Integral Human Development? Respecting human rights, aiming for participatory approaches, and cultivating respect for the dignity of the human person are not new. We could also state that the idea that human development is multidimensional may have been challenging in the times of Louis-Joseph Lebret, who had to fight against a predominantly economic understanding of development, but meanwhile the "beyond GDP"–movement has become well established (Fleurbaey 2009; Fleurbaey/Blanchet 2013). Robert Kennedy's famous "Remarks at the University of Kansas" (March 18, 1968) may have been revolutionary then, but they are widely accepted today—Kennedy made the point that

> the gross national product ... does not include the beauty of our poetry or the strength of our marriages, the intelligence of our public debate or the integrity of our public officials. It measures neither our wit nor our courage, neither our wisdom nor our learning, neither our compassion nor our devotion to our country, it measures everything in short, except that which makes life worthwhile.[10]

---

[9] In his social encyclical *Fratelli Tutti*, Pope Francis makes some observations about Integral Human Development, very much in line with Lebret's thinking. A key message of the document is a reminder of the social nature of the human person: we only achieve who we are by our interactions with others; the good of the human person is a relational good. Pope Francis asks us to reimagine ourselves "as a single human family" (8). "We need to think of ourselves more and more as a single family dwelling in a common home" (17). Specifically, there are five important claims about Integral Human Development: (a) Economic growth is not the same as Integral Human Development; we have observed growth that has resulted in increasing inequalities, even new forms of poverty (21). (b) There is a right and an obligation to Integral Human Development: "Every human being has the right to live with dignity and to develop integrally" (107). "We have an obligation to ensure that every person lives with dignity and has sufficient opportunities for his or her integral development" (118). (c) Integral Human Development is incompatible with the light-hearted superficiality that we have cultivated (113). (d) Integral Human Development is based on the recognition that the world exists for everyone (118). This limits any absolute right to private property. (e) The deepest expression of a commitment to Integral Human Development is the cultivation of friendships beyond borders; in Pope Francis's words, the cultivation of "a love capable of transcending borders is the basis of what in every city and country can be called 'social friendship'" (99).

[10] Robert F. Kennedy, "Remarks at the University of Kansas, March 18, 1968," MR 89–34. Miscellaneous Recordings, John F. Kennedy Presidential Library online.

In a sense, he expressed a concern with the integral nature of human development. This was more than fifty years ago.

Today, we have to ask ourselves, is there anything specific about the idea of integral human development? Sévérine Deneulin (2018) mentions five important aspects of Integral Human Development: inseparability of the spiritual and the material, open-ended multidimensionality, interconnectedness, reality of personal and social sin, and the need for conversion. These dimensions point to implications of the term that are clearly compatible with any understanding of development, personhood, or community.

With Pope Francis's encyclical *Laudato Si'* in 2015, the discourse on Integral Human Development has gained a new momentum (Pfeil 2018; Gianfreda 2019). *Laudato Si'* is an expression of concern with the state and the future of the planet, our common home. It provides an integral view with the explicit notion of an integral ecology. The whole document develops the thesis that everything is connected (*Laudato Si'* 16, 42, 70, 92, 117, 138, 240). This integral view comes with the obligation to think in different terms: "Interdependence obliges us to think of one world with a common plan" (*Laudato Si'* 164). The name-giving person behind the encyclical is also used as a representative for an integral view— St. Francis of Assisi "shows us how inseparable the bond is between concern for nature, justice for the poor, commitment to society, and interior peace" (*Laudato Si'* 10). Integral development requires "a conversation which includes everyone" (*Laudato Si'* 14). Both by promoting an integral view of the world and by reflecting on authentic development explicitly, *Laudato Si'* has contributed to a deepening of the concept of Integral Human Development with an ecological perspective (*Laudato Si'* 141) and with a long-term perspective that explicitly considers future generations (*Laudato Si'* 159: "We can no longer speak of sustainable development apart from intergenerational solidarity").

Integral Human Development also needs to recognize culture as an integral part of development (*Laudato Si'* 143); the disappearance of a culture can be as serious as the disappearance of a plant or species (*Laudato Si'* 145). Similar to the recognition of culture, the encyclical calls for a recognition of the contributions of religions (*Laudato Si'* 62) and wisdom traditions (*Laudato Si'* 63). In short, Integral Human Development is presented as the respect for and as an expression of the integrity of interconnectedness. The text has invited a new way to think about dignity (it even contains a line about "the intrinsic dignity of the world" in paragraph 115) and is critical of a "tyrannical" or "distorted" or "excessive" anthropocentrism (*Laudato Si'* 68, 69, 116). This is a new chapter in the discourse on Integral Human Development.

We could read *Laudato Si'* as an invitation to a two-fold transformation: (1) the ecological crisis cannot be approached with the means of technological progress;

and (2) technological challenges must be transformed into moral concerns. But we cannot stop there. The encyclical invites a further step: moral concerns are translated into spiritual questions.[11] The consideration of both moral and spiritual aspects sheds light on the meaning of "integral" in "Integral Human Development."

Two years after the publication of *Laudato Si'*, the idea of Integral Human Development was strengthened through the establishment of an official structure: the concern with "Integral Human Development" has been institutionalized in a special office of the Vatican, the Dicastery for Promoting Integral Human Development. When it was first established in 2017 through the Apostolic Letter *Humanam Progressionem*, integral human development was characterized as a kind of development that "takes place by attending to the inestimable goods of justice, peace, and the care of creation." The Dicastery was entrusted to deal with "issues regarding migrants, those in need, the sick, the excluded and marginalized, the imprisoned and the unemployed, as well as victims of armed conflict, natural disasters, and all forms of slavery and torture." This gives us a sense of the unity of development, justice, peace, and care of creation. Integral Human Development cannot be separated from these moral goods. In other words: the commitment to Integral Human Development entails a commitment to ecological integrity, structures of justice, and processes of peace.

These commitments have to be enacted with a special consideration for those who have been deprived of access to these goods, persons who have been marginalized and victimized. In the Apostolic Constitution *Praedicate Evangelium*, promulgated in 2022 to restructure the Roman Curia, the responsibility of the Dicastery was described with

> the task of promoting the human person and the God-given dignity of all, together with human rights, health, justice and peace. It is principally concerned with matters relating to the economy and work, the care of creation and the earth as our "common home", migration and humanitarian emergencies. (art.163)

In this document, we find a language that places personhood and dignity at the center of the institutional responsibility of the Dicastery. Article 165 of this document underlines the centrality of dignity once again ("to defend and

---

[11] Cf. *Laudato Si'* 202: "Many things have to change course, but it is we human beings above all who need to change. We lack an awareness of our common origin, of our mutual belonging, and of a future to be shared with everyone. This basic awareness would enable the development of new convictions, attitudes and forms of life. A great cultural, spiritual and educational challenge stands before us, and it will demand that we set out on the long path of renewal."

promote the dignity and fundamental rights of human persons as well as their social, economic and political rights") and lists those who are especially vulnerable (victims of human trafficking, forced prostitution, various forms of slavery and torture, prisoners, migrants, refugees, displaced persons). Even though lists have their clear limits, they provide a deeper sense of disadvantage and also confirm the idea that we owe special duties vis-à-vis the most disadvantaged as a key feature of Integral Human Development. It cannot be denied that the visibility of the idea and the term have been substantially elevated during the pontificate of Pope Francis.

Some Questions and Dilemmas

As any other substantial term, the concept of Integral Human Development has its challenges. It seems fuzzy and vague. With its commitment to pay special attention to the most vulnerable, the concept can lead to "vulnerability competition," pitting disadvantaged groups against each other when comparing their struggles, a dynamic that can be observed in "survivors' postwar competition for aid and compensation" (Králová 2017, 149). If people claim to be committed to Integral Human Development, they seem to claim a superior moral position, a sense of moral high ground. People have been concerned that the term comes with a sense of moral imperialism. There is a moral problem and risk, as one colleague put it, "to speak about IHD and 'traditional' international development as two separate approaches, with the former portrayed as a more enlightened, multi-dimensional approach and the latter portrayed as a one-way, top-down, often compassion-less process that only cares about income and material things." This is, indeed, an inappropriate way of thinking about development. We have to be careful not to construe "straw people" who would view the poor as charity cases, and talk at them and impose ill-conceived solutions on them. Both discourses on and practices of development have moved on since Lebret's time.

It also has to be recognized that the Catholic tradition has lost a lot of public moral authority in the late twentieth and early twenty-first centuries, and any connection of the discourse on Integral Human Development and an *ecclesia triumphans* is misplaced. There is a real concern with ever so subtle triumphalism. In an interview about Integral Human Development, a critic of the concept made the interesting remark: "Frankly, I think there is a bit of whininess in the conversation around IHD. People say 'oh the Church knows better about human beings than you technocrats.'" We want to avoid any temptation to weaponize IHD and use IHD as an excluding approach to establish moral superiority. This is simply unacceptable and against the very idea of "authentic" or "integral" discourses.

Many other critical questions can be asked and have been asked when thinking about this idea: How do we measure Integral Human Development and know if it has occurred? Is it falsifiable? How can Integral Human Development be enacted and translated into practices? What do we make of the normative import of Integral Human Development? Or, as others have put it, what if all persons do not want to "be more" and just want more stuff?[12] Integral Human Development talks about "flourishing"—but what does it mean to truly flourish? Another colleague of mine has put a major challenge to the term in the following way:

> We are at the point where the finite nature of the earth's resources, and the extent of the damage we have done to them, means that the current state of "flourishing" that has served as the gold standard—the "first world lifestyle" is completely unsustainable and must be rethought from the ground up in order to ensure that everyone around the world has even the basics of what they need to survive. Related to this, are we truly flourishing? We have terrible inequalities in our own society, and it is not difficult to argue that the highest levels of flourishing imaginable rest on the suffering and labor of others. That not everyone can flourish; we don't have the social resources in addition to lacking the physical resources. And those of us who would appear to represent peak flourishing; what does this actually look like? Are we not horribly stressed out and over-stretched? Who gets enough sleep? Who feels that they are at peace?

Additionally, some reflect on integral human development as a "good weather-term": Can IHD be enacted in conflict zones? What is the role of IHD in war? Is there room for militarism in IHD? What of those who find their meaning and flourish as defenders/soldiers? What is an Integral Human Development response?[13] Others worry about the potential restriction of freedoms imposed by the idea of Integral Human Development with its concern for creation and future generations. There is a passage in *Laudato Si'* that explicitly states that "the time has come to accept decreased growth in some parts of

---

[12] Abhijit V. Banerjee and Esther Duflo, to name one example, recount an experience in Northern Africa: "We asked Oucha Mbarbk, a man we met in a remote village in Morocco, what he would do if he had more money. He said he would buy more food. Then we asked him what he would do if he had even more money. He said he would buy better tasting food. We were starting to feel very bad for him and his family, when we noticed a television, a parabolic antenna, and a DVD player in the room where we were sitting. We asked him why he had bought all these things if he felt the family did not have enough to eat. He laughed and said, "Oh, but television is more important than food!" (Banerjee and Duflo 2011, 36).

[13] These questions remind me of a Ukrainian colleague who talked about the reality of "integral human destruction" through the Russian invasion of Ukraine in February 2022.

the world" (*Laudato Si'* 193). The Spanish version of the text with which Pope Francis has worked contains the phrase "*ha llegado la hora de aceptar cierto decrecimiento en algunas partes del mundo.*" An economist expressed concern in a conversation about the connection between Integral Human Development and special attention to the most disadvantaged since highest "return on investment" would not be yielded by focusing on the most vulnerable.

There have been "big picture"—questions attached to the term: What should we make of the anthropocentrism expressed in IHD? What is—or could be—the role of the nonhuman world in IHD? How vital are other species and the nonhuman world to Integral Human Development?

Other people are worried about the sectarian nature of the term, which does not play a major role in mainstream discourses, its religious origins, and its place in a tradition that can be seen as authoritarian and morally questionable. Colleagues have expressed concerns about the "baggage" of the term that is connected to a tradition with a clear concept of personhood that can be contested and criticized. For many anthropologists, for instance, the category of the person is always socially and historically contingent, open and malleable to transformation. The Catholic tradition has a particular "ontology of personhood" that does not have to be accepted by all. This matters since the "human" in "integral human development" is inextricably linked to a certain understanding of the human person in that tradition of origin. How can we respond to concerns about a suspicion of colonialism and the imposition of a preconceived idea of good human life?

One interesting concern that I have been confronted with is the worry about entitlements. The idea of Integral Human Development can be used as a source to justify entitlements and the claim "if you are committed to IHD you owe me the following list of services N1 to Nx." This is another example of the possibility that the idea of Integral Human Development is weaponized and used to polarize and exclude others.

I have also encountered well-justified questions about the "ownership" of the term and the discourse on Integral Human Development. Who decides what is consistent with IHD? If we accept that the discourse on Integral Human Development is not controlled or owned by the Catholic Church, we might have to accept the question: Is the Catholic community really willing to share the concept and give up ownership?[14] For example, is a "pluriversal" approach

---

[14] Let me offer a concrete example: Two colleagues have explicitly linked access to abortion to the notion of Integral Human Development: "Abortion access is freedom-enhancing, in the truest sense of the word. Consistent with integral human development that emphasizes social justice and human dignity, abortion access respects the inherent dignity of women, their freedom to make choices and to evaluate medical and other risks associated with pregnancy

to personhood and development (Hutchings 2019) compatible with Integral Human Development and its seemingly firm value basis ("the whole person," "each person")? Can IHD sustain its connection to a specific ethical and faith-based tradition while also remaining open to radical difference? Can it sustain itself in the face of having its core categories productively estranged?

These are some of the fundamental questions about the implications of Integral Human Development. Next to these fundamental questions, there are some dilemmas with which we must deal. In working with the term "Integral Human Development," we face a fundamental decision or dilemma: the more precise the term, the more exclusive the concept. In other words, the more clearly defined the meaning ("intension") of the term, the fewer cases will fall under the term ("extension"). The more precise the intension of the term, the more restricted the extension of the term. You may have a clear definition, but this clear definition will include many possible alternative ways of making sense of the term. If the term is not capacious, you will lose support from many sides. If it is not precise, it will not be able to offer much guidance. Closely linked to this dilemma is the dilemma between a "thick connection to Catholic Social Teaching" and a "thin CST connection" (either you face the reproach of being excluding or the reproach of not honoring the tradition in which the concept is embedded). Similarly, we can identify the dilemma between "standardization" (if precisely defined and translated into a metrics) and "localization" (being open to pluralism and honoring the local context). These dilemmas point to the need for proper conversations.

Both questions and dilemmas can be seen as promises of challenges and sources of discursive labor. How can we then work with the concept and idea of integral human development?

Toward Some Substantial Aspects of the Term

A major and persistent question in connection to Integral Human Development is the question of its enactment. What does IHD mean "on the ground"? What is its "cash value"? What difference does an IHD-approach make to project designs, policy making, research activities, institutional practices? What does this mean in practice? The topic of this book is the very question of the enactment of integral human development. What does "Integral Human Development" mean in

---

and childbirth." The official teaching of the Catholic Church about abortion is clear; is this a creative appropriation of the term *"Integral Human Development"* or an abuse of the word? Tamara Kay and Susan L. Ostermann, "Forced Pregnancy and Childbirth are Violence against Women—And Also Terrible Health Policy," *Salon* online, May 5, 2022.

practice, how can it be implemented, applied, realized? Is it helpful when we look at specific questions? Let me offer an example. In a course on "Integral Human Development," I ask students to grapple with a decision-making challenge. This is the assignment:

You are the Head of a Catholic Foundation that is dedicated to integral human development. You have a policy that you fund few projects, but these projects are funded to a maximum. At today's Meeting of the Board, you have to decide between five 100,000 USD projects submitted by a (predominantly Catholic) village community:

a) *A youth center: presently, the village youth has no place where they could meet on their own in a protected atmosphere*

b) *A recycling center: waste is a big challenge in the village; a recycling center could also raise awareness and generate revenue*

c) *A hospice: there is no place nearby or in the village where people can die with proper care.*

d) *A micro credit program: currently, villagers do not have access to financial services, which is a significant obstacle to entrepreneurship*

e) *An inclusion initiative to integrate children with special needs into the village school.*

Which project would you choose and why?

When students try to arrive at a decision, they have to ask deep questions about development and priorities. They have to consider the importance of the nonproductive aspects of human lives (the hospice), the challenge of integral ecology and the responsibility for the planet and future generations (the recycling center), they have to consider the central role of hope and building a future (the youth center), as well as the relevance of individual initiatives and sustainable livelihoods (the microcredit program), or the importance of a common good approach and social inclusion (the school initiative).

In these deliberations, the idea of integral human development may not provide a clear answer (even though it does help to recognize the plausibility of a hospice as an expression of human ascent), but the term serves as an invitation to ask certain questions about human needs, including "dignity needs." What is the role of beauty in community development? A student once asked, "Giving money for a nice hair salon as part of a livelihoods project is not an efficient use of humanitarian aid because it is too nice—is it?" Another one struggled with the challenge of the common good: "When we say that we do not want to leave anyone behind—are we not only wasting resources?"

In spite of (or because of) all the questions mentioned above, the term "integral human development" is a fruitful source of questions. I would also like to suggest distinguishing between the term "Integral Human Development," the different possible translations of the term ("authentic human development," "fully human development," "holistic human development"), and the idea behind the term. My claim would be that the idea of Integral Human Development can be expressed in many different ways and can be identified in many different traditions—with a concern about social change processes that do justice to the human person and the human community. As a term that is embedded in a particular tradition, the concept of integral human development implies particular commitments. We can still discuss whether these commitments hold for those who adopt "the idea of IHD" (rather than the tradition of origin).

When we take a closer look at the idea of Integral Human Development, we can identify a few important reference points: The central role of human dignity; a relational understanding of the human person; a moral understanding of development; the recognition of material needs and realities; the consideration of cultural richness, beauty, and the imagination and the importance of nonproductive aspects of human life; special consideration of the most disadvantaged and those left behind; a recognition of fundamental equality and the universal destination of goods; the recognition of interconnectedness and integral ecology;[15] a sense of "first and last questions" ("why"-questions beyond the "how"). Asking first and last questions goes beyond an instrumental understanding of rationality that is only occupied with "means" but does not ask about "ends." Pope Francis observed, "We have too many means and only a few insubstantial ends."[16]

The concept of Integral Human Development may be vague, but, as I have mentioned, it is not compatible with any and all approaches—especially not when seen in the context of its tradition of origin, the Catholic Social Tradition. Integral Human Development places human dignity at the core of any assessment of social situations; it is incompatible with a view of the human person as an "unencumbered self" and considers the person as a relational being with a history and a multidimensional existence. The conception of the human person as a complex being is close to what Charles Taylor in *Sources of the Self* had

---

[15] Pope Francis emphasizes the idea that everything is connected in his encyclical *Laudato Si'* (16, 42, 70, 92, 117, 138, 240). As a consequence, the world's problems cannot be analyzed or explained in isolation (61). This integral view comes with the obligation to think in terms of interdependence, "one world with a common plan" (164).

[16] *Laudato Si'* 203. Ignatius of Loyola points out the importance of not confusing ends with means (*Spiritual Exercises* 169) with the result that people often put last "what they ought to seek first and above all else." Strategic plans are means to an end; the end is, theologically speaking, God, the will of God, God's reign.

characterized as "interiority," a complexity of desires, beliefs, and emotions. The subject of development is not a "one-dimensional person" (Herbert Marcuse 2002); she does not live by bread alone.[17] IHD invites an understanding of the human person beyond any of the roles she may inhabit: a patient in a hospital is "so much more" than a patient; an incarcerated person is "so much more" than a prisoner; a refugee is "so much more" than a refugee; a person living in poverty is "so much more" than a poor person.[18] Integral Human Development recognizes the many aspects of human lives and is not compatible with a one-dimensional understanding of the human condition (be it materialist, be it spiritualist). The idea of the consideration of "the whole person" expresses a commitment to the multifariousness of human life and the multidimensionality of development (a claim that is hardly original, as we have seen—but a claim with implications nonetheless).

Integral Human Development is incompatible with a "neutral" understanding of development. The concept of IHD qualifies "development" with a value perspective; it encourages a view that there is no value-neutral development, a position that has been expressed by, among many others, Amartya Sen, who underlined "the essential role of evaluation in that concept [development]. What is or is not regarded as a case of 'development' depends inescapably on the notion of what things are valuable to promote" (Sen 1988, 12). Development is value driven. In Lebret's view, development "is not primarily an economic problem, nor simply the inability of social structures to meet new demands issuing from hitherto passive populations. Above all else, underdevelopment is a symptom of a

---

[17] One expression of a reductionist view of the human person is a certain version of pragmatism that does not consider the deeper and inner dimension of the person: Pope Francis quotes Joseph Ratzinger in *Evangelii Gaudium* with the warning against a "gray pragmatism of the daily life" (*Evangelii Gaudium* 83), Pope Benedict identified a specific role of the university in avoiding a reductionist reading of the human condition and promoting integral development of the person. In his meeting with young university teachers on the occasion of World Youth Day in Madrid (August 19, 2011) he emphasized a deeper sense of life: "We know that when mere utility and pure pragmatism become the principal criteria, much is lost and the results can be tragic: from the abuses associated with a science which acknowledges no limits beyond itself, to the political totalitarianism which easily arises when one eliminates any higher reference than the mere calculus of power. The authentic idea of the University, on the other hand, is precisely what saves us from this reductionist and curtailed vision of humanity."

[18] There is a beautiful scene in Lisa Genova's novel *Still Alice*. Alice, a fifty-year-old Harvard professor who is diagnosed with Alzheimer's disease, delivers a speech at a conference (speaking from the perspective of the patient): "Being diagnosed with Alzheimer's is like being branded with a scarlet *A*. This is now who I am, someone with dementia. This was how I would, for a time, define myself and how others continue to define me. But I am not what I say or what I do or what I remember. I am fundamentally more than that. I am a wife, mother, and friend, and soon to be grandmother.... I am still an active participant in society" (Genova 2019, 252).

worldwide crisis in human values; accordingly, development's task is to create, in a world of chronic inequality and disequilibrium, new civilizations of solidarity. (Goulet 1996, 9). *Populorum Progressio* 23 contains the radical statement, "No one may appropriate surplus goods solely for his own private use when others lack the bare necessities of life." This argument can be made both on an individual level and on the level of communities, even states and nations.

In his encyclical *Laudato Si'* (106–114), Pope Francis made it very clear that integral human development is incompatible with a "technocratic paradigm," that is, with an understanding that the problems we face can be solved through technological means without having to change one's life (without a change of heart, without a conversion).[19] He has expressed the same concern in his 2020 Exhortation *Querida Amazonia* where he states "that an integral ecology cannot be content simply with fine-tuning technical questions or political, juridical and social decisions. The best ecology always has an educational dimension that can encourage the development of new habits in individuals and groups" (58). A technocratic approach entails the tendency to control issues through mechanisms, technologies, objective measures. This is the default position of an organization when confronted with an issue, say sexual harassment. The organization will commission a report, establish a committee, and move toward policies and regulations.

Theodore Roszak has commented in an observation about technocracy that "those who govern justify themselves by appeal to technical experts who, in turn, justify themselves to scientific forms of knowledge" (Roszak 1969, 8). We have seen aspects of this dynamic during the COVID-19 pandemic, with all the governance challenges because of delayed and ambivalent research results (Evans 2022) or a one-sided emphasis on virological aspects of the matter. The temptation of responding to complex social (and moral) challenges through technology is pervasive. For example, in an ethnographic account about building safety in the garment industry in Bangladesh, Hasan Ashraf argues that "a narrow and technocratic focus on buildings and building safety in Bangladesh ignores and conceals the actual processes and relationships that produce shop floor risks" (Ashraf 2017, 251). The approach through emphasizing building standards in Bangladesh

---

[19] John Paul Lederach has described this temptation well: "We have a tendency to externalize responses to deep human suffering—how do we skill our way out of this, as opposed to: how do we hone the presence necessary to stay with it—we need to insist on our persistence and move away from the quick fix. We also need to be clear that patience and persistence put us in a space of constant mystery rather than in a place where we have answers for others." John Paul Lederach, "20-Minute Break with John Paul Lederach," YouTube video, https://www.youtube.com/watch?v=Syw_Efd24Dw.

tends to neglect the global nature of the industry and the power asymmetries that cannot be simply deleted by a policy change. Integral Human Development is a reminder of complexity and fragility.

Integral Human Development encourages people to ask fundamental questions about "the big picture" and "the point of economy and politics" in their value structure or the fundamental questions about first and last things, value hierarchies, and "ultimate values." These questions about values and "right living" can open doors to think not only about "underdevelopment," but also about "superdevelopment."[20] There is no doubt that there can be underdevelopment in the sense that people are forced to live in inhumane conditions without access to adequate food, safe housing, proper sanitary facilities, or drinking water. But there is also the real concern with overdevelopment. Superdevelopment is an expression of a "too much," that is, a violation of "the enough." In more classical terms, superdevelopment is a violation of temperance, of the knowledge of limits and appropriateness. The idea that there is not only a bottom but also a ceiling is also known from other areas of Catholic Social Teaching, for example, in connection to a just wage, which not only has to meet a threshold (living wage), but which also has to respect a limit, a maximum wage (Himes 2017). The interesting question, then, is the question of the tipping point. Where and when does development become overdevelopment, superdevelopment, excessive development?

Margaret Mead reflected on the notion of "overdevelopment" in a 1962 article for *Foreign Affairs*, pointing to negative indicators of development, "indices of social disorganization in those industrial countries in which political democracy and welfare-state organization have gone further than elsewhere—the indices of crime, delinquency, suicide, divorce, alcoholism and homicide. These are the current costs of overdevelopment" (Mead 1962, 86). A similar idea can be found in the thinking of Manfred Max-Neef, who reflected on human needs and human scale development (Max-Neef 1991).

In a seminar, I once asked students to give me examples of overdevelopment. They came up with examples like packaged peeled bananas, a car parked within a recreational vehicle, the city lights (and light pollution) of a major urban center, the artificial islands of Dubai. There is a "bottom" dimension and a "ceiling" dimension to Integral Human Development. Development can be excessive, wasteful, exaggerated. Lebret warned against a desire to see American levels of income as global standards: "One can live humanly with much less" (Lebret 1958, 91).

---

[20] John Paul II characterizes superdevelopment as "an excessive availability of every kind of material goods for the benefit of certain social groups" (*Sollicitudo Rei Socialis* 28); for a philosophical approach to this question, see E. Skidelsky and R. Skidelsky, *How Much Is Enough?* (New York: Other Press, 2012).

There is a beautiful Swedish term "lagom" (exactly the right amount). The term, "according to folklore, it is a contraction of laget om ('around the team'), a phrase used by the Vikings to specify how much mead one should drink from the horn as it was passed around, to ensure that everyone would receive a fair share" (Williams and Devine 2005, 19). The idea of "just enough" so that all can have enough is an important aspect of "the development of each person." One could also argue that the ability to say, "It is enough," an expression of the beautiful virtue of temperance, is part of the development of the whole person. The idea of moderated development obviously takes place within a particular culture—a student of mine reflected on the tipping point from development to superdevelopment (overdevelopment) in a little note:

> We were discussing how, in Uganda, house roofs can be made of grass or iron sheeting, but iron sheeting is expensive and grass roofs are free. We talked about how, in America, if it was to become the norm to build roofs with grass, how people would likely find a way to charge for it. That turned into a conversation of how ridiculous it is that people capitalize on very common natural resources—including a stick for sale that I found on the platform Etsy.

Probably the most important aspect of Integral Human Development is its connection with "a preferential option for the poor" and the idea that the goods of the earth are meant for all, irrespective of privilege and one's status in the birth lottery. This means that Integral Human Development expresses the commitment to the common good—it is incompatible with selective approaches that focus on majorities (e.g., "effective altruism") and also with nationalistic approaches that deny international solidarity. The common good is a principle that takes the idea of "inclusion of all persons" seriously; it implies an approach to leave no one behind. A sincere commitment to the common good (the flourishing of a community based on the flourishing of each of its members) will call for a proper consideration of all, especially those who are most disadvantaged.

Let me emphasize this point: The incompatibility of Integral Human Development with selective approaches is probably the most substantial aspect. Even if one does not accept the "background tradition," there is no doubt that integral human development, minimally and most simply understood as "the development of each person and the whole person," is not compatible with selective approaches that would pursue—for good and persuasive reasons—the best possible return on investment. The approach of "the greatest good for the greatest number" is different from the idea of thinking about the community as a whole and the development of "each person." The idea of integral human development seems naïve with the logic of a special attention to the most disadvantaged, which is a logical implication of the commitment to the development of "each person." Because of the communitarian and personalist undertones, the background theory of IHD is ultimately at odds with the idea of a meritocracy, or utilitarianism and "effective altruism."[21] The common good is a moral good that invites us to see a community as a whole with the imperative of not leaving anyone behind. This approach faces practical challenges and may serve more as a "thorn in the flesh," but it differs from perspectives that are willing to sacrifice people. The pandemic has evoked some of these debates around the primacy of dignity versus the primacy of efficiency.[22] The idea of integral human development is a common-good–based approach with the aspiration to build flourishing communities on the basis of the flourishing of each of its members. In the following chapters, we will look into fundamental questions for this approach.

Integral Human Development is a concept that invites the deep and simple questions about the point and direction, end goal and form of social change. It also invites uncomfortable questions on an existential level. We can also ask the question, which sacrifices are we asked to make in the name of IHD? For example, a colleague of mine reflected on the fact that the University of Notre Dame is built on land traditionally owned and used by Native Americans, a fact that some colleagues honor with words like these: "I acknowledge my presence in the traditional homelands of Native peoples, including the Haudenosauneega, Miami, Peoria, and particularly the Pokégnek Bodéwadmik / Pokagon Potawatomi, who have been using this land for education for thousands of years, and continue to do so." My colleague asked the question about "the flourishing of Notre Dame on land that members of the Indigenous communities consider to be unjustly usurped or occupied land. If IHD is about the flourishing of each person and the whole person, then Indigenous Peoples, as far as I have been able to understand, do not feel that they can flourish while historical injustices are not fully recognized and fractured relationships adequately repaired. What would such repair look like?"

No doubt, both concept and idea of integral human development are sources of fundamental questions, on an existential as well as on a political level. Integral Human Development is not a harmless concept; it is an invitation to ask uncomfortable questions.

---

[21] See Sandel (2020) and Bruce Wydick's reflection on effective altruism. Bruce Wydick, "Why I Cannot (Fully) Embrace Effective Altruism," *Across Two Worlds* blog, August 18, 2021.

[22] Catherine E. Bolten, "To Choose Life or Solvency? Fear as a Pre-Existing Condition in COVID-19 Mortality in the United States," *News & Events—Dignity and Development*, Keough School of Global Affairs online, April 27, 2020.

Here is a brief summary of the profile of the term:

Integral Human Development (IHD) implies...	IHD is incompatible with...
The central role of human dignity	A view of an "unencumbered self"
A relational understanding of the human person	A one-dimensional understanding of the human condition
A moral understanding of development including a concept of "overdevelopment"	A neutral understanding of development
The recognition of material needs and realities	An understanding of development without limits
The consideration of nonproductive aspects of human life and the idea of flourishing	A technocratic paradigm
A special attention to the most disadvantaged	Selective utilitarian approaches
A commitment to universal destination of goods and the global common good	Forms of nationalism and "closed common goods" that are not open to the global context
The recognition of interconnectedness and integral ecology	A disregard for future generations
A sense of first and last questions	A mere instrumental understanding of reason

The idea of integral human development invites us to think about the point of life, its direction, the meaning of a "good life," reasons for change, foundations of community, responsible engagement with resources. These questions are relevant whatever term we want to use for "development."

Even with the short formula "development of each person and the whole person" the real significance of "integral human development" still needs some more work. What does it mean to enact integral human development? What difference does this understanding make "on the ground"?

Enacting Integral Human Development:
The Project of This Book

A major challenge of lofty concepts like "human dignity" or "common good" or "integral human development" is the question of proper enactment. What is the "cash value" of the concept? What difference does the application of the concept make in reality and on the ground? This is a challenge that is also familiar from "applied ethics." What does it mean to "apply" the concept of integral human development? The word "apply" refers to French *plier*, which means "to fold." What does it mean, then, to "fold integral human development into reality," to adapt it to practices and local contexts?

This question is the research question of this book: what does it mean to enact Integral Human Development?

Des Gasper and Lori Keleher observe that "Lebret's influence is recognizable in many aspects of Catholic Social Teaching, including for example the integral human development policies of organizations like Catholic Relief Services (CRS)" (Gasper and Keleher 2021, 116). CRS makes use of a framework based on integral human development.[23] The approach works with an analysis of assets, systems and structures, and strategies, and it pays attention to power dynamics (influence and access), risks, and vulnerabilities. Projects developed on this basis will be monitored and evaluated. CRS describes its way of proceeding as "a holistic approach to helping people improve their livelihoods" by taking into account the contexts in which people live. Since CRS is a major humanitarian organization, the experience with Integral Human Development in specific projects is significant.

Participation is a major aspect of enacting IHD. With its focus on human-centered development, the concept of IHD can be seen to invite a proper reflection on community-based approaches and the ownership of decisions; Lori Keleher articulates this point well:

This understanding of development radically shifts the development paradigm away from one in which aid, charity, or service, flows one way: from the rich "givers" to the poor "beneficiaries" or "takers." Instead, within the integral human development perspective, authentic development integrates each and every person in a humanizing process of standing in relationships of solidarity as we strive together towards promoting the common good. (Keleher 2018, 31)

---

[23] Geoff Heinrich, David Leege, and Carrie Miller, *A User's Guide to Integral Human Development (IHD): Practical Guidance for CRS Staff and Partners* (Baltimore: Catholic Relief Services, 2008); "Integral Human Development Overview," Catholic Relief Services online.

IHD is, then, a particular way of identifying needs, of designing and planning social change, of implementing and evaluating projects. It is a contextually sensitive, community-centered approach. That is why the concept underlines the importance of accompaniment models (Pope 2019) and the importance of encounters and experience (Desierto and Schnyder von Wartensee 2021, 1525). The experience of being listened to can be life-giving, a sign of recognizing that a person is truly a person. The simple perception that a person is a person (and not a problem or a project) makes a huge difference. Kimberly White talks about the huge impact of the simple idea to treat people as if they were people (White 2018). Integral Human Development, we could say, is not so much a strategy, but a way of "seeing" and a way of "looking," a way of perceiving the world. This perception also refers to the structural side of things.

Integral Human Development emerges as a fundamental attitude. This attitude can be translated into more tangible exhortations. The concept of integral human development, understood as "development of each person and the whole person," can be translated into two imperatives: Do not leave anyone behind! Make sure that each dimension of the person counts! These two imperatives correspond to two important concepts: the concept of the common good and the idea of "a full human life." This book will reflect on both concepts in conversation with concrete examples and life realities.

The approach of this book is "source sensitive" and "nonauthoritarian." The former means that the concept of Integral Human Development is rooted in a particular tradition: the Catholic Social Tradition; it is not a product of academic research, and it reflects a particular "context of genesis" and a particular "background tradition." This context is a rich source of principles and practices but can also give reasons for concern—because of the contents of the tradition or because of the contested credibility of the Catholic community in promoting inclusive approaches.[24] The book will engage with this tradition and try to show its fruitfulness and wealth. The latter ("nonauthoritarian") refers to the fact that the Catholic Social Tradition does not "own" the discourse on Integral Human Development; given the global challenges we face, any well-meant creativity that comes out of pluralism, any commitment to integral ecology and a dignified life for all are valid and important. In the spirit of intellectual integrity, it will, in fact, be important to democratize the discourse on Integral Human Development. This also means that the approach of this book is critical in the sense that it engages with important concerns about IHD (the term and its approach have

---

[24] I was once asked, how can the Church reconcile the teaching on homosexuality with the commitment to the development (and flourishing) of "each person and the whole person"?

been called unrealistic, vague, authoritarian, and anthropocentric). This engagement should happen in a respectful and constructive way.

The idea of Integral Human Development is not original in the sense that it could only be found in the Christian tradition. The predominantly Buddhist country Bhutan has embraced the idea of "Gross National Happiness" (Schroeder 2018), an integral vision of ultimate values that are relevant for discussions about the limits of growth (Masaki 2022). One could argue that Integral Human Development, with its insistence on the immaterial dimension of the human person, is well in line with Buddhist thinking and its emphasis on spiritual enlightenment.

Deep insights into human flourishing can also be found in the Islamic tradition. A Muslim colleague shared: "A term in Islam I see as analogous to IHD is *Ihsan*. Its multiplicity of meanings in English can be translated as excellence, beauty, perfection. Muslims are called to do all things with *ihsan*. It reflects an inner dimension of faith but manifests in right action. Ihsan, however, is not something that can be mandated, it is the highest spiritual level one can attain." The Islamic tradition can offer a deep understanding of human flourishing, for example through the concept of a good life (*"hayatan tayyibah"*), which can be related to *"falah,"* defined by Islamic Relief Service as "a comprehensive state of spiritual, moral, cultural, political and socio-economic well-being in this world and success in the Hereafter" (Aminu-Kano and FitzGibbon 2014, 12). The principles of trusteeship (*khalifa*), well-being (*falah*) combined with growth and purification (*tazkiyyah*), can be understood "to provide a comprehensive understanding of human enrichment and flourishing in Islam" (Aminu-Kano and FitzGibbon 2014, 12).

This book is organized in three parts. The first part ("A Dignity-Centered Approach") discusses the enactment of human dignity (through three negative approaches and a reflection on three areas of concern) in chapter 1 and offers an account of "dignity needs and the desire for a full human life" in chapter 2. The third chapter is dedicated to the topic of respect, and the fourth chapter introduces the idea of microtheories as a specific approach to learning from unique settings. The second part ("Integral Human Development, Dignity, and Development Projects") discusses development projects through a chapter on dignity-centered change and a chapter on the ethics of project management. Chapter 7 reflects on what it means to do justice to a local context, and chapter 8 illustrates the idea of a "moral biography of projects." The third part ("Common Good-Oriented Policies") moves from a chapter on the moral relevance of policies and political decisions to fundamental discussions on freedom, dignity, inequality, and the "point" of development. Chapter 11 looks at the process of policy making, and the final chapter, chapter 12, discusses attempts to institutionalize integral human development in organizations, and IHD-based institutional practices such as accompaniment. As said above, the book is an invitation to have conversations about the idea of integral human development, not the attempt to offer a definitive answer to the question what is IHD.

Concluding Remark

In his beautiful essay, "Why Read the Classics?" Italo Calvino characterizes a classic as a book that never finishes saying what it has to say. This is a beautiful line that can be applied to a key concept like "integral human development" as well. The term "integral human development" is a concept "that has never finished saying what it has to say." Or, to further paraphrase Calvino: Integral human development is a concept to which you cannot feel indifferent, that helps you to define yourself in relation to it, even in dispute with it.

PART I

A DIGNITY-CENTERED APPROACH

Late at night on December 9, 1948, Emil St. Lot, a descendant from slaves and the first ambassador of Haiti to the United Nations, presented the final draft of the Universal Declaration of Human Rights. It was a symbolic moment, since St. Lot's commitment to freedom and equality had special weight given his own history. In a way, he represented an important chapter in the book of the moral history of humanity. The draft resolution on human rights, he said, was "the greatest effort yet made by mankind to give society new legal and moral foundations."[1]

The moral history of the twentieth century is full of darkness and atrocity, as Jonathan Glover showed in his remarkable study *Humanity: A Moral History of the 20th Century.* The Universal Declaration of Human Rights (UDHR) was a milestone in this moral history, a statement of hope and moral commitment in the aftermath of two world wars. The venue, the Palais de Chaillot, is itself a representation of the moral history of the twentieth century. On June 23, 1940, Hitler was pictured on the terrace of the Palais with the Eiffel Tower in the background. On May 8, 1945, the US Army celebrated their victory right there. And three years and seven months later, the Palais became the official place of birth of the Universal Declaration of Human Rights, with its message of global and universal moral standards based on the dignity of the human person. The Syrian representative to the United Nations at the time observed that the Declaration was not the work of the General Assembly, but "the achievement of generations

---

[1] Office of the High Commissioner for Human Rights (OHCHR), "Universal Declaration of Human Rights at 70: 30 Articles on 30 Articles," United Nations Human Rights, online press release, November 9, 2018.

1

of human beings who had worked to that end."[2] René Cassin, who had written an early draft, noted that

> "the chief novelty of the declaration was its universality, [and because it was universal,"] he said, "it could have a broader scope than national declarations;" "he articulated what many of his colleagues also felt, namely that with the Declaration 'something new ha[d] entered the world.' It did not simply express the values of some of the great spirits of our age, but it was 'the first document about moral value adopted by an assembly of the human community.' It was therefore universal in origin and aim." (Morsink 1999, 33)

Thanks to the efforts of smaller nations, Human Rights became part of the UN discourse after 1945 (Glendon 2001, 11–18). We should, however, not be tempted to claim that the ideas expressed in the UDHR, the principles of inalienable universal human rights as based on the inherent dignity of all human beings, were "invented" in the twentieth century: "Equivalent moral decrees and ideas existed … in the intellectual systems of the indigenous peoples of the Americas long before the arrival of the European invaders" (Pharo 2014, 147).[3]

The Declaration is the recipient of many moral traditions and conveys a sense of history and moral development; its preamble contains a reminder of the fact that "disregard and contempt for human rights have resulted in barbarous acts which have outraged the conscience of mankind." The preamble also refers to the UN Charter from June 1945, which, in its preamble, reaffirmed "faith in fundamental human rights, in the dignity and worth of the human person, in the equal rights of men and women and of nations large and small." The Universal Declaration of Human Rights was drafted by representatives with different philosophical, legal, and cultural backgrounds from all regions of the world. Thanks to the tenacious Indian drafter Hansa Mehta, the French phrase "all men are born free and equal" became "all human beings are born free and equal." Even though the Declaration was promulgated before the decades of decolonization and the attempts to bring the Global South more fully into international decision-making processes, the fifty-eight member states of the

---

[2] OHCHR, "Universal Declaration of Human Rights at 70."

[3] In fact, going back to the moral sources of indigenous peoples could lead to new nuances or even amendments of the Universal Declaration of Human Rights: "Indigenous peoples have an intimate relation to nature where all life and every being are equal. There is a value of 'one dish, one spoon' where humans are responsible in a moral eco-philosophy of equity.… The universal value of dignity connected to nature is not expressed in the UDHR" (Pharo 2014, 152).

United Nations in 1948 included Asian nations (Burma, China, India, Pakistan, the Philippines, and the Union of Soviet Socialist Republics), countries of Central and South America (Argentina, Bolivia, Brazil, Chile, Colombia, Costa Rica, Ecuador, El Salvador, Guatemala, Honduras, Paraguay, Peru, Uruguay, Venezuela), Middle Eastern countries (like Egypt, Iraq, Lebanon, Saudi Arabia, Syria, Yemen), and also African nations like Liberia and the Union of South Africa. The Declaration cannot light-heartedly be called a Western document. There is a perception of universality—it is not surprising that Nelson Mandela, in an important address to the General Assembly of the United Nations in 1998, stated that "the values of happiness, justice, human dignity, peace and prosperity have a universal application because each people and every individual is entitled to them."[4]

The World Conference on Human Rights (Vienna, June 1993) underlined the universal claims of the Declaration in the Vienna Declaration and Programme of Action (June 25, 1993) by emphasizing "that the Universal Declaration of Human Rights ... constitutes a common standard of achievement for all peoples and all nations."[5] Abdulaziz Abdulhussein Sachedina has argued that "the Declaration of Article I of the international document that 'all human beings, are born free and equal in dignity and rights' captures the essential characterization

---

[4] Nelson Mandela, "Address by President Nelson Mandela at 53rd United Nations General Assembly, New York—United States," *Speeches by Nelson Mandela*, South African Government Information Website, September 21, 1998; It may be of interest, in this context of universal claims, to mention the "United Nations Millennium Declaration," based on the largest-ever gathering of world leaders to that date (September 6–8, 2000); the Declaration cited six values fundamental to international relations for the twenty-first century: freedom, equality (of individuals and nations), solidarity, tolerance, respect for nature and shared responsibility. The term "dignity" is explicitly mentioned in paragraph 2 ("we have a collective responsibility to uphold the principles of human dignity, equality and equity at the global level"), paragraph 6 in connection to the value of freedom ("Men and women have the right to live their lives and raise their children in dignity, free from hunger and from the fear of violence, oppression or injustice"), and paragraph 26 when talking about refugees and their right to safety and dignity. General Assembly Resolution 55/2, "United Nations Millennium Declaration," United Nations Human Rights online, adopted September 8, 2000.

[5] The same document also addressed the general question of balancing universal and cultural claims with this compromise language in article 5: "All human rights are universal, indivisible and interdependent and interrelated. The international community must treat human rights globally in a fair and equal manner, on the same footing, and with the same emphasis. While the significance of national and regional particularities and various historical, cultural and religious backgrounds must be borne in mind, it is the duty of States, regardless of their political, economic and cultural systems, to promote and protect all human rights and fundamental freedoms" The World Conference on Human Rights in Vienna, "Vienna Declaration and Programme of Action," United Nations Human Rights online, adopted June 25, 1993.

of human wisdom that has been transmitted under different historical circumstances when humans have fought and killed fellow humans, having denied them their dignity" (Sachedina 2009, 7).

The claim to universality can also be strengthened by the design of the deliberation process. The deliberation process was based on broad participation with many structured opportunities to shape the text (Morsink 1999, 1–35). Each state was invited to submit its own version—Chile, China, Cuba, Ecuador, France, India, Panama, the United Kingdom, and the United States followed this invitation (Morsink 1999, 10). The eighteen members of the Human Rights Commission (established on June 21, 1946, through the Economic and Social Council) were carefully selected. During its first session, Eleanor Roosevelt (United States) was unanimously elected chair with P. C. Chang (China) as her deputy and Charles Malik (Lebanon) as Rapporteur. The Canadian John P. Humphrey (as newly appointed director of the Human Rights Secretariat) was asked to join the group as well; he suggested a first draft. In a next step, eight nations formed a drafting committee (Australia, Chile, China, France, Lebanon, Union of Soviet Socialist Republics, United Kingdom, and United States), which appointed a three-person working group (René Cassin from France, Charles Malik, and Geoffrey Wilson from the United Kingdom). René Cassin, as mentioned above, submitted a first draft that accepted about three-quarters of Humphrey's text (Morsink 1999, 8). During the second session of the Human Rights Commission in December 1947 in Geneva, the committee consulted with a series of experts from different international organizations. This "Geneva draft" received feedback from fourteen member states. During the third session of the Human Rights Commission in May and June 1948, the text was moved closer toward finalization. It was a truly collaborative effort.

The Universal Declaration of Human Rights sets out that human rights derive from "the fact of existing" (as Chilean drafter Hernán Santa Cruz observed) and that human rights are not granted by any state. This goes beyond the citizens' rights declarations from 1789 (Déclaration des droits de l'homme et du citoyen). The UDHR advanced from rights restricted to citizens to the rights of humans, equal for all whether they belonged to a particular country or not, which is particularly important in the case of totalitarian states or the condition of statelessness.[6] The demands articulated in the Declaration claim universal status and ask for global recognition.

Even though the Universal Declaration of Human Rights, with its commitment to human dignity, was designed to be accessible to secular and religious

---

[6] See Spiegelberg (2020).

groups and was understood to express universal moral claims,[7] we can identify a particular anthropology and a particular understanding of the good life in the background of the Declaration. The criticism echoes the skepticism (mentioned in the introduction) that some people express with regard to the idea of Integral Human Development (or IHD): there is a concern, for instance, that "Integral Human Development" (understood as the development of each person and the whole person) conveys a certain understanding of personhood and individual identity. A critic of the discourse on human rights, Makau Mutua, articulates epistemological, representative, and imperialist reservations: "the human rights corpus views the individual as the center of the moral universe, and therefore denigrates communities, collectives, and group rights. This is a particularly serious problem in Africa, where group and community rights are both deeply embedded in the cultures of the peoples and exacerbated by the multinational nature of the postcolonial state" (Mutua 2008, 34).

It may be interesting to note that some of the reservations articulated vis-à-vis the idea of the universality of human rights resemble the doubts about the concept of Integral Human Development, as the introduction has shown. IHD faces similar criticism as the Universal Declaration of Human Rights and the subsequent discourse on Human Rights with regard to the reservations about political and conceptual imperialism and epistemological colonialism. Human Rights–skepticism and IHD-skepticism share important concerns—the common ground of reservations based on worries about imperialist universalism, individualism, vagueness, and ineffectiveness. This also means that the questions that have to be negotiated (questions about universal aspects of the human condition and an overlapping consensus on aspects of a desirable mode of coexistence, and aspects of the good human life) are similar. The two discourses (Integral Human Development, Human Rights) can form and enter a "learning partnership." It is also worth noting that, at the time when the concept of Integral Human Development was articulated in the 1960s, the Catholic Church had officially recognized the importance of the Universal Declaration of Human Rights.[8]

---

[7] "[T]he drafters thought that human rights are part of people's moral DNA and ... they wanted to keep the declaration a secular text accessible to religious and nonreligious people alike" (Morsink 2022, 1); cf. Morsink (2017).

[8] Pope John XXIII endorsed the Universal Declaration of Human Rights (after the well-known reservation of the church vis-à-vis the discourse, especially with regard to religious freedom) in his encyclical *Pacem in Terris*, published shortly before his death in 1963, when he praised the United Nations: "A clear proof of the farsightedness of this organization is provided by the Universal Declaration of Human Rights passed by the United Nations General Assembly on December 10, 1948. The preamble of this declaration affirms that the genuine recognition and complete observance of all the rights and freedoms outlined in the

Both approaches are dignity centered. And, in both cases, it is useful to substantiate the claim that there is a non-Western and non-Christian way of approaching the dignity of the human person. The Islamic tradition, for example, provides reference points to understand, defend, and enact human dignity. Miklós Maróth identified the Arabic expression *karamat al-insan* as an equivalent to "human dignity" (Maróth 2014, 155): "In Surah 17, one can find the word in its basic meaning, when we read that Allah commanded the angels to prostrate to Adam, which they did" (Maróth 2014, 156). The idea of the special status of the human person in creation is also expressed in Surah 17:70: "We have honoured the children of Adam and carried them by land and sea; We have provided good sustenance for them and favoured them specially above many of those We have created." Clearly, God is the source of human dignity, but the idea of dignity and the belief in the special dignified status (elevated position) of the human person is explicitly articulated. Human dignity is linked to freedom,[9] and the human person has a status higher than the status of angels, as Surah 17:70 indicates. It is God given, based on God's dignifying action, and has to be reflected in a proper form of life, in accordance with the divine commandments.[10]

The Cairo Declaration on Human Rights in Islam (August 5, 1990) states in article 1a:

> All human beings form one family whose members are united by their subordination to Allah and descent from Adam. All men are equal in terms of basic human dignity and basic obligations and responsibilities, without any discrimination on the basis of race, colour, language, belief,

---

declaration is a goal to be sought by all peoples and all nations" (*Pacem in Terris* 143). The text also alludes to some of the compromises the Declaration had to accept: "We are, of course, aware that some of the points in the declaration did not meet with unqualified approval in some quarters; and there was justification for this. Nevertheless, We think the document should be considered a step in the right direction, an approach toward the establishment of a juridical and political ordering of the world community. It is a solemn recognition of the personal dignity of every human being; an assertion of everyone's right to be free to seek out the truth, to follow moral principles, discharge the duties imposed by justice, and lead a fully human life. It also recognized other rights connected with these" (*Pacem in Terris* 144). Mary Ann Glendon has demonstrated that the Catholic Social Tradition had exercised a certain influence on the UDHR (Glendon 2013); Samuel Moyn has argued that the rise of human rights after the Second World War was inspired by a defense of human dignity that can be traced to Christian churches and religious thought in the years just prior to the outbreak of the war (Moyn 2015).

⁹ Cf. Quran 21; 19–30.
¹⁰ See Kamali (2002); Waardenburg (2002, 160–85).

sex, religion, political affiliation, social status or other considerations. The true religion is the guarantee for enhancing such dignity along the path to human integrity.[11]

The text confirms the importance of the idea of human dignity in the Islamic tradition, but leaves in its last sentence the question open whether "true dignity" can only be found in Islam. For our purposes, it can be argued that the plausibility of the idea of human dignity is not restricted to the Judeo-Christian tradition. It can be also shown, for example, that Confucianism offers a virtue-based understanding of human dignity (Li 2019; Ni 2014), grounded in the idea of benevolence and one's capacity to connect with others (An'xian 2014). Buddhism has important contributions to make to the discourse on human dignity, especially through the idea of a distinctively human capability for "awakening" and self-liberating (Wong 2017; Sevilla-Liu 2022). The religious and moral tradition of Hinduism, to establish a further reference point, offers insights onto a tension between inherent dignity of all living beings and the lived tradition that dignity appears in degrees in the social realm (Braarvig 2014).

Many religious traditions and philosophical schools enrich and deepen the discourse on human dignity, which emerges as a colorful concept that is not owned by Western intellectual history; the key challenge of the Declaration, however, is and remains the question of its implementation, since it was meant to respond to the experience of human destruction. Eleanor Roosevelt famously observed in 1958 that universal human rights begin "in small places, close to home—so close and so small that they cannot be seen on any maps of the world. Yet they are the world of the individual person; the neighborhood he lives in; the school or college he attends; the factory, farm, or office where he works."[12] The enactment of values has to shape the everyday life of citizens in their daily actions and interactions. Nancy Rosenblum made the same point in her book about democracy, a political form of human coexisting based on the ability of being good neighbors (Rosenblum 2016).

The human rights discourse suffers from a concern with elitism. There seems to be a disconnect between the moral universe of the human rights theorist and activist, on the one hand, and the moral universe of ordinary, especially vulnerable, citizens, as Michael Ignatieff had observed, on the other:

---

[11] The Nineteenth Islamic Conference of Foreign Ministers, *Cairo Declaration on Human Rights in Islam*, University of Minnesota Human Rights Library online, adopted August 5, 1990, UN Doc. A/CONF.157/PC/62/Add.18 (1993). See also article 6a: "Woman is equal to man in human dignity."

[12] United Nations, "Teaching Guide and Resources: Human Rights," un.org.

> In the moral universe of the human rights activist and the global
> ethicist, the object of ultimate concern is the universal human being.
> Human differences—of race, class, or situation—are secondary. In this
> conception of moral life, one's primary duty is to be impartial, to regard
> the distinction, for example, between a citizen and a stranger as morally
> irrelevant. In our conversations surrounding the moral universe of the
> ordinary virtues, on the other hand, the universal human being was
> rarely, if ever, the object of ultimate concern. The most striking feature
> of the ordinary virtue perspective is how rarely any of our participants
> evoked ideas of general obligation to human beings as such; and how
> frequently they reasoned in terms of the local, the contingent, the here
> and now—what they owed those near to them and what they owed
> themselves. (Ignatieff 2017a, 10)[13]

To offer another example of the same point. A student reflected on an encounter
she had had in Ireland. She asked a business-owning father of four about his take
on dignity and Integral Human Development, and his response was short, swift,
and honest: "I don't care about dignity, I care about taking care of my family." He
explained that many "common people" do not think of dignity. They simply try
to survive day to day.

The project of enacting universal and rather abstract ideas of dignity and
human rights is in need of proper translations from abstract ideas to "ordinary
virtues" and "everyday practices." The ideals have to be brought closer to human
agency. Catherine Bolten, for example, has shown that the introduction of the
idea of children's rights in Sierra Leone has changed the patterns of interactions
between children and adults, partly eroding traditional care-taking structures
(Bolten 2018, 2020).

Even though the discourse on human dignity reveals some major theoretical
concerns (definition of dignity, justification of dignity and rights, range of dignity
and rights), the key challenge to human dignity and human rights remains the
enactment. Nelson Mandela made this point very clear in his above-mentioned
address to the United Nations in 1998, fifty years after the promulgation of the
Universal Declaration of Human Rights. He asserted that "the very right to
be human is denied every day to hundreds of millions of people as a result of
poverty, the unavailability of basic necessities such as food, jobs, water and shelter,

---

[13] See also Ignatieff (2017a)—Ignatieff shows that the moral language that reso-
nates with most people is that of everyday virtues such as trust, tolerance, forgiveness.
These "ordinary virtues" serve as the moral fabric of global cities and obscure shanty-
towns alike.

education, health care and a healthy environment."[14] And he points to human agency when he claims "that all these social ills which constitute an offence against the Universal Declaration of Human Rights are not a pre-ordained result of the forces of nature or the product of a curse of the deities. They are the consequence of decisions which men and women take or refuse to take."

One limit of Human Rights is clearly the politics of human rights and the agency of policy makers: "human rights are limited by the realities of power and interest. Human rights matter when, and only when, powerful actors say they do" (Reus-Smit 2019, 121). And he adds, "historically this has been rare."[15] Samuel Moyn has identified human rights as the last utopia, a source and projection of hope, built on the ruins of earlier political utopias (Moyn 2010). Furthermore, this utopia has lost political power in the context of neoliberalism and is reduced to minimal tasks: "human rights have remained chiefly rhetorical in their inroads into the socioeconomic domain, whereas neoliberalism has transformed the globe profoundly" (Moyn 2014, 168).[16]

This observation brings us back to the question about Human Rights skepticism. It cannot be denied that the Universal Declaration of Human Rights was promulgated against the background of gross atrocities, even genocide; it was not primarily concerned with or sensitive to everyday suppressive structures. It was not meant to change the international order and the economic structures. So, the question "What does it mean to enact human dignity, human rights, integral human development?" becomes even more pressing.

---

[14] "Address by President Nelson Mandela at 53rd United Nations General Assembly," New York, September 21, 1998.

[15] The concern about vagueness and ineffectiveness has similarly been articulated by McCann: "if rights are so light and supple [in order to gain support], they must also mean very little and carry little weight as a challenge to the status quo; they are merely the superficial 'um' and 'ah' of social and political banter, mere talk rather than action with sufficient material consequence to compel respect" (McCann 2014, 256).

[16] See also Moyn's *Not Enough: Human Rights in an Unequal World* (Moyn 2018) with the thesis that the evolution of human rights into the prevailing legal, political, and moral response to global problems changed the nature of justice seeking, from a concern with equality (including and especially material equality) to a contentment with a lowest common denominator and minimal standards, that is, a form of sufficientism.

1

Enacting Human Dignity

Dignity has many faces—respect for dignity can be expressed on a microlevel of interactions and on the macrolevel of structures and policies. An approach that puts dignity at the center can make a tangible difference, for example, in education, recognizing the "somebody-ness" of students and educators (Irby et al. 2022). Respect for the dignity of the person can be shown in everyday life as well as in emergency situations. Dignity matters for the highly vulnerable person and for the privileged one. In spite of its multifariousness, dignity is, at the same time, quite simple.

Irina Mosel and Kerrie Holloway's research works to understand what dignity means to refugees, internally displaced people, and returnees in six different countries (Afghanistan, Bangladesh, Colombia, Lebanon, the Philippines, and South Sudan) "and whether (and how) they feel that their dignity has been upheld in displacement" (Mosel and Holloway 2019, vi). Key aspects of the experience of dignity that emerged in the study were respect and self-reliance. These two main themes emerged in all six case studies. Respecting a person means accepting the person as a source of normative claims and expressing this acceptance in the real effort to honor these normative claims through the consideration of the unique needs and contributions of the person, and through properly polite ways of interacting with this person. Self-reliance means the experience of being in a position to make decisions about one's life and to exercise agency in providing for oneself and for one's family. Even though the concept of dignity seems lofty, the enactment can seem quite simple with the emphasis on respect and promoting self-reliance.

Human dignity is precious, since it is inherent and inviolable, and it cannot be diminished or taken away. Yet human dignity is fragile, since it can be trampled upon, violated, not properly respected. The concrete experiences of persons and groups have to be taken into account: "any satisfactory conception of dignity should ... not be detached from concrete occurrences and interpretations in social life" (Kaufman et al. 2011, 2). In the above-mentioned study, statements like "Respect is so important to my dignity that I would trade all of the luxuries of life for it" or "dignity means receiving respect in the same way as everyone else and without discrimination" or "working hard and earning your own livelihood is a big part of our idea of dignity" (Mosel and Holloway 2019, 7) are important contributions to an understanding of dignity and respect.

Three Negative Approaches

There is also a *via negativa*, a negative way, to understand dignity. Ways of disrespecting a person's dignity can tell us a lot about the enactment of human dignity. The world is full of concrete occurrences of dignity violations. This section discusses three: infantilization, instrumentalization, and humiliation. Following a *via negativa*, enacting human dignity can occur through a very basic triad of *noninfantilization*, *noninstrumentalization*, and *nonhumiliation*. Conversely, the infantilization, instrumentalization, and humiliation of persons are three major ways of disrespecting human dignity.

Firstly, *infantilization*. Infantilizing a person means treating a person as if she were not capable of making decisions, of exercising agency. Forms of (government) paternalism are especially strong vis-à-vis vulnerable groups or in moments of crisis, as the COVID-19 pandemic has shown, where many citizens felt infantilized by the deprivation of civil rights. Totalitarian regimes create a climate of infantilization by taking away the motivation for initiative and agency (Dobko 2022, 255). Similarly, in terms of power dynamics, the colonized have been infantilized (Goerg 2012; Studer 2021). The model of adult and child has also been transferred to global relations with the image of the adult North and the young South, implying a patronizing attitude toward "nations allegedly not able to take care of their own citizens. This leads to a kind of infantilized dependency ... established and reproduced through ... fundamentally unequal and interrelated relationships" (Valentin and Meinert 2009, 23). An experience of the North/ South divide:

> As a Peace Corps volunteer, I was sent to Zambia to integrate fish farming into the Zambian agriculture system, with only my environmental science bachelor's degree as proof of my "expert" status. This status allowed me to be a teacher to subsistence farmers who had farmed their entire lives. All I had was a theoretical understanding of the science behind agriculture and ecosystems. Who was I to tell these men and women how to actually farm the land they grew up on and had an intimate understanding and connection to?

No doubt, the dynamics of infantilization are compatible with good intentions and general human decency. There is also an undeniable contextual element at play. Entry points for the dynamics of respect-denial through infantilization depend on the local context and the status of the person within this context. In an article in *The Guardian* on the situation of women in Qatar from 2021, Harriet Grant reports that women complained to her that they are treated as children, depending on men for permission to travel, to pursue higher education, marry, or make decisions about their own children.[1]

Entry points for infantilization are especially present in the case of people with a higher vulnerability status. For example, a person who does not speak the language or does not know the culture of a particular context can easily find herself in child roles. In a research project on a Humanitarian Corridor that brought five hundred African refuges on a safe and legal pathway to Italy, I could observe similar dynamics: whereas the children of some families picked up Italian and knowledge of the local cultures quite rapidly, the parents had to be accompanied and guided as if they were children; even more so, the parents had to rely on their children for translation purposes in their interactions with bureaucracies, thus pushing children into adult roles and infantilizing the parents, which created challenges for the culturally established family hierarchy patterns.[2] Infantilizing refugees has been recognized as a means of political dominion (Avramidis and Minotakis 2017); women refugees have been described as "infantilized" and "de-matured" in gender-insensitive refugee camps (Manchanda 2004),[3] and the concerns about infantilizing refugees also refers to the representation of refugees in the public.[4]

---

[1] Harriet Grant, "'We're Treated as Children,' Qatari Women Tell Rights Group," *The Guardian* online, March 29, 2021.

[2] A social worker described the challenges in these terms: "Da un lato si trattano queste persone come bambini bisognosi di tutto, anche di quello di cui non hanno bisogno" ("On the one hand they treat these people like needy children, even in situations where this is not necessary"). On the other hand, they are disappointed by the passivity of the adult refugees: "Ci sentiamo molto sollecitati a rispondere a tutti i loro desideri, a tutte le loro esigenze e cosi, ma li sentiamo molto passivi" ("We try hard to respond to their desires and needs, at the same time we see them as quite passive"). See Sedmak et al. 2021, 130.

[3] One example from South Asia: "The protection regime in the camps trivialises gender-based violence as reason for flight and domestic violence in the camps. The mechanisms for grievance redress and the camp decision-making structures are both gender insensitive and tend to infantilise women. 'Sometimes I was beaten so badly I bled. My husband took a second wife. I didn't agree. He said, "if you don't allow me to take a second wife, then the ration card is in my name, and I'll take everything." I have asked my husband for the health card and ration card and he doesn't give it to me. I have not got approval to get a separate ration card.' Geeta M (alias) Bhutanese refuge" (Manchanda 2004, 4183).

[4] Manea Dragoș and Mihaela Precup observe: "In an analysis of Michael Winterbottom's

Another group that is particularly vulnerable to the deprivation of respect through infantilization is the elderly; Nina A. Kohn refers to "the tendency to infantilize the elderly by attributing child-like characteristics to them" (Kohn 2009, 1108). Sonia Mina Salari (2005) presented a study about US American adult day centers and their patterns of infantilizing their clients in the form of speech infantilization (baby-talk, nicknames, reprimands), activity infantilization (use of toys, games, teacher-student learning format), and environmental infantilization (child-oriented décor, limitation of movement). Additionally, loss of privacy regulation, autonomy, and choice lead to the disrespectful experience of infantilization and deprivation of adult status. This is connected to treating old age as a second childhood, based on a perceived lack of independence (Salari and Rich 2001, 116).

The experience of infantilization is connected to the vulnerability status of a person or group, especially in institutional settings; homeless persons in a shelter are residents; a study from the United Kingdom revealed that "residents [of the shelter] felt that they lacked ownership over their own space, and they weren't permitted to embark on do-it-yourself projects or use other skills that they may have had. They generally felt like they were being 'treated like a child'.... Excessive rules and regulations perpetuated the notion of infantilization" (Stevenson 2014, 137). The experience of homeless persons of being treated like children leads to a sense of not being respected, even humiliated (Hoffman and Coffey 2008).

Poor people experience infantilization in personal interactions as well as in institutional settings and in their interactions with the government. There are politically heated debates about the appropriate way of supporting especially vulnerable people without infantilizing them, for example, with regard to conditional cash transfers with their in-built reward structure.[5] We also find

---

2002 film *In This World*, Bruce Bennet critiques "the over-determined humanitarian representation of the refugee as a helpless, infantilised and feminised male figure." Similarly, Nando Sigona notes that "humanitarian, academic, and media discourses ... tend to privilege a one-dimensional representation of the refugee which relies heavily on feminized and infantilized images of 'pure' victimhood and vulnerability." While such depictions of refugee men tend to be grounded in the best of intentions, they are nevertheless shadowed by an older Orientalist representational tradition that has willfully framed such men as childlike in order to bolster Western claims to superiority. Exploring the endurance of such constructions, Sophia Rose Arjana notes that "[w]hen not vilified, Muslims are infantilized and feminized, much as they were in the past" (Dragos and Precup 2020, 482).

[5] In a 2007 article, Dafna Izenberg frames conditional cash transfers as political means of infantilization and offers examples like these: "Last summer, an Italian mayor promised $75 to townspeople who lose three kilograms, and another $150 if they keep the weight off after five months. In September, the U.K. government announced that, beginning in 2009, all pregnant women, regardless of income, will be given $250 if they refrain from smoking and drinking

observations that enduring infantilization can lead to patterns of "learned help-lessness." A religious sister who worked in an Asian country for a number of years commented on the *imbalance of relationships.*

> *The giver vs. the receiver, the savior vs. the saved, the poor vs. the rich, the developed vs. the undeveloped. In my experience, I saw this dynamic play out so clearly. The people I worked with have been subjected to a dole out mentality for far too long that any foreigner is seen in terms of bringing gifts, money, opportunity. So much so that, when I invited a group of women to think together and come up with a plan, they found it strange that I did not tell them what they needed to do.*

Obviously, this is a singular experience and observation that cannot be generalized, but it does raise some questions about respecting agency and responsibility. There are also concerns that infantilization strategies justify the paternalistic treatment of minority group members with the consequence that they may be "kept in their place" as dependent inferiors (Arluke and Levin 1984). This will lead to the erosion of agency and the underestimation of a person's contribution to knowledge and insights.

In a nutshell: Respecting a person's dignity requires the effort to give space to the person's agency and decision-making power, and to avoid patterns of infantilization that undermine a person's self-reliance and self-perception as an (adult) agent. Integral Human Development (or IHD) is a dignity-centered approach that is sensitive to entry points for infantilization.

A second pattern of depriving a person of the respect that is due is the reality of *instrumentalization.* Instrumentalizing a person is part of what we do every day—a teacher, a plumber, a doctor, a lawyer are "also" means to an end, instruments for our projects. The important point to note is that they are not to be treated *merely* as a means to an end.[6] A person is treated merely as a means to an end if her rights are violated or if she is confronted with the denial of the claim that she has equal practical standing in virtue of her humanity (Pallikkathayil

---

and agree to receive professional advice on nutrition. And since 2001, the Canadian federal government has been testing a program called learn$ave, similar to the one in Washington, that matches money saved by low-income earners provided they only use the funds for education, training or a small business start-up." She concludes that "rewarding good behaviour is best known as a parenting strategy for managing tricky times—problems with toilet training, sibling rivalry, kids refusing to sleep at night. It isn't much of a leap, then, when critics argue that incentive programs … patronize even infantilize, the disadvantaged" (Izenberg 2007, 37).

[6] Immanuel Kant's classical version from his *Groundwork of Metaphysics*: "So act that you treat humanity, whether in your own person or in the person of any other, always at the same time as an end, never merely as a means" (Kant 1785, 429).

2010, 141). A person is instrumentalized if she is unable to consent to another agent's use of her and her inability to share the agent's end (Kerstein 2009, 180). Sadly, instrumentalizing persons as merely a means to an end is not uncommon.

The experience of being instrumentalized is not infrequent in institutional settings that impose role expectations and employee status on a person. A study of Swedish nurses and mental health workers, for instance, showed that these care providers suffer from the experience of being instrumentalized (Kristiansen et al. 2010). A young development worker who worked with a particular nongovernmental organization (NGO) complained that the NGO

> *viewed their students as products that could have positive results that would further increase their funding and reputation. This is sort of contrary to the notion that dignity is inherent, implying that the students were treated as a means to an end.*

Similarly, a volunteer teacher reflects on her experience:

> *We were trained to focus on the deliverables: how were the children testing? Was there an increase from the baseline to the final grades each quarter? What was the fail rate? It seemed to reduce the children to numbers and the teachers to performers.*

The introduction of standardized assessment mechanisms, however well justified, can make it more difficult to see "the whole person."

Seeing others as instruments is not a rare occurrence. Kimberly White observed that we frequently see the other persons as instruments for our projects and that it might actually be revolutionary to treat people as if they were people (White 2018). We can recall the migration politics of Aleksandr Lukashenko's Belarusian regime in 2021, when Belarus began actively attracting migrants from Syria, Iraq, Afghanistan, Yemen, and other countries, before encouraging and even forcing them to cross the borders into the European Union, putting pressure on the neighboring countries of Poland, Lithuania, and Latvia. Migrants were instrumentalized by the Belarusian regime to respond to EU sanctions imposed following the regime's rigging of elections in 2020. A Declaration by the High Representative on behalf of the European Union from July 2021 starts with the sentences: "The instrumentalisation of migrants and refugees is utterly unacceptable. Using human beings in need to advance political goals violates fundamental European values and principles."[7]

---

[7] Council of the European Union, "Belarus: Declaration by the High Representative on behalf of the European Union on the Instrumentalisation of Migrants and Refugees by the Regime," *Consillium Europa* online press release, July 30, 2021.

Here, instrumentalization and exploitation (of people with increased levels of vulnerability and despair) go hand in hand. Exploitation means to take unfair advantage of another person, to use another person's vulnerability for one's own benefit, without considering the well-being of the other person. The dark reality of contemporary slavery tells thousands of stories of instrumentalization. People are treated as objects and instruments. Francis Bok, from South Sudan, was captured and enslaved in May 1986, at the age of seven, during an Arab militia raid on his home village Nyamlel. He was held for ten years as a slave by a man called Giemma and his family; he recounts his first experience of being treated like an object, when, after his arrival at his new "home," he was beaten by the slave holder's children:

> The man's children, including the boy my age that I wanted to be my friend, chanted and laughed and struck me from all sides.... Why were they beating me.... I had done nothing wrong.... I rubbed the marks on my arm and legs, still burning from the blows from the sticks. But something else stung me even more. I realized that if the bearded man and his wife did not try to help me, then they didn't care about me. (Bok 2003, 18–19)

A human person is sometimes reduced to a source of labor. One of the most atrocious ways of instrumentalizing a person is sexual exploitation. The sexual instrumentalization of persons typically happens in a structural setting, with power asymmetries and a lack of accountability. Sexual abuse happens in the aid sector and the humanitarian "industry" as well. The Oxfam scandal in Haiti in 2011 is only the tip of the iceberg as we have been confronted with scandals with the UN peacekeeping troops,[8] Peace Corps,[9] and the World Health Organization.[10] Factors like the following contribute to the systemic violations of dignity: power disparity and dependency,[11] working with vulnerable people and in exceptional circumstances (postdisaster context, remote areas); moral claims and a sense of moral superiority; personal factors like stress, pressures, experience of displacement and alienation; a particular work culture combined with

---

[8] Skye Wheeler, "UN Peacekeeping Has a Sexual Abuse Problem," *The Hill* and *Human Rights Watch* online, January 11, 2020.

[9] "Peace Corps Hearing Details Abuse of Volunteers," Women's Congressional Policy Institute online, 2011.

[10] Claire Parker, "Report Details Sexual Abuse Allegations against WHO Staffers during Congo Ebola Outbreak," *Washington Post* online, September 28, 2021.

[11] An Oxfam report identified four top drivers: hierarchy, gender, power over resources, race (Bangura and Sierra 2019, 27)—hierarchy issues have become more relevant with the "corporatization" of the aid sector.

mechanisms of institutional reputation protection and internal processes. Charlotte Lydia Riley argues that the aid industry exists in a historical, social, and political space that is particularly volatile and that the abusive behavior of men in the sector is shaped and enabled by inequalities of race, class, and gender (Riley 2020). Abuse undermines the stated aims of international aid programs. The credibility gap has been named "the nonprofit paradox" by David La Piana, who makes the claim that "nonprofits tend to recreate within their own organizational cultures the problems they are trying to solve in society" (La Piana 2010, 23). The abuse of people through those involved in "dignity work" is particularly shameful because of the disconnect between explicit value commitments and the agency on the ground.

One does not need to commit to Integral Human Development to condemn abuse and instrumentalization, for any decent and dignity-sensitive approach will invest in resisting the temptation to reduce persons to roles and services.

A third way of grossly disrespecting a person's dignity is *humiliation*. The Colombian artist Emma Reyes, to offer one example, was maybe seven years old, when she was deeply humiliated in her convent school, where she was educated after having been abandoned by her mother:

> One day, at recess…. I was alone, standing with my back against a wall…. A group of girls played together, spinning in a circle, all holding hands. I'm not sure how I found myself suddenly in the middle, and they began to close in around me while the girls shouted, "Dirty little girl, shitty, dirty little girl!" The circle closed, and they threw me to the floor and took off the only pair of underwear I owned. Of course it was dirty…. One of the girls, a very fat one, cross-eyed like me, hung my underwear on a broomstick. They marched along, the broomstick held high, forming a long procession through the courtyards, shouting in a chorus: "The New Girl's dirty underwear!" (Reyes 2017, 80)

Emma's experience is humiliating. Humiliation is a strong language of dignity violation, and nonhumiliation can be suggested as a minimum standard of dignity respect. Humiliation is a form of debasing a human person. It challenges the public persona of a person, her reputation, her status; it calls into question the right of a person to be respected. Since it touches upon layers of human identity, it is a deep experience. It is a deeply emotional experience as accounts of the Middle East can tell us (Fattah and Fierke 2009). The damage done through humiliation is very difficult to repair. Hans Blix, the well-known diplomat who served as the head of the International Atomic Energy Agency, observed after decades in international diplomatic service:

In all situations do not humiliate the other side because you don't get anywhere; you make them furious. There are many examples of this, even in vocabulary.... In human relations, humiliation is very dangerous ... don't humiliate, don't ever humiliate. I think it is underestimated how important dignity is between people and how important it is not to humiliate.[12]

A simple translation of dignity in practical terms is nonhumiliation. "Humiliation is any sort of behaviour or condition that constitutes a sound reason for a person to consider his or her self-respect injured" (Margalit 1996, 9). Self-respect is the kind of respect that I owe to myself on the basis of being human. Humiliation erodes the foundation of a person's source of self-respect. Avishai Margalit has identified different ways of humiliating a person: treating persons as if they were not human; performing actions that lead to a loss of basic control, especially control over bodily functions; excluding a person from the human family (Margalit 1996, 144).

People are treated as if they were objects or animals when a person is reduced to a number or treated like a nonhuman animal. Concentration camps were designed as laboratories for dehumanization. Primo Levi, in his famous book, *If This Is a Man*, where he gives an account of his experience in the concentration camp of Auschwitz, mentions all kinds of humiliation, including the way of treating humans as if they were animals:

The Kapo comes to us periodically and calls: "*Wer hat noch zu fressen?*" He does not say it from derision or to sneer, but because this way of eating on our feet, furiously, burning our mouths and throats, without time to breathe, really is "*fressen*," the way of eating of animals, and certainly not "*essen*," the human way of eating, seated in front of a table.... "*Fressen*" is exactly the word and it is used currently among us. (Levi 1959, 85)

Experiences of dehumanization are, sadly, not matters of the past. A case study about domestic service relations in a neighborhood of Pietermaritzburg revealed that Black domestic workers feel dehumanized in their day-to-day interactions with their Indian employers (Murray et al. 2022). This dehumanization also referred to the provision of food:

More specifically, perhaps because routines of food provision are part of the daily interactions between domestic workers and their employers,

---

[12] "Hans Blix: The Most Important Lesson in Diplomacy Is Not to Humiliate," Détente NOW! online, January 29, 2019.

their cumulative effect is also humiliating and dehumanizing. In both extracts, for example, interviewees make explicit links to experiences of animalistic dehumanization. Buhle asserts that both the nature of her employer's communication surrounding food provision ("they'll say 'eat'") and the quality of food provided (stale "crusts") deprives her of full human status by signalling "you are a dog to them." It is important to emphasize how this process is dynamically enacted through negative contact experiences. (Murray et al. 2022, 1059)

Obviously, there are structural issues behind these microinteractions. Humiliation on a microlevel can also be seen as a stage of macrodynamics.

It is also humiliating to make a person lose control over her body—for example, by denying her access to a bathroom or by refusing to establish structures that would enable a person to control her body. For example, the European Court of Human Rights, in the case *Vincent v. France* (October 24, 2006) had to assess whether a paraplegic person, who was serving a ten-year prison sentence and who was detained in different prisons that were not adapted to his disability, was humiliated. The court held that there had been a violation of article 3 of the European Convention on Human Rights (prohibition of inhuman or degrading treatment) since the applicant could not move autonomously around the prison and had this loss of control over his body. A similar scenario (with a similar assessment) was dealt with in the case *Grimailovs v. Latvia* (June 25, 2013). Supporting a person's control over her body is a minimum level of showing respect. Institutions can create detrimental conditions through their power over body politics, which has been analyzed by Michel Foucault, especially in his lecture series *The Birth of Biopolitics* (Foucault 2010).

Humiliation also occurs if a person is given the message that she is not, or at least not fully, a member of the human family (as in the examples of racist regimes, an apartheid setting). Desmond Tutu recounts an experience of humiliation from South Africa's apartheid regime days:

My family was having a picnic on the beach. The portion of the beach reserved for blacks was the least attractive, with rocks lying around. Not far away was a playground, and our youngest, who was born in England, said, "Daddy, I want to go on the swings," and I said with a hollow voice and a dead weight in the pit of my stomach, "No, darling, you can't go." What do you say, how do you feel, when your baby says, "But Daddy, there are other children playing there?" How do you tell your little darling that she cannot go because though she is a child, she is not that kind of child? And you died many times and were not able to look your child in the eyes because you felt so dehumanized, so humiliated, so diminished.[13]

Desmond Tutu felt denied full membership of the human family. The experience of humiliation goes deep and can be transmitted intergenerationally. Another way of humiliating a person through exclusion from the human family is invisibilization in which certain persons are treated as if they were invisible (the experience of many custodians and cleaning personnel (Rabelo and Mahalingam 2019), or certain groups are invisible in the public because they lack public presence or representation (Herzog 2018). If people are not seen or heard, they are denied recognition (Honneth 2001).

Humiliation can happen on an individual level, on the level of groups (e.g., a whole group can be humiliated by the humiliation of a group representative),[14] and also on the international level. Franziska Dübgen has reflected on the humiliation of Africa through the lack of equality in relationships of international cooperation, through resource-driven paternalism, through implicit or explicit power divides, and through formal or informal hierarchies determining the content and form of "cooperation" (Dübgen 2012). Livie Onyebuchi has offered some guidance with regard to dignity-sensitive approaches to aid in Africa. Such an approach will ask questions such as

to what extent can the aid be said to be genuinely developmental, such that its beneficiaries are able as a result to become efficient architects of their own future development? ... What is the extent to which the aid upholds and promotes in real and practical terms authentic human development in Africa, particularly the dignity of its beneficiaries? ... How sincere are the aid programmes in the face of the prevailing and clearly unfair global economic and political equation in which Africa is regularly made to negotiate from an enfeebled position? (Onyebuchi 2000, 414)

---

[13] Desmond Tutu, "Archbishop Desmond Tutu Reflects on Working toward Peace," Markkula Center for Applied Ethics, Santa Clara University, online, 2014.

[14] Neuhäuser (2011) distinguishes three ways of collective humiliation: direct group humiliation (humiliation because they are members of a group) / symbolic group humiliation (a symbol of the group is defiled) / representative group humiliation (selected members representing the group); and it is against this background that he pleads for social dignity; without social dignity someone is not recognized as a fully respected member of a society (Neuhäuser 2011, 33).

This is not to be taken for granted. In many instances, local people feel misrecognized in being judged according to the parameters of Western actors within the international community. Aminata Traoré, quoted by Dübgen, analyzes the unequal power dynamics that determine the international context of Mali's cotton industry. These dynamics have led to constellations where, in the words of former President Mamady Touré, "people that have never seen a single ball of cotton come to teach us lessons on cotton." Such a relationship cannot be classified as a partnership, for it is the relationship "between teacher and student" (Traoré 2009, 194). There are serious issues of recognition in the development industry, and local knowledge is not infrequently ignored.

Lack of respect for local knowledge and local circumstances can lead to detrimental effects. The irrigation system of Bali, for example, was tragically misinterpreted by colonial and governmental powers. It is predicated upon an interdependent hierarchical system of *subaks* that weaves religious and economic affairs together. This system was valued by the Balinese for imparting necessary social order, provided by the religious authority, the *Jero Gde*. Based on the regulations and verdicts issued by the *Jero Gde*, the *subak* units cooperate effectively in managing water flow and optimizing crop yield. Due to this order, the Balinese understand their hierarchical water temples as the "[defining] connection between productive groups and the components of the natural landscape that they seek to control," a notion the Dutch overlooked as they subjugated the land for resources (Lansing 2009, 52). The Dutch colonizers misinterpreted the system as "theocracy because of ignorance" and disrupted it; so did the Indonesian government in the name of farming efficiency when instituting the Green Revolution in the 1970s. The enforced use of chemical fertilizers, pesticides, and new cropping patterns through the Green Revolution initially galvanized rice production but quickly proved itself unsustainable (Lansing 2009, 111). In seeing "the proposal to return control of irrigation to water temples as religious conservatism and resistance to change," the government consultants and proponents of the Green Revolution failed to recognize the doubly practical and social value the *Jero Gde* maintains (Lansing 2009, 115); officials failed to acknowledge the interwoven system of agriculture and religion. Disrespecting local knowledge creates patterns of epistemic injustice and denies epistemic status to certain people, which can be read as humiliating, as not offering full membership in the human family, which is also a community of knowers.

The structures of "aid" and "cooperation" can lead to institutionalized humiliation. Cheikh Tidiane Diop has argued that colonialism is a thread that binds past and present together, for all aid happens within the framework of an economic system the foundations of which are not called into question (Diop 2006). Dübgen observes,

The present imbalances are often grounded in previous and more fundamental injustices, inherited from the period of colonialism and slavery.
In addition, the euphemism of "partnership" veils the actual power
divide that inhibits the recognition of "partners" as equal counterparts:
If a program is not accepted, it can easily be enforced by the donor due
to the recipient's fiscal and economic dependence on financial resources.
(Dübgen 2012, 73)

There is a political dimension to humiliation as an instrument of power that
has been used and can be used as a means of control and coercion, especially in
public and staged settings (Frevert 2020). The experience of humiliation is also
powerful in international relations; it can be argued that the humiliation of states
(like the humiliation of Germany after the First World War) erodes the possibility
of stable peace. Joslyn Barnhart claims that states that experience humiliating
events are more likely to engage in international aggression aimed at restoring the
state's image and reputation in the eyes of its citizens and also in the eyes of other
states (Barnhart 2021). NATO's eastern enlargement in 1993–1995 (Radchenko
2020), the US experience of and response to 9/11 (Saurette 2006), and aspects of
China's historical memory (Wang 2012) can be framed in the language of humiliation. Forms of club-based diplomacy that deliberately exclude others and form
internal clubs (like the G7, G8, G20 groups and summits) can be seen as use of
humiliation (Badie 2014). Which countries from the Global South are presented
in these "clubs?"

We can identify many historical events that have been humiliating for groups
and countries of the Global South; enacting human dignity is not ahistorical (as
the reflection on the Universal Declaration of Human Rights, which is a product
of a particularly cruel history of atrocities) but sensitive to the richness and depth
of history and histories. Integral Human Development in this sense also includes
a commitment to historicity and the awareness of the past. That is why there is
also a diachronic perspective to international development. Such a perspective
opens the space for arguments that European countries owe more to African
migrants because of Europe's colonial history and persistent Afrophobia.[15]

Integral Human Development can be presented as an approach that is particularly sensitive to dignity violations and to the ways and forms in which respect
for the dignity of persons, especially the most vulnerable persons, are expressed.
The negative reference points of infantilization, instrumentalization, and humiliation provide minimum standards for dignity cultures. These forms of dignity

---

[15] Nils Muižnieks, "Afrophobia: Europe Should Confront This Legacy of Colonialism
and the Slave Trade," Council of Europe—The Commissioner for Human Rights online, July
25, 2017.

violations are relevant on the microlevel of individuals and projects, the meso-level of programs and policies, and the macrolevel of international relations. On each of these levels, Integral Human Development means (positively) respect and promotion of self-reliance and (negatively) noninfantilization, noninstrumental-ization, nonhumiliation.

Three Areas of Concern

With regard to respect for human dignity and a dignity-sensitive approach to the person, we can identify three areas that are especially important: vulnerable groups and their dignity, vulnerable moments and the human body, institutional settings and individual powerlessness.

Vulnerable groups need higher dignity support structures. People are vulnerable to the extent they cannot protect what is dear to them. Structural arrangements can mitigate, cause, deepen, or consolidate the vulnerability of populations. David Hulme offered a case study from Bangladesh about a two-person household (a mother with health issues and son with a disability) that fell into chronic poverty after the death of the husband/father whose illness had depleted the family resources. Additionally, the relatives of the deceased took away their piece of land, the only asset of the small household. The educational system, the health care system, and also the legal system (loss of land was illegal, but not corrected) had increased the vulnerability levels of the household (Hulme 2003).

Figure 1: Minimally Respecting Human Dignity

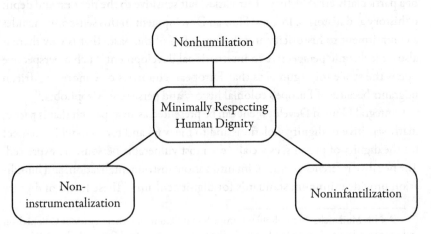

Vulnerable groups (in the Bible, literally and metaphorically listed as "the orphans and the widows") face vulnerability frequently for social reasons. Social pathologies produce "pathogenic vulnerabilities" that could be avoided with different social and legal settings (Mackenzie et al. 2014, 7–9). People are vulnerable for social and structural reasons. Even a natural disaster like an earthquake (or a global challenge like a pandemic) has a social face. Jon Sobrino, for example, has shown that the "natural disaster" of an earthquake in San Salvador was very much a social disaster due to the facts that ambulances could not access the poorer parts of the city and that the dwellings of the poor are much more fragile (Sobrino 2004, 1–11). We learned the same lesson during the COVID-19 pandemic—the virus does not know of borders and social stratification, and does affect the vulnerable populations more deeply.

These structures must reach a formal and official level. In May 2022, for example, the Supreme Court of India issued a much-noted set of directives that acknowledged voluntary sex work as a dignified profession and mandated freedom from violence for the sex workers. The judgment talks about "the constitutional regard for human decency and dignity" and observes that the Court

> extended the meaning of the right to life beyond the protection of limb or faculty to include the right to live with human dignity and all that goes along with it, namely, the bare necessities of life such as adequate nutrition, clothing and shelter and also the right to carry on such functions and activities as constitute the bare minimum expression of the human-self.

It also added,

> Needless to say, this basic protection of human decency and dignity extends to sex workers and their children, who, bearing the brunt of social stigma attached to their work, are removed to the fringes of the society, deprived of their right to live with dignity and opportunities to provide the same to their children.[16]

The Court made use of an important aspect of autonomy (by distinguishing between voluntary and nonconsensual sex work), but the dignity language clearly adds depth to the judgment that a discourse solely based on autonomy could not give. The judgment can be considered a milestone in establishing a culture that respects "each person" in her dignity.[17] The Court's approach reflects an approach

---

[16] Budhadev Karmaskar v. The State of West Bengal, Supreme Court of India, May 19, 2022.

[17] Kavita Chowdhury, "India's Supreme Court Recognizes Sex Work as a Profession," *The Diplomat* online, June 13, 2022.; Outlook Web Desk, "Explained: The

very much in the spirit of Integral Human Development, with its commitment to leave no one behind and unprotected. It is remarkable that the judgment explicitly mentions the children of sex workers and the social stigma that undermines the possibility of a dignified life, that is, a life in accordance with the dignity of the human person. Children are explicitly considered as stakeholders and agents of dignity. This is an encouraging example of a dignity-protected legislative response to vulnerable groups with structural implications.

A second area of concern is the *human body*, especially issues like nakedness, exposure and bodily shame, restraints and restrictions, loss of control over bodily functions, and (the infliction of or management of) pain. As we have seen above, the vulnerability of the human body is dignity relevant. Mistreatment of the body can involve humiliation and reducing of a person to an object. Emma Reyes, whom I had mentioned above, recounts degrading treatment based on a loss of control of a bodily function:

> I wet the bed. . . . I didn't tell anyone, and, and made the bed very quickly so the nun wouldn't see the stains on the sheet, but when I went to the chapel to pray, Sor Teresa saw that my legs were all reddish. . . . Without giving me even a moment to open my mouth, she struck me, punching and slapping me all over. Then she took me by the ear and with giant steps dragged me to the dormitory, where she had me strip the bed. The smell of urine-soaked hay was piercing. Sor Teresa yanked my braids once more and started rubbing my face against the mattress, the same way they did with the cats ... when they peed outside their litter box. When we went back to the chapel the mass had begun, and all the heads turned to watch me. (Reyes 2017, 118)

Emma was treated as if she were an animal, exposed to corporal punishment, and publicly humiliated. This instance evidences how humiliation can engage with the intersection of a material and an immaterial dimension of the person. Corporal punishment that uses the body for the purpose of immaterial humiliation is indeed a dignity violation and not only a concern of the past: A Peace Corps volunteer shares a particular experience: *Once, when my teacher heard that my class had misbehaved, a fellow teacher took the "bad children" into the supply closet and slapped their hands with a ruler. I could hear the slaps across the room and it truly shocked me.* How the body is treated is a window into the dignity culture of an institution.

Supreme Court Order on Sex Work, How It Changes Things, and Laws on Sex Work," *Outlook* online, June 2, 2022.

The management of bodily needs is a good indicator of dignity-respecting cultures. Sanitary facilities are windows into dignity cultures. A young researcher who worked in Haiti collected experiences with sanitation:

> *One woman told a particularly humiliating tale that exemplifies the vulnerability of inadequate sanitation, "I remember I have been to Harbicot (market in neighboring town) and I asked someone to use a toilet. The man took a machete and started to dig a hole in the ground. He told me to go in the hole and that he would walk away and come back when I finished. With no cover, no privacy, they just dig a hole and expect you to go! After you finish, they cover it with soil. He said they do that for everyone. I had no other choice."*

Even though dignity can seem to be a lofty concept, it is inextricably linked to bodily realities and mundane structures like restrooms in public spaces or single occupancy bathrooms in institutions.

The ways in which the needs of menstruating persons are accommodated in an organizational setting is a useful example. In this context, Elizabeth Cooper (2021) talks about menstruation-related dignity violations, such as failure to include menstrual products in emergency-preparedness or response packages; not supplying public school students with free access to quality products; denying free and ready access to such products to people who are incarcerated or detained through our country's immigration policies; imposing state and use taxes on such products as though they are "nonessential" goods; not permitting menstruators to bring their own products into the bar exam. There may be a stigma and an invisibilization attached to menstruation; words and the available language matter.[18] The ability to manage one's periods safely and affordably affect a person's ability to engage fully with the external world. "Period poverty," defined as being unable to afford menstrual products, as well as having inadequate access to toilets, washing receptacles, and hygienic waste management (Cooper 2021, 49–50), is an affront to the idea of a dignified life. It makes sense to call bags with products supporting menstruating persons to maintain proper hygiene "dignity kits."[19]

Connected to this second area of concern is the third one, the issue of the *power disparity between individuals and institutions.* The kind of dignity that is referred to in the Universal Declaration of Human Rights is inherent and equal. It does not come in degrees, and it cannot be lost. The institutional apparatus

[18] Erza Selmani, Becca Reisdorf, Oluwatoyosi Ayodele, Laura Nyiha, and Eunice Kilonzo-Muraya, "Breaking 'Code Red': Why Words Matter When Talking about Menstruation," *Think Global Health* online, December 17, 2021.

[19] GBV Sub-Cluster Turkey (Syria), *Dignity Kits Guidance Notes*, online, 2015.

can offer "dignity encounters" (dignity-promoting experiences) and "dignity events" (opportunities to promote dignity), but it can also further dignity violations. Institutions are dignity challenged in the sense that they create hierarchies in which there exists the persistent temptation to confuse dignity with honor/status/rank (as in the status of "dignitaries"). It is tempting to think of dignity in terms of "the honor of dignitaries." The idea of social honor contrasts dignity and points to a phenomenon that is competitive and unequal, mutable since it can change over time, and extrinsically attributed. Luis Cabrera has pointed to this tension between intrinsic dignity and social status in a reflection on the work of Indian constitutional architect and anti-caste champion B. R. Ambedkar (Cabrera 2021). He asks the excellent question, can a concept, such as dignity, with roots in hierarchy and exclusion, serve as the constitutional basis for advancing egalitarian justice within a democratic political community?

The power of institutions is real in the interactions between institution and individual. An individual can feel helpless vis-à-vis and within an institutional setting, be it a border control structure, a police station, or a mental health facility. A dignity-centered approach can transform institutions. In a hospital setting, for instance, the practice of dignity can be linked to respect for privacy, the appropriate physical environment and infrastructure, and dignity-affirming interactions that make the patient feel valued and in control (Baillie 2009). Entry points for humiliation can increase the likelihood of dignity violations in an institutional setting. This is especially the case for vulnerable groups like people struggling with mental health challenges (Husuma et al. 2019). A case study of clients with multiple problems (such as chronic mental health challenges, substance abuse, poverty, debt, difficulties in sustaining housing or work) accompanied by social workers in the Dutch city of Utrecht, identified different ways in which service users experience their dignity being violated: being seen or treated as an object, an empty space, a child, or even a monster (Schmidt et al. 2020).

A hospital is a context that is particularly sensitive to entry points for humiliation—persons can be reduced to occupational objects; they may find themselves in delicate situations with fragile body conditions and limited control over the body. There are issues with bodily shame, nakedness, standardized clothing (Bergbom et al. 2017), and a loss of control over basic bodily functions; there are issues with privacy and personal control over the environment and interactions; there are challenges with the objectification of persons by reducing a person not only to the role of a patient, but even to the body part(s) under treatment. Patients are at high risk of being humiliated and experiencing shame because of the perception of diseases as defects and the necessary exposure in a medical context (Lazare 1987); there is a risk that societal inequalities and social hierarchies are translated into "microinequities" in a hospital setting that can become normalized and part of the hospital culture (Subramani 2018). This is especially relevant in societies with an understanding of strict hierarchies like a caste system.

These findings are clearly relevant for any organization working with vulnerable populations. A major contributor to disrespectful behavior in a hospital setting is "production pressure," which again points to a culture of nonmoderated efficiency (Leape et al. 2012). Organizational settings can lead to toxic constellations that obstruct a culture of respect. Phenomena like moral stress (being forced to act against one's own beliefs and values), institutional double standards (disconnect between official institutional values and institutional practices), power dynamics, lack of accountability, and distorted value priorities (with efficiency taking precedence over dignity) undermine a dignity culture. Even if there is good will and an intuitive understanding of human dignity, there can be institutional pressures, such as lack of resources and time constraints, that can still create "undignifying institutions" (Seedhouse and Gallagher 2002). From an IHD perspective, the challenge of "compassionate professionalism" (as opposed to "cold professionalism" or "warm dilettantism") also exists; a challenge that can also be identified in the humanitarian or aid sector.

In this chapter, we have identified three special areas of concern from a dignity perspective: vulnerable groups, the human body, and institutional power. The three areas of concerns cannot be neatly separated. Identity checks in France (*controles d'identité*), for instance, can target vulnerable groups (migrants) and subject them to lengthy questioning, bag searches, and intrusive pat-downs. These interactions with the police are experienced as humiliating by minority youth and have a deep negative impact on the relation between young people and the authorities (Sunderland and Ward 2012). Dignity is inviolable, but at the same time fragile. People have needs beyond their bodies. They want to be respected.

2

Dignity Needs and
the Desire for a Full Human Life

The human person does not live by bread alone, even though bread is necessary. The cellist Vedran Smailović became famous for his concerts during the 1,425 days of the siege of Sarajevo, when he played Albinoni's Adagio in G Minor in the ruined square of downtown Sarajevo for twenty-two days. Canadian author Steven Galloway remembered this heroic gift of music in his novel *The Cellist of Sarajevo*. Music is neither necessary nor nourishing in a calorie-sense of the word. But it adds beauty and depth, it offers consolation, it appeals to the soul, it creates community, it is a reminder of a peaceful life. Vedran Smailović reminded his people of the fullness of life beyond bodily needs, even beyond personal safety and public security. The concerts nurtured and stretched the imagination and inspired people and even social change (Thompson and Ibrahimefendic 2017). Atka Reid and Hana Schofield, in their moving book *Goodbye Sarajevo*, mention the Cellist of Sarajevo: "Since the first big massacre at the end of May, when a Serb shell killed twenty-two people queuing for bread, few dared to go out into the streets any more. A brave cellist from the city symphony orchestra played daily in that spot in memory of those who had been killed" (Reid and Schofield 2011, 24). There is no doubt that limited access to basic services is dignity relevant; if a person cannot meet her basic needs, her dignity is not respected (Manomano and Mundau 2017). But if a person is not respected, a basic need is not met.

The idea of Integral Human Development comes with an image of the human person as a multilayered being that cannot be reduced to a "one-dimensional" existence, as Herbert Marcuse described a one-sided and reductionist development (Marcuse 2002). We could add that even a consumer may not necessarily be a one-dimensional materialist but could express social commitments, even love, through purchasing decisions. We do not live one-dimensional existences. There is no "culture-free space" in the human condition. Even basic aspects of human life, such as sanitary facilities, have a critical cultural dimension, for latrine adoption is influenced by cultural conceptualizations of purity, pollution, and space (Juran et al. 2019). The life of the human person shows inner depth as well as external complexity. As we have seen in the introduction, Louis-Joseph Lebret introduced the idea of "dignity needs," a class of personal needs that allow a person to live a dignified life. Attempts to fulfill dignity needs (e.g., spiritual needs, needs for a transcendent connection) do not necessarily mean that a culture of dignity is being built—religious fundamentalism speaks to "the ambivalence of the sacred," as Scott Appleby has powerfully shown (Appleby 2000). Sometimes, in the spirit of fighting for the dignity of the despised, religious leaders can undermine peace and encourage violence (Appleby 1997). There is, as we can see, a structural and political component to dignity needs.

The idea of dignity needs points to a simple and, I suggest, universal aspect of the human condition: people want to feel respected; people want to be affirmed in their dignity and recognized as human beings.

> Consider Dalit women and Dalit feminism in South Asia. Dignity is at the core of their demands for social change. Their primary experience of caste discrimination is one of humiliation. It is not enough to address the demands of these women by addressing practical needs— water, housing and education—though that must be part of it. Programs also need to consider how they are aiding or diminishing Dalit women's possibility for advocacy, for collective action and for gaining respect in their communities.[1]

Dignity needs include *space*—a space to which one can retreat and contemplate, perhaps also a space to entertain friends or to ponder a literary work or other artistic evocations of one's inner life. Virginia Woolf recognizes how having a space that you can shape, where you can invite people in, but also close the door, is a deep expression of personhood in *A Room of One's Own*. There may be cultural nuances to the understanding of space, but the general point transcends specific traditions. The space Woolf talks about is both literal and figurative. In order to be respected and supported in their self-respect, human beings need space to develop. This is not desirable, it is necessary—not a "dignity desire," but a "dignity need."

A dignified life is more than a struggle for survival. Carolina Maria de Jesus, a single mother of three children dwelling in a favela in São Paulo in the 1950s and author of a published journal, describes her life as a constant battle: "Here in

---

[1] Duncan Green, "Why Do We Keep Forgetting about Dignity? 4 Ways to Address Dignity in Development Programs," *From Poverty to Power*, Oxfam online, March 23, 2022.

the favela almost everyone has a difficult fight to live" (de Jesus 2003, 28). "I felt I was as a battlefield where no one was going to get out alive" (de Jesus 2003, 58). "My battle of the day was to fix lunch" (de Jesus 2003, 166). "Hard is the bread that we eat. Hard is the bed on which we sleep. Hard is the life of the favelado" (de Jesus 2003, 33). She talks about her lack of rest ("The poor don't rest nor are they permitted the pleasure of relaxation" [de Jesus 2003, 4]) and deprivation of beauty (de Jesus 2003, 35, 129). Her journal is a vivid testimony of the struggle to meet basic needs, including the need for beauty, space, tranquillity, and peace. In short, she describes poverty as a deprivation of material and immaterial goods.

Dignity needs point both to tangible and intangible infrastructure. Social change is as much about the intangible infrastructure as it is about the tangible infrastructure. Experiments with façade coloring in Tirana, Albania, demonstrated ways the two are intertwined. Edi Rama, mayor of Tirana from 2000 to 2011, created colorful façades in his city as a political intervention, announcing the end of the old oppressive times. A number of Soviet-style buildings were painted in many colors, creating a sense of newness in happy public spaces. Obviously, new colors do not change the infrastructure, but they do change the spirit. The Albanian artist Anri Sala commented:

> Colour has an accelerating impact on the rhythm of breathing. It allows the dusty veil to be lifted and creates a new era for the city. It is a paradox because it is the poorest country in Europe, riddled with problems, and I do not think you can find another one in Europe, even among the richest where they also discussed colour so passionately and collectively. The biggest debate, from my point of view, in cafes and on the street was: What will come along with the colours?[2]

No doubt, "the capital city needed hope and joy.... Colour can help and contribute in the city rehabilitation.... Urban requalification encourages people for a better life, less pollution and social awareness. As such, the colour is more than decoration" (Abazi and Dervishi 2014, 12). Even decoration as such is a reminder that life is more than surviving. Beauty may seem fragile, but it is, at the same time, powerful and a source of resilience because beauty matters.

The Italian architect Raul Pantaleo fights for the ethically justified claim for beauty in emergency settings.[3] In Pantaleo's experience, aesthetic needs are real, and displaced people need beauty, since the absence of beauty can trigger and aggravate psychological pain, which is largely compounded with the already-present

---

[2] Anri Sala, *Dammi i colori* (Film 2003), quoted after: Conte 2016, 248–49.
[3] Raul Pantaleo, "Un'etica che è già estetica," *il manifesto* online, August 27, 2016.

physical and emotional discomfort.[4] Beauty is healing. If a patient in a hospital has a room with a window and can see a tree, this access to natural beauty can reduce medication and days in the hospital when compared to patients facing a brick wall (Ulrich 1984). The experience of Carolina Maria de Jesus further points to the fact that access to beauty (beautiful buildings, beautiful nature sites) is a good that is, as is the case with most goods, not equally distributed.

Beauty and access to beauty matter on so many levels. However, we do not want to deny that there is a politics of beauty and that "selling beauty," as Annie M. Elledge and Caroline Faria argue with regard to certain developments in Uganda, can be (ab)used for nationalistic purposes and a neoliberal agenda (Elledge and Faria 2020). We also do not want to overlook the pressure that beauty ideals can impose on individuals and entire communities, serving as a vehicle of neocolonialism through an imposition of a particular (but globally impactful) ideal of beauty (Mckay et al. 2018; Murray and Price 2011; Kaziga et al. 2021). Even these worrisome aspects show the significance of beauty as a dimension and the power of the discourse on beauty.

Integral Human Development is an approach that honors dignity needs, "needs of the soul." Beauty, space, rest, and tranquillity are examples of deep needs. Access to beauty and creativity is access to a sense of dignity. Arts programs, for example, can contribute in many different ways to international development, for example, through healing and recovery from trauma, deeper empathy, development of cognitive skills, social connections and the sharing of new skills and ideas, inspiration of agency and creativity, promotion of important messages (health, peace), reconnection to traditional culture, and even provision of new economic opportunities (Ware and Dunphy 2020). Music can be a means of advancing social justice, as the example of El Sistema, a music-education program, founded in Venezuela in 1975 by José Antonio Abreu, can show (Strother 2013). The arts can bring communities together for shared experiences, promoting political reflection and dialogue and supporting an increase of capacity for innovation.

A young development worker shares the dance team initiative, Kawpi Pacha, in the province of Pichincha, Ecuador. The dance team was founded by a long-time human rights activist and local youth worker. He sought to provide the people of his town with a "safe-space" to come together and express their creativity, working toward the realization of personal and community identity. After some time, the team was also performing in local festivals or celebration of the town's holidays.

---

[4] Institute of International Humanitarian Affairs, "Beauty: The Forgotten Necessity in Disaster Relief Contexts," *HumanitarianPulse* medium online, July 2, 2019.

The idea was simple. Teach a group of people, of all varieties of ages, body types, knowledge bases, etc. to dance together. He had seen firsthand the positive effects of art on a person's self-esteem, critical thinking and enhanced personal development, as well as the strength of community it had the potential to build. It started slowly, with group practices two times a week in a small room of the local art studio; and encompassed the salsa and bachata, as well as multiple forms of national and indigenous dances.... Practices entailed a sense of discipline and focus in the memory and mastery of dance moves and steps. They also worked on a member's physical health, including cardiovascular and joint/muscle flexibility.... Not only did the small dance community continue to master a new craft, but they gained greater self-understanding and self-confidence. They had somewhere to belong to and this showed in their relationships and in their participation in local activities.

No one will claim that these activities will lead to systemic change and structural adjustments, but, clearly, the arts open the door to many opportunities for showing respect and building self-respect and self-esteem, a sense of belonging, thus strengthening resilience. The arts can also create a "safe space" that does not push people into a certain direction.

In a local example, two professors from the University of Notre Dame offered the "big books" course to residents of the Center for the Homeless in South Bend, Indiana.[5] One of the founders, Professor Stephen Fallon, observed,

> We have a strong belief that humanities are important politically speaking. Not in terms of right or left, but in terms of enfranchising people to join the public conversation.... We believe that students who are empowered by reading classic texts will gain more of a voice and confidence to address issues in the public. We have found that students report growing in self-confidence and in the sense of belonging to a larger intellectual community.[6]

The approach of the course, not wanting to push the students in any political direction, was much appreciated. There was a mutual learning experience involved in that setting. Some of the students' lives resembled the tragedies they were reading, and the professors learned from the life experience of their "not so usual students":

---

[5] Ethan Bronner, "For the Homeless, Rebirth Through Socrates," *Notre Dame News* online, March 6, 1999.

[6] "World Masterpieces Seminar at the South Bend Center for the Homeless," *Humanities for All* online.

The students whom we have at the Homeless Center have all sort of washed up on the shore after a tempestuous period. That has been particularly interesting for texts like the *Odyssey*. . . . There is a strong sense of homelessness and searching in the *Odyssey*. . . . Their experiences are in some ways more easily connectable to the texts than the experiences our traditional undergraduates have had.[7]

Processing one's life experience and reconciling oneself to one's biography is an important aspect of self-respect and, in this sense, dignity.

Integral Human Development is a way to think about the human condition beyond bread alone, an approach "beyond basic needs." The "not for profit dimension" (Nussbaum 2016) of the humanities, of reflexivity and wisdom, can be seen to respond to a dignity need. Henning Mankell's memory book project, inviting women to tell their life stories and share their wisdom, is a response to a deep-seated need (Mankell 2005). The language of dignity needs points to an understanding of the person beyond the physical dimension. Language matters, and careful speech matters in creating a culture of respectful relationships (Kowalski 2022).

Beyond Basic Needs

The human person does not live on bread alone—all the examples mentioned remind us of this simple lesson. We might add that even bread and so-called basic needs are culturally shaped. Shelter, food, and clothing may be basic in the sense that many other aspects of a human life depend on this foundation, but even these fundamental needs are not basic in the sense of "simple." They are culturally sophisticated and call for an integral approach.

Shelter is, by most accounts, a basic need; but, even with a roof over one's head, this basic need is not necessarily met in a way that respects people's dignity. The basic need to "have shelter" can be culturally translated into the dignity of "having a home"; constituting an environment for family living and fulfilling various functions like protection, the forming of emotional and social ties with family members, friends, and neighbors; the expression of cultural traditions and religious preferences; the ability to make choices about space, time, and company; and the establishment and communication of social status. A home contributes to the private order as well as to the effectiveness of a person as a citizen and member of the public. A home fulfills self-expressive functions and can be a space with minimal—or at least reduced—role expectations. A home is

---

[7] "World Masterpieces," *Humanities for All.*

a bridge between the private/personal and the more communal/public. It is also a stage that reflects the drama of the wider social and political life. A home has personal, physical, and social dimensions (Sixsmith 1986). A home is part of a social and cultural context that gives richness and depth to a human life.

When the inhabitants of Poletown, a neighborhood in northeast Detroit, had to move in 1981 because their neighborhood was razed to provide land for the construction of a General Motors plant, they lost much more than shelter. Indeed, they were bought out or relocated and had "a roof over their heads." But, due to the land-clearing, they lost the familiarity of a built environment, a certain microgeographical way of living, with neighbors and routines, including patterns of worship (Wylie 1989). The neighborhood that had to make way for an automobile plant formerly contained 1,500 homes (and about 150 businesses and 16 churches). In Taguig, Metro Manila, the Fort Bonifacio Tenement further illustrates how losing a place can mean losing part of one's life. The seven-story concrete maze of 671 apartments was built in 1963. The building was basically given up after the government condemned it and revoked lease agreements in 2010. The residents, however, refused to move to the government-designated shelter thirty miles outside of the city. They stayed, holding on to the life they built, including an iconic basketball court.[8] The basic need for shelter can be translated into the dignity need for a home.

In the case of temporary shelters after a disaster, for instance, key concerns, such as privacy, quality of sanitation, attention to cultural and religious views, have to be considered. Otherwise, there are grounds to assume that the dignity of persons housed in temporary shelters is not properly upheld (Khaji et al. 2019). The concept of "habitability" is more complex than "having a place to stay." The concept includes the aspect of safety and also the dimensions of sociality, cultural appropriateness, and comfort; in order for a place to be called (even temporarily) "home," there has to be the basic possibility of "inviting people in" and "keeping people out," that is, the ability to control access and a threshold.

In its *Emergency Handbook* the United Nations High Commissioner for Refugees defines emergency shelter as "a habitable covered living space providing a secure and healthy living environment with privacy and dignity." Even here, in the case of emergency housing, the explicit dimension of dignity cannot be separated from the basic need for shelter: the above-mentioned dignity need for space, a room that is owned. An indicator of appropriate shelter is the question whether people can carry out their daily activities with ease and whether people

---

[8] Wayne Drehs, "From an Eviction Notice to a Kobe Bryant Tribute, How the Philippines' Tenement became Hallowed Ground," *ESPN*.com, February 9, 2020.

can function well, given their family constellations, health needs, and cultural traditions. A case study of temporary disaster shelters in Pohang (South Korea) after an earthquake in 2018 has shown that "in personal living spaces, the biggest problem was uniform accommodations without considering the family composition of survivors. Failure to consider sex, disability, number of family members, age, etc., eventually leads to invasion of privacy" (Kim et al. 2021, 13).

Inclusion and participation are particularly important in response to these challenges in the spirit of a dignity-centered approach. Indonesia's Central Sulawesi province was hit by an earthquake in September 2018. Findings from the response to the disaster showed that

> diverse groups should be involved in the entire life cycle of post-disaster recovery—regardless of age, ability, and gender. Addressing inclusion at the outset helps reduce future barriers for vulnerable groups and mitigates social issues. For example, the original design of the housing unit for disaster-affected communities in Central Sulawesi afforded limited privacy. After capacity-building on inclusive design standards, stakeholders modified the design to include an internal partition.[9]

People want to make choices about their spaces since they want to express their preferences and values. People want to live by their own rules; this is why, in many instances, homeless people prefer to stay on the streets rather than move into a shelter.

A shelter is also much more than just an isolated space; it is a place within a legal and cultural space. An investigation by a Haitian NGO has shown how emergency shelters distributed by a British organization in the mountains above Léogâne after the 2010 earthquake in Haiti remained uninhabited six months after they were built.[10] Families preferred to live in tents or makeshift huts and did not move into the eighteen-square-meter, two-room houses, built from plywood on a cement base, with a tin roof. The issue in this case was not so much the design of the tangible infrastructure but the design of the intangible infrastructure; that is, the access and distribution. In order to get a shelter, "a family had to have proof it owned land or had a long-term lease. Over two-thirds of the post-quake refugee families—some 200,000 families—were renters, meaning they were not eligible

---

[9] Muhammad Halik Rizki, Jian Vun, and Andre Bald, "Three Years On: Four Lessons Learned from Post-Disaster Recovery in Central Sulawesi, Indonesia," *World Bank Blogs*, February 18, 2022.

[10] Inter Press Service (IPS), "Shelters Don't Shelter Haiti's Needy," *reliefweb.int*, March 15, 2012.

for the structures."[11] The situation generates the impression that the British organization did not have adequate knowledge of the local context and was ill-advised in some of its choices. The basic need for shelter is embedded in cultural dynamics that shape an understanding of dignified living in a space.

An integral perspective of the person will move "beyond basic needs." This point is not spectacular, but it has implications for the way we look at and think about the needs of people. The same invitation with shelter, connecting a basic need to dignity needs, can be made for food. It is well known that food is surrounded by a myriad of rules and regulations, cultural codes and religious traditions. As much as dignified shelter is so much more than "roofs and walls," dignified food is so much more than "calories and nutrients." Food-supported dignity and dignity-informed food rules are ideas that are also expressed in religious traditions. The recommendation to "eat of all wholesome things which are lawful to you" is a recurring sentence in several Surahs in the Quran (e.g., 2:170, 5:5, 20:81). Food is a blessing to be enjoyed and shared (24:61). The book of Acts in the New Testament contains an important scene of Peter's vision of unclean food being declared clean by God, asking to renegotiate the distinction between "in place" and "out of place" (Acts 10:9–16). Furthermore, food is culturally coded. Attitudes toward food shape eating habits and patterns of food production and consumption. Michiel Korthals recounts an incident from Mali:

> Normally, in times of lesser yields of the national staple crop sorghum, people eat wild plants and certain insects. However, because of the lesser value that nowadays is attached to these plants and insects, and the higher respect that Western foods garner, plus the ease of getting food from international charities, people do not collect these foodstuffs anymore.... The standards that determine which things are perceived to be edible and which are not depend not only on information and knowledge—metaphors play a role as well in differentiating the edible from the not edible. (Korthals 2012, 105)

Bread is more than bread—another reason why the person does not live on bread alone.

The same point can be made with respect to the basic need for clothing—there is a dignity dimension to clothing as well. Kemi, a Nigerian refugee to Britain, was granted refugee status and secured her first job interview:

> Unsurprisingly, she had nothing to wear. Instead of having to scrabble or beg for something appropriate, however, she was referred to a small social enterprise ... which asked her size and what kind of clothes she

---

[11] IPS, "Shelters Don't Shelter Haiti's Needy."

liked. "And they gave me three beautiful shirts. Those clothes were like gold to me.... They asked me what I actually wanted. That makes you feel valued."[12]

Here again, the access to material goods as much as the material good itself reflects dignity relevance. After a clothing donation in the Gorom Refugee Settlement in South Sudan, Becky Alimas Ondoa, a community-based protection associate for UNHCR, observed a similar significance: "Giving them clothes, we have given them dignity.... Dignity is all about feeling on top, that you are in the right place, and you have the right things that you are putting on, and that everyone will look at you and say 'wow.' That is very important."[13] While her statement may be criticized, it does further illustrate the connection between a basic need, cultural codes, and dignity. There are also countless stories of clothing donations going wrong that illustrate these significant connections (Norris 2012).

The way we cover our bodies expresses and confirms a sense of who we are. Clothes express aspects of a person's identity in very peculiar ways. I, for example, like to wear ties. I wear ties out of a certain sense of respect for my work, respect for the students I work with. It is also a habit and a soft "identity marker" in the sense that people know that I am a tie-wearing person. When I buy a tie, the purchasing decision is based on rational and emotional factors connected to who I am or who I think I am or who I would like to be. The ties I buy are simple, without images and messages. This says something about my self-understanding. I see myself as a member of the social group of university teachers and intellectuals. I find it appealing to dress in a way that is appropriate in the context of lectures, seminars, public talks, meetings.

The idea that our purchasing decisions depend on our self-understanding (our identity and our understanding of group membership) has been developed in the approach of "identity economics," first introduced in a seminal paper by George Akerlof and Rachel Kranton (Akerlof and Kranton 2000). Drawing on Gary Becker's and Erving Goffman's works from the 1950s (Becker 1957; Goffman 1959), Akerlof and Kranton take the concept of identity to refer to "a person's sense of self" and establish this "sense of self" as the foundation of economic decisions. Identity is a construction on the basis of social categories whereby each category is associated with social expectations that people seek to meet. "Individuals' behavior depends on who they think they are," they argue (Akerlof and Kranton 2010, 28). People make decisions based on the groups they

---

[12] Esther Addley, "'Those Clothes Were like Gold': Fashion Donors Give Refugees Dignity of Choice," *The Guardian* online, September 14, 2022.

[13] Tim Gaynor and Gift Friday Noah, "Dressing to Impress Gives Lift to Refugees in South Sudan," *UNHCR News* online, May 11, 2022.

think they belong to and that they want to belong to, including the social categories that shape these groups.

Material objects, then, are more than "things." The watch I was given for my Confirmation cannot be valued in tangible cash terms: it is intangibly priceless and invaluable beyond its face "value" or significance as a timepiece. Things have something to say. They have both message and meaning beyond their tangible surface. The material objects we deal with, like shelter, food, and clothing, are partially shaped by a symbolic sphere. An object is so much more than an object. Daniel Miller (2009), studying the objects in many households in a south London street, has shown that (most of) the "things" that can be found in a certain home have a history, a meaning, a status beyond the material value or function. There is "a comfort of things," a consolation they can give. Things can even be seen as "extensions of the self" (Belk 1988), becoming part of the human identities they help create. Recognizing this reality, Integral Human Development warns against a one-dimensional view of living beings and objects alike. An African colleague once stated such a view succinctly: a cow can be a living being to take care of rather than something with a monetary value.

When we see the objects in people's households, we see more than things. Dignity needs point to the need for beauty, and the desire for beauty tells stories about the brokenness of the world and the imagination of a different world. In his Easter Sunday, 1999, "Letter to Artists," Pope John Paul II emphasized the importance of the beautiful:

> In so far as it seeks the beautiful, fruit of an imagination which rises above the everyday, art is by its nature a kind of appeal to the mystery. Even when they explore the darkest depths of the soul or the most unsettling aspects of evil, artists give voice in a way to the universal desire for redemption. (Letter to Artists, 10)

The human imagination shapes the way we "see" things and, in that sense, the very question of what kind of "thing" any material object may be. Visible beauty speaks to an invisible dimension of the human condition.

Interiority and the Imagination

Development is as much about external change as it is about internal resources. The idea that development is to enhance people's freedoms (Sen 1999) can be understood on the visible level of external freedoms (e.g., political freedoms, material freedoms) and on the invisible level of internal freedoms (e.g., freedom of the imagination, the ability to protect an inner space).

The Ukrainian poet and teacher Irina Ratushinskaya survived harsh conditions in a Soviet gulag through the power of poems. She was arrested in 1982, only to be released from the gulag in 1986. She described conditions in the "small zone" of the camp in a moving memoir, *Grey Is the Colour of Hope*. She was committed to (the power of) writing. In November 1983, after seven months in prison, where she was subjected to beatings and solitary confinement under freezing conditions, she wrote a beautiful poem "I Will Live and Survive." The poem is a testimony to the power of beauty and speaks to the ability and effort to find beauty through and in a frost-covered window in prison. She found a source of strength in the imagination and the beauty and power of poetry:

> While imprisoned Ratushinskaya sometimes managed to write down her poems on four-centimeter-wide strips of cigarette paper, which were then tightly rolled into a small tube "less than the thickness of your little finger" ... that were sealed and made moisture-proof by a method of her own devising. These "capsules" were then secreted out of the prison when an opportunity presented itself. She would write poetry in her head while sewing gloves on sewing machines that made a racket like "machine-guns": "After arriving at the final version of five or six lines, I jot them down on a bit of paper which is concealed under a pile of unsewn gloves. When the poem is complete, I commit it to memory and burn the paper." (Dennen 2017, 175)

Sometimes, when she was deprived of paper or other materials, she would scratch her poems on a bar of soap, with a matchstick. She learned the verses by heart and then washed them away. During her four years in confinement, she wrote (and remembered) some 150 poems. She was also asked by fellow prisoners to recite poems; her poetry was in high demand.

Irina Ratushinskaya's poems and the fact that she learned them by heart also point to another important dimension of the human person: interiority. Having an inner life, having inexhaustible depth, is a motif that the Western history of thought has worked with for a long time (Taylor 1989).

Irina Ratushinskaya cultivated her inner life—"as a young person, before her imprisonment, she had loved airplanes and dreamed of flying one.... She continued to fly in her imagination and was able to preserve a sense of inner freedom during her imprisonment" (Dennen 2017, 173). She also believed in the power of prayer as another inner source of inner strength. In deep gratitude and recognition of the significance of shared inner strength, she dedicated her 1987 poem "Believe Me" to all who had taken part in the campaign for her release.

In the spirit of Integral Human Development and the intentional effort to respect "the whole person in all her dimensions," the proper consideration of a person's interiority is crucial. We can see the importance of interiority and the enhancement of freedoms in Francis Bok's above-mentioned account of how he survived ten years as a slave and worked on his flight. Francis Bok explains the role of his inner life in his resistance and resilience. He had discovered a space that was his and his alone: "No one could see what went on inside your head and heart" (Bok 2003, 83). Charged with looking after animals, he had a lot of time to cultivate his inner life:

> I lived much of the day and night in my own head, and it was there in my thoughts—my memories of life with my family, and my dreams of escape—that I discovered freedom. Giemma and his family could beat me; they had total control of what I did every day. But they could not touch my thoughts and dreams. In my mind I was free, and it was there in that freedom that I planned my escape. (Bok 2003, 47f.)

He lived by his dreams, both day dreams ("Escaping was my dream" [Bok 2003, 32]) and night dreams: "I often dreamed of my family: In these dreams, I would wake up in the morning and my mother would be there" (Bok 2003, 52). "I always knew I would escape. That dream was the only thing that made my heart smile. Some days I would treat my loneliness by thinking of a reunion with my family" (Bok 2003, 65). He survived by cultivating his imagination; imagining how Giemma would come looking for him in the morning, and he would be gone. He survived beatings after an attempt to flee because of his dream and his inner freedom: "I had nothing to say to this man who was beating me with a whip. I still had my dream. I knew what I wanted. Giemma had control of me now, but my mind was free" (Bok 2003, 71). Giemma probably underestimated Francis and his rich inner life because he "did not think that I had any mind at all. He treated me as an animal, and animals do not think" (Bok 2003, 83).

The inner life of dreams was not just the vague imagination of how things could and would change. Bok demonstrates that there is disciplined hope in the inner life of dreams. Hope can be defined as the perceived capability to derive pathways to desired goals and motivate oneself via agency thinking to use those pathways (Snyder 2022). Francis Bok followed this pattern by identifying pathways for getting closer to his goal of escaping:

> I was learning the language. That would help me find help among these Arab people. But I also had to learn the area. I decided that each day I went out with the animals I would go a little farther in every direction. I

would look around, investigate the roads, see who lived where, remember where there were men riding on horseback checking on their slaves. To escape I had to know that. And my primary goal in life was to get away from Giemma Abdullah and his family. (Bok 2003, 47)

He made plans and developed a long-term perspective ("My plan was to do the work and be as cooperative as I could be.... I wanted to build on Giemma's trust" [Bok 2003, 65]). He also had a serious prayer life. A rich inner life emerged through his imagination, his memories (particularly lessons from his parents), and his vivifying hope toward freedom. His inner life, dynamic as it was, served as the ultimate source of agency in his response to enslavement.

Hope is an important aspect of development efforts, for, in genuine hope, we can experience the power of the imagination and the importance of a sense of what is possible. Bok's example illustrates the power of cultivating interiority alongside hope and a sense of the future and alternative worlds. In a study on the effects of religious messages of hope in the context of a microfinance project with indigenous women in Oaxaca, one of the poorest states in Mexico, Bruce Wydick, Robert Dowd, and Travis Lybbert have shown that "developing hope and its components represents a fundamental process in the cultivation of human dignity and human flourishing and that this is possible through spiritually based interventions that can accompany other kinds of 'tangible interventions' such as those related to women's empowerment and microfinance" (Wydick et al. 2020, 156). Fazle Hasan Abed, the founder of the world's largest NGO, BRAC in Bangladesh, has recognized the importance of hope and the dramatic effects of hopelessness, as his biographer reconstructs: "It is likely that psychological factors, including a sense of despair rooted in generations of lived experience, will remain an obstacle.... Activating people's confidence and giving them hope can lead to material improvements that cannot otherwise be accounted for" (MacMillan 2022, 11). Recognizing the significance of hope and imagination, development work must cultivate intangible infrastructure just as much as it builds up tangible infrastructure. Hope and the imagination play a major role in improving people's lives. Many a challenge people face can only be solved "by nurturing their ability to imagine a better future, to cast aside fatalism and believe that one's destiny is, at least partially, in one's own hands" (MacMillan 2022, 214). Self-efficacy as a sense of one's agency is the basis of a belief that that the world can be changed, can be changed through one's own decisions (Bandura 1997).

Inner life matters. Having discussed the devastating effects humiliation can have on individuals and groups, we have already recognized the immaterial dimension of the human person; categories like "honor" and "identity" matter.

Reflecting on the role of "honor" as a significant intangible in the lives of people living in poverty, Martin Kämpchen has described how people will protect and defend their honor to the point of throwing their family into debt for a wedding or funeral (Kämpchen 2011). Intangible infrastructure, as Kämpchen's research suggests, like "honor" or "hope," is ultimately ambivalent. Honor can be a source of agency and a motivation to act, but it can also become an obstacle toward flourishing when enacted in particular ways. Hope, likewise, can nourish a rich inner life, but it can also delude someone into thinking that things may one day get better in ways that are inconsistent with reality. In this way, hope is a major factor in contemporary slavery and debt bondage, where labor migrants travel in the hope of securing income opportunities and become prey to usury or abusive labor conditions. They persevere under inhumane conditions in the hope of receiving a full wage one day. Empty promises and unfounded hopes consolidate a person's misery; false hopes are very much part of the drama of labor trafficking and sex trafficking (Kara 2018). This tragic observation, however, strengthens the point that the immaterial dimension of our lives matters.

Issues like reputation and image and identity have significant impacts on the design of social change. Following is an example from West Africa:

> *As the Business Operations Manager, I took the team to implement the first phase of the project that would empower over fifty local farmers in setting up their organic farms. The long-term goal was to develop and train one hundred young farmers. During the project implementation phase, we noticed a large percentage of the farming activities were carried out by farmers aged 50 and above. . . . It was discovered that the majority of the youths were not interested in farming and all things agricultural-related because of the general perception that the profession is crude and farmers are regarded as poor people. This has greatly influenced the production of food in the community, as young people do not want to be associated with the profession.*

Taking "the whole person" seriously means honoring the immaterial dimension of a person's life, her hopes and her imagination, and also her sense of honor and identity. The properly cultivated imagination and *docta spes*, hope based on reasons, emerge as major inner factors of human development. Respecting a person's dignity cannot be done without acknowledging what is dear to the person. This is like an intangible environment the person operates in: "honor as well as dignity can be seen as constituted by a symbolic sphere surrounding a person to which others have to pay attention in their behavior and which can easily be threatened by the actions of others, namely by their symbolic actions"

(Kuch 2011, 50). That is why conflict and peace can be seen in terms of symbols and rituals (Schirch 2005). Both the material and the immaterial dimension matter in respecting a person.

There is also a more fundamental dimension to "the development imagination." If we understand imagination as the sense of what is possible, any intentional social change requires the imagination. John Paul Lederach discusses the moral imagination in peace-building as the ability to embrace inclusive complexity without falling into the trap of simplification (Lederach 2005). Martin Kämpchen, mentioned above, worries about the lack of a sense of possibilities with many poor people he has met in India (Kämpchen 2011); they are caught in a prison of limited and truncated imagination. Writing about debt bondage in the same context of India, Siddarth Kara argues that the lack of a sense of possibilities "burrows into the consciousness of a society and, despite all best intentions, disassociates the equality of being between those with servants and those who serve. This is the exact mind-set that those who exploit servants in debt bondage or slavelike conditions use to justify their treatment" (Kara 2018, 181). The imagination matters because it attends to the presence of possibilities.

Persistent poverty and persistent inequality can also be linked to a deprivation of a sense of possibilities. "Perceiving that inequality is inevitable and cannot be changed leads to psychological reactions ranging from becoming 'resigned,' to justifying existing inequalities as coping mechanisms" (Pellicer et al. 2019, 283). Mohammad Yunus (2007) and Amina Mohammed (2015) have articulated that "it may be a lack of the imagination that does not enable us to conceive of "a world without poverty." Paul Farmer simply observes, "Failures of imagination are the costliest failures" (Farmer 2011). Cultivating the "development imagination," the sense of what is possible (beyond what has been considered possible before), is as much a moral as an educational task in the spirit of integral human development.

3

On Respecting a Person

In a moving scene in the 2004 movie *Sideways*, one of the main characters describes his love for Pinot Noir, emphasizing its delicacy as a grape: it's hard to grow, thin-skinned, it cannot grow anywhere, it cannot thrive when it is neglected, it needs constant care and attention. In fact, it can only grow in specific little corners of the world. "And only the most patient and nurturing of growers can do it." With such patient nurturing, its flavors are "most haunting and brilliant and thrilling and subtle."

Leaving aside the fact that this movie had a positive impact on Pinot Noir sales and a devastating impact on Merlot sales, Paul Giamatti's character Miles offers an interesting message. There is a grape that is hard to grow but will give you amazing results, rewarding the effort. There is so much more to great wine than "grape + climate." You need to find the right soil, look for the appropriate space, offer care and accompaniment, and show patience and attention. Only then, the outcome will be stunning.

Integral Human Development (or IHD) is an approach that articulates the commitment to each person and the whole person. As in the case of Pinot Noir, it may take a lot of intensive accompaniment and effort to see the flourishing of a person. But the results could be amazing. Some persons may be "Cabernet people," growing almost anywhere. Other people are "Pinot Noir" persons, requiring higher levels of care and attention. The thought that so much talent remains unrecognized underscores the importance of the invitation, and challenge, to leave no person behind. For example, the immense talent of Ugandan chess player Phiona Mutesi was discovered by chance when she happened to enter an after-school program in Kampala.[1] The probability for this journey to happen was decidedly low. Realizing that talents that are overlooked or unsupported are not just a loss for the many persons whose talents are unseen, but a loss for all of us, is a motivation to look deeper.

---

[1] Tim Crothers, "Chess Queen of Africa," *The Guardian* online, August 28, 2016.

Enacting human dignity is, in a sense, very simple: seeing the person for who she is. The approach of "dignity therapy," an accompaniment model for terminally ill patients developed by Harvey Chochinov and colleagues, intends to ensure that the uniqueness of the person is properly acknowledged. Dignity therapy invites patients to discuss issues that matter most or that they would most want remembered (Chochinov et al. 2005). This makes it easier for care-giving professionals to "see the person." The category of uniqueness means that each person is "*sui generis*" (forming her own class); each person is beyond comparison—and also beyond measurement. In the study by Mosel and Holloway mentioned in Chapter 1 about the experience and perception of dignity among refugees and internally displaced people, one result is the connection between respect and seeing a person in her uniqueness: "Dignity as respect relates to how people are treated, and specifically whether they perceive themselves as being treated as individual human beings" (Mosel and Holloway 2019, 6).

Each person is so much more than the role she inhabits. A professor is so much more (and so much less) than a professor; take a professor out of the classroom or conference setting, place him next to a flat tire on the road, and you might find a helpless individual; fluent in ancient Greek, but in desperate need of help on the road. An inmate in a correctional facility is much more than "a person serving a term." Respecting a person means more than respecting the role that the person inhabits. The point may seem trivial, but it has many implications.

Respecting a person means recognizing the person as a source of unique demands on me, given their uniqueness as a person. Respecting a person means seeing and confirming the unique space the person inhabits in the world in the deepest sense, appreciating the person's contribution to the world. This may require some deep effort to engage with the person and her context. Let me offer an example from an American volunteer teaching English abroad:

> *Part of the curriculum at junior high school instructed that I conduct individual speaking exams to students. On test day, most students performed well and the exams went smoothly. However, there was one student who didn't speak during his exam. No matter what I said or asked him he provided no response. Taking his attitude as rude and a waste of our time, I gave him a 0% on his speaking exam. . . . Following up from test day, this student's homeroom teacher approached me in the staff room after school. She explained to me that the student was unable to speak and requested that I reconsider the grade I had given him on his test. My reaction was understanding at first, assuming the boy was mute and had some kind of damage to his vocal chords. However, when his homeroom teacher*

explained that his issue wasn't physical but psychological, and that he spoke at home but never at school, I found myself frustrated. How will he ever function in society? Is it fair to the other students in his class who study and perform well on the exam?

In spite of these doubts, the American teacher showed flexibility and empathy and changed his approach:

Prior to the next speaking exam, I asked this student's homeroom teacher if she could inform him in private that I would allow him to take the speaking exam under the same guidelines as other students, except he would be able to give his responses by writing them down. She agreed, and on test day the student sat down for his speaking test with a pen and scratch sheet of paper. I conducted the exam in precisely the same manner as I had with other students, and sure enough, as soon as I asked him a question, he moved his pen with lightning speed and then proceeded to show me the answer on his paper. His answers were correct at a similar level, if not better, than what I would have expected most of his peers to perform at. Following the exam, the student's homeroom teacher approached me again in the staffroom after school, but this time she thanked me for accommodating the boy on his speaking test. After all, the slight alteration of the test was effortless on my part. She also informed me that he seemed happy after class and that he felt encouraged to continue studying English.

The example shows the hard work involved in respecting a person; this will take time, and it will be difficult to scale it up and make respect "more efficient." We could think of structural arrangements that create a respect-conducive environment (e.g., by providing sufficient spatial and temporal resources), but a culture of respect stands and falls with the people involved. Integral human development is a dignity-centered and a person-centered approach. Maybe the basics of this approach are actually quite simple.

The Complexity of Respect and the Simplicity of a Single Imperative

Maybe we overthink the term "Integral Human Development." Maybe respecting a person is quite simple. One simple way of thinking about IHD in these personal terms is the idea of not being an asshole. Aaron James pays attention to that concept and the question of when we are justified in using this word (James 2012, 2016). Assholes can be characterized in three aspects (thoughtlessness, indifference to others' sensitivities, and unawareness to social contexts). Aaron James suggests that an asshole allows himself to enjoy special advantages, does so systematically out of an entrenched sense of entitlement, and is immunized by his sense of entitlement against complaints of other people (James 2012, 5). In other words, assholes do not consider others as morally equal. And you can be quite successful by doing that (Pfeffer 2016), even though it can also be argued that dominant-aggressive behavior may well be positively predicted for those attaining higher power, while less generous behavior undermines a person's influence at the same time (Anderson et al. 2020). Simply, assholes can make a workplace very difficult (Sutton 2007).

I like to translate the lofty concept of IHD into the simple imperative: Don't be an asshole! Or maybe, do not act like an asshole! It may be helpful to distinguish between persons being assholes and persons acting in particular situations in an asshole-like manner.

The encounter with assholes is familiar to many (as may be the experience of having occasionally acted in an asshole-like way). A volunteer talks about one particular encounter with an asshole that had a humiliating aspect:

The green and clean campaign was one of the monthly activities of the team. Each month one part of the city was chosen for cleaning, the aim was to encourage the community to keep their environment clean. In this team most of us were girls. So many times, we were humiliated by men, making fun of us and throwing empty drink bottles in front us, while we were collecting the trash on the street and walking areas. I do remember very well the day I was collecting the trash from a walking area when a young man who was driving an expensive black car threw his energy drink bottle to me, laughing: "collect this one."

Talking about assholes is not an attempt to fish for a punch line. It can be quite demanding to consider others as moral equals.

Treating humans as if they were humans can be a revolutionary idea. Kimberly White's *The Shift* reflects on this new paradigm. More often than not, we treat other people as a means to our ends, as instruments that help us realize our plans. Exceptions to this strategy are eye-opening. White describes a custodian in a nursing home named Jason: "His primary job was running the floor machine. It was run every day in all the hallways and large rooms, and that's what he was paid for; that was his entire shift, all day, every day" (White 2018, 3–4). In the standard narrative of labor, this job does not require special qualifications or skills. White notes, however, that Jason "does more than he's strictly paid for. He knows every single last resident of the facility" (White 2018, 4). Jason explains his particular way of inhabiting the job by pointing to the residents of the nursing home as his family. "Every day," White continues, "Jason can be seen to push wheelchairs to and from dining and activities or carrying blankets to an old lady who caught a chill or filling a water jug for an old man who can't fill it himself. None of these tasks are technically his job, but they are part of the job to him" (White 2018, 4). Jason's approach invites a perspective that allows each person to be a special person, to be "my mother (or son or father or daughter)." This shift allows for a perspective where another person's needs are not less important than my needs.

Respecting a person means that she is seen as a person with an equal right to dignity and rights, ideally with the kind of benevolence that prefers a person's existence to the person's nonexistence. Dignity needs also include social space, a space where a person is known, respected, honored. These aspects of respecting people's dignity is, frankly, a major challenge in academic research. A young researcher told us about intrusive interviews when working with refugees:

> *To evaluate their socioeconomic situation we needed to ask very detailed and personal questions such as how much is their income. What do they eat? How many meals do they eat per day? We had to be very careful in how we asked the question to make sure not to insult them or make them feel that their dignity was stripped from them.*

In research, the temptation to reduce human persons to epistemic objects, that is, to representations of a particular category that serves the goal of a tangible research result is a major challenge to a human-centered and dignity-sensitive approach. The creation of epistemic objects typically happens in laboratories, but it can also move beyond that when reducing unique living beings to data points (Latour and Woolgar 1986; Amann 1994; Knorr Cetina 1999). Epistemic objects are deprived of their uniqueness, for epistemic objects lack agency. Many examples exist of research about children, patients, refugees, and poor people that does not recognize the agency of the persons involved. A young researcher recalls,

> *Participants in research studies can be left vulnerable and humiliated; an example of this would be a research study that I witnessed in Ghana where women were asked personal questions in an open space using an English-speaking researcher without a proper interpreter, or in Syria when the participant's names were added to the research document and not properly protected (later endangering their lives), or in Palestine when refreshments were provided to the researchers but not to the participants who had been waiting for hours. In these instances, the participants became only viewed as a source of answers and data.*

It is tempting to reduce a person to an epistemic object. An IHD-approach, with a commitment to "the whole person," would be sensitive to dynamics that lead to the creation of epistemic objects. Let me offer an example, making an attempt at "an exercise in deconstruction."

An Exercise in Deconstruction

In *Voices of the Poor: Can Anyone Hear Us?* (World Bank report from forty-seven countries in 1999) we read:

> The boy died of measles. We all know he could have been cured at the hospital. But the parents had no money and so the boy died a slow and painful death, not of measles, but out of poverty.—A man from Ghana (Narayan et al. 2000, 36)

We can ask a number of questions: Who is the nameless man? Does he represent Ghana? Did he speak on behalf of the poor? Has this man become an "epistemic object," that is, an element of a research paper where the flesh and blood person has been reduced to a quotation? What was the journey like from the mouth of the man to page 36 of the report? What got lost on the way? Is this what he said? What else did he say? What did he not say, even though he could have said it? And why? Or why not? We could also ask who the interlocutor of this man from Ghana was: The author of the Ghanaian country report? A member of a research team for the country report for Ghana? Would it make a difference to know who the interlocutor was? Was it a dialogue?

Robert Chambers discussed the challenge of this report in 2013 in terms of "the ethics of soundbites:"

> All of us who have been editors are familiar with the power to fashion quotations through deletions so that they support an argument or our own view. With policy influence, there can be ethical dilemmas and choices, with a tension between a more complete and contextual, but longer, quotation and one which is shorter and makes a point more sharply. An example was a quotation from a woman in Ethiopia.... Part of the quotation was: "A better life for me is to be healthy, peaceful and live in love without hunger. Love is more than any-thing. Money has no value in the absence of love". The speech writer for Wolfensohn left out the last two sentences.[2]

---

[2] Robert Chambers, "'Voices of the Poor' and Beyond: Lessons from the Past, Agenda for the Future," lecture (The Hague: International Institute of Social Studies, October 11, 2012), 11.

We can ask, what has been left out of the words of this "man from Ghana?" Tens of thousands of people have been interviewed for this project; relatively few quotes have been selected—on which basis? Here again the question is, what was left out?

The study claims to be participant driven: Was the research agenda, as Stephen Matthews asked, set by the participants? Matthews observed that "the researchers asked people to define our concepts, such as ill and well-being. If the definitions are implicit in the questions, and indeed the approach, then are we merely legitimizing our established understanding?" (Matthews 2002, 201). What does it say about the status of the report?

There is a concern, voiced by John Pender, that the research agenda was not set by the participants:

> Rather, it was predetermined by World Bank staff and the study researchers. For example, the theme of wellbeing was one of four aspects of inquiry. The researchers had previously decided to explore this theme.... Further, the researchers actively intervened in the study process to elicit answers that they regarded as more desirable. For example, while the study claimed to ask the poor, impartially, for their problems and priorities, the study report notes that they "changed the sequencing of methods as needed." Changing the sequencing to first asking about problems rather than priorities, for example, was justified on the ethical grounds of not unreasonably raising the hope of the participants.[3]

Pender also worries about the emotional impact of the research project and its method on the participants:

> The most damning indictment of this study, however, relates to its proposal to reconceptualise development on the basis of the "authenticity" of the voices of the poor. The study report notes the "emotional stress, grief and despair that was sometimes unleashed among participants" as they were encouraged to relive painful memories of living in poverty.[4]

A report on "the poor" inevitably works with broad and homogenizing categories. The Acknowledgements of the Report contains the line: "This review would not have been possible without the openness of the poor, whose voices we have tried to convey." This man's voice is framed as a "voice of the poor." Does this man see himself as "poor?" What is his understanding of "being poor?" Would he like

---

[3] John Pender, "Voices of the Poor—Who's Talking?" *Spiked* online, May 4, 2001.
[4] Pender, "Voices."

to be categorized as "poor?" Is Simon Maxwell right when he comments "that all this talk of 'the poor' makes it look like poor people always agree and have the same priorities"?[5]

The "Consultations with the Poor" (Narayan et al. 2000) claims the authenticity of the voices of the people involved in it, who come to be cast as "the true poverty experts." "But a number of questions rise about the ways in which the perspectives of those involved in this exercise on their own circumstances and their identification as 'the poor' were framed by the way in which the exercise was designed, conducted and distilled" (Cornwall and Fujita 2012, 1752).[6]

What should we make of the remarks of Anne Rademacher, a team member of the *Can Anyone Hear Us?* exercise, when she says that "the book tells us more about struggles within the Bank as an institution than it does about what those at the margins have to say about poverty"?[7] In a footnote to their article "Retelling Worlds of Poverty," Anne Rademacher and her coauthor Raj Patel mention that "the press release accompanying the launch of *Can Anyone Hear Us?* claimed that 60,000 poor people had been consulted. In a different press release, the number was a more modest 40,000" (Rademacher and Patel 2002). Does it matter? What difference does it make? How much can the art of slow listening be practiced with tens of thousands of people? Robert Chambers, who was involved in the research, admitted, "I became aware of the extent to which time pressure made it harder to be open to new categories or framings."[8] Chambers also asked the following questions: "Isn't listening to, and repeating, voices just legitimising and not changing? Could one consider the voices as disembodied—as purely cosmetic to make the World Bank look good?"[9] Is Chambers right when he asks,

Could the deprivations of poverty and powerlessness confront the responsibilities of wealth and power? Dare we hope for a new self-critical awareness and a redefinition of the goal of development as responsible well-being for and by all, stressing the well-being of the poor and weak, and the responsibilities of the rich and strong? Could we … follow "Voices of the Poor" with "Choices for the Rich?" (Chambers 2001, 306)

---

[5] Robert Chambers, "Were the 'Voices of the Poor' Really Heard?" *ODI* online, November 29, 2000.

[6] See also Andrea Cornwall and Mamoru Fujita, "The Politics of Representing 'The Poor.'" In J. Moncrieffe and R. Eyben, eds., *The Power of Labelling: How People Are Categorized and Why It Matters* (New York: Routledge 2007).

[7] Critical Voices on the World Bank and IMF, "Voices of the Poor Study Oversold by Bank," *Bretton Woods Project* online, April 15, 2000.

[8] Chambers, "'Voices of the Poor' and Beyond," 11.

[9] Chambers, "Were the 'Voices of the Poor' Really Heard?"

A dignity-centered approach to data gathering and data processing will, of course, not be opposed to the generation of big data. It will, however, be sensitive to a dynamic of data processes and their interpretation that would be oblivious to the fact that they refer to human beings. Acknowledging the uniqueness and the epistemic authority of a person has to do with humanizing the other. The "perceptual shifts ... that occur when one becomes interested in another's distinct subjective perspective are central to rehumanization (Halpern and Weinstein 2004, 565)." It is dehumanizing to deny the uniqueness claim of a person; and even global poverty studies must not forget or downplay the fact that (1) each person is unique and (2) a poor person is primarily a person and not primarily "poor."

4

Learning from the Unique: Microtheories

Global scale perspectives, including macroframeworks and big numbers, are indispensable tools for analysis and policy planning. Big data are necessary for macropolicy decisions and poverty monitoring, making frequent and accurate poverty measurements key to any undertaking. Big data provide raw data to monitor Sustainable Development Goals; they affect policies and policy outcomes. They allow comparisons (both synchronic and diachronic) and lay the foundation for overviews. Global phenomena require global data on the respective macrolevel in order to inform and justify policy responses. Macroconsiderations, however, run particular epistemological risks.

Big data have to begin with questions, and these questions have to have a clearly justifiable origin and foundation (Coppola et al. 2014). There are issues of access and ownership that must be considered. Furthermore, the need exists for a robust and stable infrastructure in generating and managing big data. Additionally, a healthy intellectual community is challenged "to develop knowledge infrastructures that serve the diversity of ideas, questions, methods, and resources that each contributes to scholarship. Across the spectrum, scholars agree that the enthusiasm for big data puts smaller scale scholarship at risk" (Borgman 2015, 15).[1] Consequently, David Hulme has argued for the place of a microperspective in the world of megadata (Hulme 2003). In a longitudinal in-depth study of one particular household in Bangladesh, he offered an analysis of the factors contributing to the chronic poverty situation of mother and son (Hulme 2003; Hulme and Moore 2010). This approach does justice to the uniqueness of a setting and allows for both a long timeline and depth. Finally, such an approach allows for the identification of structural factors and contextual issues that transcend the particular case.

---

[1] See also Berlekamp (2012); Gamazon (2012); Siminovitch (2012).

The Idea of Constructing Microtheories

I call an approach that offers an in-depth analysis of a particular dynamic a microtheory. Microtheories open the space for an encounter with a reality. In Pope Francis's words, "True wisdom demands an encounter with reality" (*Fratelli Tutti* 47). The category of "encounter" plays a major role in the pontificate of Pope Francis, who invites us to invest in "the growth of a peaceful and multi-faceted culture of encounter" (*Evangelii Gaudium* 188). An encounter respects the uniqueness and even mystery of the other. Microtheories are special ways of encountering reality. They will nourish and stretch the imagination.

A microtheory is an *interest-guided systematic analysis of a thick descrip-tion of a person's life and her experiential horizon.* The idea of thick descriptions was introduced by British philosopher Gilbert Ryle, who described a situation where only a thick description would render a proper account of what was going on; a description considering details and background information and a "depth grammar" not available to an external observer or an outsider (Ryle 1971, 480–96). The term was appropriated for ethnographic and anthropolog-ical purposes by Clifford Geertz, who described the anthropologist's stance as approaching

> more abstract analyses from the direction of exceedingly extended acquaintances with extremely small matters. He confronts the same grand realities that others—historians, economists, political scientists, sociologists—confront in more fateful settings: Power, Change, Faith, Oppression, Work, Passion, Authority, Beauty, Violence, Love, Pres-tige; but he confronts them in contexts obscure enough—places like Marmusha and lives like Cohen's—to take the capital letters off them. These all-too-human constancies, "those big words that make us all afraid," take a homely form in such homely contexts. But that is exactly the advantage. (Geertz 1993, 21)

Thick descriptions require "knowledge by acquaintance" and a substantial and significant immersion experience. They offer colorful and fresh accounts of social situations, providing a sense of the plasticity of the social.

Microtheories work with rich and detailed examples. Examples serve different purposes. Ludwig Wittgenstein saw the role of examples in their demonstrative value, for they "show" something (Wittgenstein 2007, 373). Examples work in areas where general rules are not available, and they enable us to learn a language, a learning process that is based on exercise and examples. Aristotle discussed the capacity of the tragedy to "show" something—possible if the characters in a tragedy are exemplary people living exemplary lives,[2] lives that stand for something that transcends that individual's life and takes on features that can be used to say something about life as such. There is a universal dimension at work here; because of the particularity of characters in a tragedy, tragedies are able to evoke emotions.[3] Here again, we could confirm that examples "show" something and that this showing calls for a specific response on the part of the audience. Examples do specific work—they express an application of a theory or concept that cannot be expressed with this theory or this concept alone.

Microtheories work with thick examples and "show" the insights of a discourse that a theory or a macrostudy could not render. From the perspective of ethics, microtheories, with their forms of "thick" and "small" knowledge, could be seen as providing a counterbalance to the large discourse on global justice (Schweiger 2016). They complement the macrolevel. One could also say that microtheories complement the analytical process in a similar way that Pascal's thinking style complements a Cartesian thinking style: whereas Descartes pursued (in his *Discours de la méthode*) an analytical approach, Pascal cultivated (in his *Pensées*) a "politeness in thinking" that would not directly approach an issue with analytical means but would approach it from different perspectives, slowly and tactfully. Policy decisions may require both—Cartesian analysis and Pascalian politeness, macrodata and microtheories.

Obviously, microtheories slow down the thinking and research process and provide an exercise in slow thinking. "I think it takes time—it took me time—to realise just how very different people are from each other," comments Stephen Grosz after twenty-five years of practicing as a therapist (Grosz 2013, 2). "Seeing a person" takes time. Time is one of the major demands of integral human development. The added value is a dignity-centered way of showing respect for the person in her uniqueness and "depth," that is, a sense of details that would remind the attentive observer or listener of the irreducible complexity and diversity of social situations and the many factors that can become relevant in policy decisions. Microtheories help to identify good and disturbing practices; they do *not* produce anecdotal knowledge—this is evidenced by the epistemological status "If X worked in situation S, it is not possible to say: 'X never works.'"

There is a hermeneutical circle at work that is useful for the translation from microtheories into macromeasures. Microtheories start with a preknowledge

---

[2] Aristotle, *Poetics* 1448a2, 1454a17.
[3] Aristotle, *Poetics* 1453b11; cf. Aristotle, *Politics* 1342a6ff.

that provides perceptual and analytical categories with which a text or situation can be approached in depth, elaborating these categories and changing the semantic thickness of the concepts used while enabling the identification of different key concepts and key questions. In other words, microtheories are developed against the background of salient aspects. Salient aspects are perspective-defining aspects that emerge in a particular discourse. This discourse is enriched, deepened, and slowed down by microtheories that will make it more difficult to make generalizing and sweeping statements. Microtheories offer deep insights into narrow contexts. The result, then, can be used to inform macropolicies that, in turn, can help to identify starting points and framing conditions for microtheories.

Constructing microtheories can be compared to the project of constructing contextual and local theologies, making use of locally available concepts and considering the context while, at the same time, putting more universal and more global categories to use.[4] Similarly, the project of exploring local economic practices can be seen in the light of this dialectic between the macrolevel and the microlevel (Gibson-Graham 2014). Microtheories, presented here as complementary to macropolicy considerations based on a concept of reflective equilibrium, will follow a more "personalist approach" in global ethics. If the limits of microtheories are properly respected, this approach has the double advantage of (1) expressing respect for the person and the local in a particular way and (2) identifying less obvious and more implicit factors of social situations that are relevant for structural and policy issues.

"Poverty-Eradicating Innovation": A Microtheory

Microtheories are developed against a background of salient aspects, those perspective-defining features that emerge in a particular discourse that I discussed above. Child poverty discourse has suggested a particular emphasis on factors of "keeping in" and "leading out of" poverty (Schweiger and Graf 2015). Here, I put forward a microtheory following an analysis that identifies (1) child poverty-causing and child poverty-consolidating factors, (2) child poverty-alleviating factors, and (3) child poverty-eradicating factors. The first aspect is built along the question what causes child poverty? What are the factors that make child poverty persist? What are the obstacles standing in the way of alleviating and eradicating child poverty? There is not only the need to ask "Why are people poor?" but also to pose the questions "Why does poverty persist?" and "Why do

---

4   See Bevans (2002).

people remain poor?" The second aspect is concerned with factors that make the poverty situation less unbearable, factors that ease the strain and take off some of the pressures without overcoming the actual condition of poverty per se. The third aspect explores those factors playing a decisive role in lifting people out of poverty, in breaking cycles and persistent patterns of poverty.

A microtheory requires an appropriate and valid source that unfolds a relevant experiential horizon with honesty and in some depth. In exploring aspects of child poverty through a microtheory, I will make use of the autobiography of William Kamkwamba. Kamkwamba, born in 1987, is an internationally known Malawian inventor who works now as a consultant for human-centered innovations. Even though he had to drop out of secondary school for economic reasons, he managed to build his own windmill to produce electricity in his village. In 2007, Sarah Childress published a *Wall Street Journal* article about "a young tinkerer who built a windmill." This was an important step in discovering the importance of William Kamkwamba for the development discourse. The most important source to understand his childhood and youth is William's autobiography, published with Bryan Mealer under the title *The Boy Who Harnessed the Wind* (Kamkwamba and Mealer 2010). I will use the abbreviation "WK" for this book. I explore the autobiographical account using the above-mentioned lenses of poverty-consolidating, poverty-alleviating, and poverty-eradicating factors. A close and careful reading of William Kamkwamba's text reveals the following ("thick") factors contributing to William's poverty situation.

Poverty-consolidating factors in his case were many. First, *poor governance*, in what could be called "blind politics," combined with "empty promises" and "position politics" was significant. "Blind politics" was succinctly summarized by William's father, commenting on an interview in which the president of Malawi had denied any hunger-related deaths at the height of the famine: "'Some men are blind,' my father replied. 'But this one just chooses not to see'" (WK 139). A particular lifestyle can lead to a particular way of perception within a "bubble of self-deception" (Arbinger Institute 2010). Politics without "feet on the ground" will suffer a similar fate as was experienced by William on the occasion of a presidential visit in the midst of the food crisis:

> The day of the rally, several thousand people stood in the sun, hoping to hear what the president had to say about the crisis. But instead of answers, they got dancing and speeches that dragged on for hours, speeches about how the president was a great and powerful man, and how he was kind enough to approve new development in the area, such as building new toilets in some villages and digging a few wells. (WK 95–96)

A local authority who humbly challenged the president was beaten up. "Empty promises" as a second element of poor governance were made by the president, who promised to assist the farmers at the beginning of the food crisis and did not fulfill the promise with action on the ground (WK 77). "Position politics," a third indication of poor governance, consists of politics dedicated to generating and administering material and immaterial position goods, such as visible signs of prestige or reputation management, leading to distorted decision-making processes and poor decisions about priorities. When Muluzi became president, he "wanted to be different from Banda in every possible way, and this included stopping all subsidies and making the farmers fend for themselves" (WK 55). The market drove the prices down, and the small farmers were priced out. A fourth factor in the poverty-consolidating force of poor governance is corruption. William Kamkwamba describes a number of entry points for corruption and experiences of corruption, including loans with 300 percent interest rates during the times of hunger (WK 124). According to William's analysis, corruption was one of the reasons for the food crisis in Malawi.

> A few months before, President Muluzi's people had sold all our surplus grain for profit. Much of it had gone by lorry over the border to Kenya. In addition, millions of kwacha were missing, and no one in the government was taking responsibility.... Much of the good maize was sold to prominent traders with government connections—men who'd foreseen the food shortage and wanted to take advantage of this dire situation. (WK 87)

Entry points for corruption can also be identified in bureaucratic practices like a list of names of those farmers who would be supported by the government ("A government list then appeared in the trading center of those who'd receive packs. My father's name was missing, along that with many others" [WK 77]). William experienced corruption firsthand when he was cheated selling maize in a government center: "The worker who measured my maize then cheated me. He filled my pail very quickly then tossed it onto the scale, causing the needle to bounce wildly from one end to the next. But before it could settle, he whipped it off and emptied it into my sack" (WK 110). Poor governance is the opposite of pro-poor governance.

A second poverty-consolidating factor to be identified is *destructive customs*, that is, customs that erode personal and communal well-being and advancement. William's economically deprived childhood can be traced back to a destructive tradition: After his wealthy uncle, John, on whose property William's family had worked, died, custom required the oldest son to take over. William's father gave the estate to his nephew, Jeremiah, who showed no interest in the work. "As soon as Jeremiah took control, he spent most of the season's profit in the bars of Lilongwe and Kasungu" (WK 53). Within a few months, the inheritance had been wasted away, all assets lost. Another destructive custom in William's childhood was faith in magical beliefs and practices, including the dangerous and exploitative practices of wizards "curing" people's health problems (WK 244–45) and beliefs that attached a stigma to HIV/AIDS.[5] "There was such a stigma attached to AIDS," he wrote, "that most people who suffered from it didn't seek any medical help beyond what they could get from the *sing'anga*" (WK 245). William himself was considered a "madman" and "crazy" for trying to create electricity on the basis of physics (WK 189–90). He lacked both institutional and personal support with few exceptions (his friend Gilbert and his father who supported his self-study). Furthermore, once he had successfully constructed a working windmill, people did not cease to be suspicious. During a weeks-long dry period, rain clouds began to gather, but no rain fell. Instead, a strong wind began to blow, dispersing the clouds. The windmill, logically, worked visibly hard because of the wind, and a crowd that had gathered suspected the windmill to have blown the rain clouds away. The situation became dangerous. William writes, "I became very afraid these people would collect a mob and tear down my windmill, or worse" (WK 243). Changing people's belief is a long-term and far-reaching project.

Third, poverty in William's life was consolidated because of *humiliation* rooted in powerlessness and resulting in a lack of self-esteem. His father was humiliated when he could not pay the school fees William had asked him for: "My father looked down at the dirt the same way he'd looked at those sacks of grain in the storage room—as if waiting for it to tell him something. He then gave me the look I'd grown to fear ... 'You know our problems here, son,' he said. 'We have nothing'" (WK 132). Sitting in the school without having paid the fees was humiliating for William. "Once in class, I sat in the back corner of the room with my head down. I was so scared of getting caught, I never asked questions for fear of looking suspicious" (WK 180). He returned to school after having to drop out for financial reasons, only to find out that he would have to pay the fee for the entire year and not just the term. His father unsuccessfully pleaded with the headmaster. In a crucial memory for William, he writes of his father's return.

---

[5] "Others visited magic men who recognized the HIV symptoms right away, but still told the patient, 'You're right, brother, you've been bewitched. Luckily, I have just the thing'" (WK 244).

I was sitting on a chair in the yard when my father returned with this bad news. His eyes were pale and troubled, as if he'd wrestled with a ghost.... He kneeled down to face me. "Please understand me, son. *Pepani, kwambiri.* Your father tried...." My education meant everything to my father. That night he told my mother he'd failed his only son. "Today," he said, "I'm a failure to my whole family." (WK 182–83)

His father, who had been a proud man in his youth, was a prisoner of poverty for many reasons and suffered immensely under repeated humiliations. William described his father's life in terms of humiliation and hopelessness, writing, "Thin and dirty, with hands as rough as animal hides and feet that knew no shoes" (WK 183). If William had been forced to live his father's life, "my life would never be determined by me, but by rain and the price of fertilizer and seeds.... Most of the time, I knew, there would be hardly enough to simply survive" (WK 183). The lack of choices, options, and freedoms is humiliating. It was humiliating for William to see his father sell their goats in the period of hunger, to be called a madman by the other villagers, to be kicked out of school because he could not afford to pay the fees. It was humiliating for the entire family to have to cut back to one meal per day and maybe even more humiliating to have to eat this one meal in the same room thus breaking with a deep-rooted element of their culture. "My father gathered us all in the living room," making it the first time we'd ever eaten together as a family.... In our Chewa culture—at least in the village—the daughter *never* eats with the father, and the son *never* eats with the mother. It's not considered polite" (WK 99).

We have seen before that entry points for humiliation are important windows into social structures. A humiliating experience can change a person's self-perception and perception of the social world; it can erode a person's sources of self-esteem; it can even contribute to a person's decision join a terrorist group.[6] William's self-esteem declined further as he witnessed his parents' suffering after his uncle's death. "It was the first time I'd ever seen my parents suffer, and the sight of it frightened me" (WK 50).

A fourth factor contributing to William's experience of poverty as a child was *asset vulnerability*, usually caused by the lack of food security and the dependence on nature, especially rains. "I saw my father rounding up our goats to sell in the market. Like many people in Malawi, our livestock were our only wealth and stature on this earth, and now we were selling it for a few pails of maize" (WK

---

[6] The latter is seen in the example of Eamon Collins, who engaged in terrorist activities in Northern Ireland after he had seen how his father was humiliated by British police officers. Eamon Collins and Mick McGovern, *Killing Rage* (London: Granta Books, 1997).

90). This was an unwise action—but in the absence of options, poor choices are the only ones available. William's family could not protect their assets; it was similarly foolish and even short-sighted to exhaust all financial assets by using up the family savings: "My father managed to withdraw our family's entire savings—about a thousand kwacha—and used it to buy another pail of maize, which he milled and sold the next day. We'd eat another week" (WK 127). But again, this action only allowed the family to survive a further week. William saw the extent of asset vulnerability firsthand when he observed how people sold their dishes, their roofs, their grains, even their children[7] during the famine months. He also saw how people resorted to eating seeds in exasperation:

> Others resorted to eating the seeds from government starter packs, scrubbing off the pink and green insecticide that kept off the weevils. But it was impossible to get all the poison off, and many suffered from vomiting and diarrhea, which only made them weaker. Plus, having now eaten their seeds, they had nothing left to plant. (WK 135)

Again, an unwise decision but one born of despair, without the freedom to choose. Asset vulnerability comes to light in connection with deforestation, as was the case here, too, and identified by William Kamkwamba as a poverty-consolidating factor:

> Few people realize this, but cutting down the trees is one of the things that keeps us Malawians poor. Without the trees, the rains turn to floods and wash away the soil and its minerals. The soil—along with loads of garbage—runs into the Shire River, clogging up the dams with silt and trash and shutting down the turbine. Then the power plant has to stop all operations and dredge the river, which in turn causes power cuts. And because this process is so expensive, the power company has to charge extra for electricity, making it even more difficult to afford. So with no crops to sell because of drought and floods, and with no electricity because of clogged rivers and high prices, many people feed their families by cutting down trees for firewood or selling it as charcoal. It's like that. (WK 82)

In summary, assets like land, seeds, capital, forests, and livestock are threatened by fragile socioeconomic conditions and cannot be used to build up and sustain an existence. There is no sense of advancement or "life-building." Food insecurity takes control over asset allocation.

---

[7] "A man in the trading center was caught trying to sell his two young daughters.... People were becoming desperate" (WK 113).

A fifth factor consolidating William's child poverty was *lack of access to infrastructure*, including no access to proper sanitation facilities (WK 149) or free secondary school education. In addition to not being able to afford the school fees, having to buy a school uniform and exercise books would have been an additional burden. Furthermore, he was not fully able to "access" the school, even though he was physically present. He was unable to concentrate because he was starving:

> Despite what I'd imagined earlier, the hunger was just as painful in class as it was in the fields. Actually, it was worse. Sitting there, my stomach screamed and threatened, twisted in knots, and gave my brain no peace at all.... During the first week of school, enthusiasm among my fellow classmates had been high, but only two weeks later, the hunger had whittled away at all of us. A gradual silence soon fell over the entire school.... Most just wanted to go home to look for food. (WK 131)

Yes, there was a physical school (albeit without desks or any helpful equipment) and yes, he did finally manage to get there and be physically present, but he was mentally absent because the sheer agony of being hungry was so great as to rob him of any interest and energy to focus. It is not enough to provide an infrastructure. One must also provide "access." It is not enough to provide physical access. One must provide "integral access," that is, access for the whole person to be present as a person. Otherwise, the access is "ambiguous."

Lack of access to infrastructure becomes visible in the lack of access to electricity, an experience of deprivation that shaped William's life in remarkable ways. A lack of electricity has many poverty-consolidating implications.

> Only 2 percent of Malawians have electricity.... Having no electricity means no lights, which meant I could never do anything at night, such as study or finish radio repairs.... Once the sun goes down, and there's no moon, everyone stops what they're doing, brushes their teeth, and just goes to sleep ... seven in the evening! (WK 81)

An absence of electricity means the absence of the possibility to read when the sun goes down, less study time, less social time, less business time. It consolidates poverty. Poor governance (blind politics, empty promises, position politics, and corruption), destructive customs and beliefs, humiliation, asset vulnerability, and lack of nonambiguous access to infrastructure were key poverty-consolidating factors in William Kamkwamba's childhood.

Poverty-alleviating factors in William's childhood included local appropriating skills, local social capital, his father's entrepreneurial spirit, and spiritual resources. *Local appropriating skills* are the skills needed to appropriate the local context, for example, hunting. "My family never had much money, and trapping birds was often our only way of getting meat, which we considered a luxury" (WK 58). William was taught how to set traps and catch birds by his peers: "Hunting with my cousins had taught me the ways of the land" (WK 59). During the famine, in early 2001, people had to develop survival strategies such as selling the husks from the maize kernel normally used to feed animals or eating plants (WK 88). His mother taught them to "stretch" the food they were given during the famine with water. These are locally specific resilience and alleviation techniques.

A second poverty-alleviating factor in William's life was his *local social capital.* William's relationships with his peers and extended family were vital. He spent time with his cousins and friends, learning from them, playing with them, easing his experience of poverty and opening useful networks for resources. He learned how to play "bawo," a game requiring strategy and quick thinking, and chess (WK 66). He started his first business on the basis of these contacts, which provided him with a business partner (his cousin) and suppliers (his relatives).

A third poverty-alleviating factor was his father's *entrepreneurial spirit.* His ingenuity and willingness to take risks saved the family from starving. William recalls a particular instance, when his "father announced a brilliant plan—a gamble, a roll of the bones even riskier than magic.... 'We're selling all our food,' he said" (WK 102). His father's plan was to process food, sell it, make a profit, buy food, process it, eat some, sell some, and make a profit. The plan worked, easing the impacts of the most severe and most extreme poverty. It was not an escape route or road out of poverty, but it was a way to alleviate poverty-induced pressures. His father's strategies for his family to organize food distribution patterns during the famine and his sense of priorities in a time of crisis helped the family survive.

A fourth poverty-alleviating factor in William's life were *spiritual resources.* Faith and religion did not lift the family out of poverty, but religion did provide a source of hope ("Hopefully God has a plan for us" [WK 134]) and an additional "measure" to alleviate the pain of the situation such as his sister's suffering due to the food shortage ("'Pray for your sister,' my mother said. 'She's very sick'" [WK 153]). His mother tried to console her children with her faith ("'We can only trust in God,' my mother said" [WK 87]), and she also encouraged them—a source of "epistemic resilience"—to think about positive things to distract themselves from the pain of hunger (WK 152).

We can also identify *poverty-eradicating factors,* factors lifting William out of poverty. William had a *sense of possibilities* ("Whereas most people saw garbage in

those [cigarette] cartons, we saw treasure and possibility" [WK 19]). He had the
gift to see the potential of objects. William learned to "see" in a particular way,
interpreting his environment in terms of opportunities. His trips to the scrapyard
were educational and profitable: "It was an environment where I learned something each day. I'd see strange and foreign materials and try to imagine their use"
(WK 187). His encounter with a bicycle dynamo sparked possibilities, giving
him "a small taste of electricity," he wrote (WK 81). Seeing the dynamo made
him think about electricity and radio sets and how the one might enable him
to listen to the other. "That made me want to figure out how to create my own"
(WK 81). Looking at reality in terms of possibilities is a gift, a skill that can be
learned in an appropriate environment. William happened to read about a windmill in a book and was inspired and encouraged to believe in the possibility of
building one himself. "I knew if windmills existed on the cover of that book, it
meant another person had built them. After looking at it that way, I felt confident
I could build one, too" (WK 169).

Secondly, there were *sources of education* that, at least in William's case,
turned out to be the key to his poverty-overcoming knowledge. Games he played
with his friends helped to exercise and develop his mind, and books became his
main source of knowledge.

> I remembered that the previous year a group called the Malawi Teacher
> Training Activity had opened a small library in Wimbe Primary School
> that was stocked with books donated by the American government.
> Perhaps reading could keep my brain from getting soft while being a
> dropout.... For the next three weeks, I began a rigorous course in inde-
> pendent study, visiting the library in the mornings, and spending the
> afternoons reading in the shade. (WK 161)

William overcame an obstacle that is a reality for millions of children in developing countries: to study and read, one must often do so in a foreign language.[8]
William made good use of books on physics and energy, crediting the library as
the source of his idea for a windmill (WK 172).

A third poverty-eradicating factor was William's remarkably *inquisitive
mind*. Driven by curiosity and a desire to make connections, William recognized
that he had "become very interested in how things worked, yet never thought
of this as science. In addition to radios, I'd also become fascinated by how cars

---

[8] "Reading on my own was often difficult. For one, my English was very poor, and
sounding out words took a lot of time and energy" (WK 162); he also would have needed a
mentor: "Plus, some of the material was confusing, and it would've helped to have a teacher to
explain things" (WK 162).

worked, especially how petrol operated an engine.... I stopped the truckers in the trading center and asked them, 'What makes this truck move? How does your engine work?' But no one could tell me" (WK 71). Though William lacked a proper mentor and his hope to find proper opportunities in secondary school were frustrated because of the poverty-consolidating lack of access to infrastructure, his inquisitive mind encouraged his pursuit of answers and deeper questions.

A fourth poverty-eradicating factor in William's life was the fact that he had *access to investment,* especially to an "investor" providing risk capital. His friend Gilbert acted as an investor.

> Gilbert's father had given away all their food during the famine, and he wasn't farming as much because of his health. I was pretty sure their money was low. Still, Gilbert had bought my nuts and bolts for the rotor, and he now reached into his pocket and pulled out two hundred more kwacha—two red paper notes—and handed them to the man. After some messing around to get the dynamo and bulb off the bike, I was holding them in my hand. (WK 193)

William's father invested in another way, giving him the time to study, experiment, and work on his electricity project.

A fifth factor was William's *longing for a better life.* His deep desire shaped dreams and motivated efforts. Of course, this poverty-eradicating factor is connected to the earlier factor of a "sense of possibilities" as a "sense of how life could be." He dreamed of becoming a scientist. "To me, being a scientist was worlds better than farming, which by then had started taking up a large part of my time" (WK 72). As soon as he saw the bicycle dynamo, he began dreaming about electricity. His dream was to have a different life from his father's life, which he found depressing: a life determined by himself, by his choices, and by his decisions.

Sense of possibilities, sources of education, an inquisitive mind, access to investment, and longing for a better life are five poverty-eradicating factors in William Kamkwamba's case that worked together toward a path that would lift him out of poverty. The key concept that summarizes these factors could be the ability to create and use opportunities.

This example could encourage a deeper discussion on opportunities. Opportunities are not simply "vague possibilities." They are invitations to exercise agency that is connected to a clear pathway of that agency. William's approach shows how an encounter with reality shapes a person's desire and ability to change the world. He was able to identify resources as resources and put them to use. He also used the opportunity to create opportunities, which is an important gift. Having an entrepreneurial spirit means that you can create jobs, creating opportunities for employees. Being an educated person means that you have the gift of transforming situations into opportunities. What lifted William Kamkwamba out of poverty was his ability to transform situations into opportunities. He showed a spirit of innovation based on "(1) his own desire to tinker (with engines, radios, go-carts), (2) his ability to use the materials at hand to perform the tinkering, and (3) his access to textbooks containing essential principles of physics, magnetism, and electricity" (Wilbanks and Wilbanks 2010, 1009).

William was able to work with opportunities, but he had to overcome poor governance, destructive customs and beliefs, humiliation, asset vulnerability, and lack of nonambiguous access to infrastructure. His second-order skills were helped by local appropriating skills, local social capital, role models for entrepreneurial spirit and resilience, and a sense of inner resources. One important factor worth mentioning is the role of mentoring. Mentoring has been identified as a crucial factor in a child's development (Lai 2014). William Kamkwamba had limited, but nonetheless some, access to mentors: his cousins, his friends, his parents, his teachers, his books (as virtual mentors). He experienced some accompaniment on the way. We will revisit this category at the end of the book as an important expression of integral human development.

The example of William Kamkwamba confirms important insights of the idea of integral human development—each person counts and can contribute, also in unexpected ways; it is "the whole person" who is the agent, and many factors contribute to agency that brings about social change.

PART II

INTEGRAL HUMAN DEVELOPMENT, DIGNITY, AND DEVELOPMENT PROJECTS

Integral Human Development (or IHD) focuses on "each person" and on "the whole person." The approach would specifically make a difference when considering the most disadvantaged or ignored persons and when considering aspects of the human person that are not being addressed. The commitment to the development of "each person" can be seen in projects that walk the extra mile to reach the most vulnerable and those hardest to reach in the spirit of "leaving no one behind."

Matiullah Wesa's initiative *PenPath* tries to reach children in remote Afghan areas to provide them with books, pens, and schools.[1] The initiative works with a mobile library, hundreds of volunteers, and is particularly committed to providing education for girls and orphans.[2] *PenPath* practices the integral human development value of "deep inclusion." Deep inclusion often requires explicit and additional efforts outside prevailing patterns of operation. This is one of the reasons that deep inclusion is challenging. The "Leave No One Behind" project of the UN Development Program, a four-year program that aims to empower vulnerable persons in Albania (particularly persons with disabilities and members

---

[1] Namrata Biji Ahuja, "An Afghan NGO [nongovernmental organization] Is Determined to Educate Girls Despite Taliban's Return," *The Week* online, August 20, 2021.
[2] VOA News, "Afghan Man Fights for Women's Education," *VOANews* online, April 21, 2022.

of the Roma and Egyptian communities), and the Gaza Risk Reduction and Mitigation (GRRAM) Project are other examples.[3]

The GRRAM project was implemented by Catholic Relief Services and was designed to target women from various backgrounds and literacy levels in Gaza, opening doors for them to become community leaders. The project was run by the Palestinian Red Crescent Society from October 2011 to February 2013. It sought to create a pilot disaster reduction project that identified and addressed risks from natural disasters and armed conflict through participatory methodologies, thus creating a sense of ownership in the communities.[4] The project faced a series of challenges and restrictions. The political fragility and restrictions in Gaza made it generally hard for organizations to realize projects on the ground. Women found it difficult to participate because of their limited availability and mobility as a result of cultural and gender norms. The project resulted in extra work for women who were already stretched with household responsibilities. The evaluation of the project stated that the project would not be sustainable without the proper involvement of the entire community, including male stakeholders.[5] The reality of "leave no one behind" is complex. Committing to the development of "each person" seems simple and deceptively straight forward, but doing so successfully requires sophisticated strategies in practice.

The commitment to "the whole person" can be illustrated by holistic efforts or efforts to address neglected dimensions of the human person. One such dimension can be human sexuality, which is often surrounded by taboos and restrictive discourses. That is why, in order to break traditional taboos, a young African development worker decided to address the silence about female sexuality on a radio show. It is why the Bolivian Campaign for the Right to Education offers workshops to create spaces to talk about sexuality, the physical changes of adolescence, and domestic violence.[6] And this is why the National Council of Churches in the Philippines (NCCP) is creating safe spaces for discussing human sexuality and working on sexuality modules.[7]

The sexuality of youth has been recognized as a challenge of the development discourse. Patrick Fine and Kristin Lord have argued that "the

---

[3] United Nations Development Programme, "Leave No One Behind," *UNDP.org*, Albania Projects.

[4] Humanitarian Innovation Fund, *Final Report: Gaza Risk Reduction and Mitigation* (Catholic Relief Services/United States Conference of Catholic Bishops [USCCB], 2017).

[5] Erik Rottier, *Final Evaluation Report: Gaza Risk Reduction and Mitigation (GRRAM)* (Jerusalem: Catholic Relief Services, 2017).

[6] Malene Aadal Bo, "Story of Change—How to Break the Taboo around Sexuality in Bolivia," *Education Out Loud: Advocacy and Social Accountability* online, October 6, 2021.

[7] NCCP, "Sexuality Is Taboo in the Philippines. Here's How the Church Is Breaking That," *National Council of Churches in the Philippines* online, August 20, 2018.

international development community loves children—but it is surprisingly disengaged when it comes to youth, their needs, and the whole issue of sex."[8] The tendency to overlook one dimension of the human person (sexuality) has led to a tendency to overlook a particular group (adolescents). "Even as development organizations have prioritized children, they have consistently overlooked youth and young adults.... Adolescence, it turns out, is not just an awkward and vulnerable stage. It is a difficult phase for development organizations to deal with."[9] A commitment to Integral Human Development is a commitment to the road less traveled, to the awkward issues and difficult topics and neglected dimensions.

In addition to "invisible" or neglected dimensions, the whole person approach seeks to address the person beyond role and label. The "Graduation Approach" for refugees, adopted by the United Nations High Commissioner for Refugees (UNHCR), is designed to address the economic and psychosocial vulnerabilities faced by refugees. Developed by the Bangladesh Rural Advancement Committee (BRAC), it is a program for asset creation, individual capacity and skills-building, and sustainable development. It was designed as a training program for people struggling with extreme poverty and food insecurity. In the program, they complete an accompaniment process with different inputs (coaching, networking, savings, consumption support, skills training, employment support) and "graduate" from the program after its completion. The approach is holistic in the sense that it considers the many structural elements in a society that impact a person's quality of life, and it moves beyond a sole focus on generating income opportunities for an individual (Abdul Azeez and Subramania Siva 2019). The approach aims to deliver dignified assistance for people to become self-reliant and resilient, to develop an orientation for employment and entrepreneurship. The UNHCR has adopted the Graduation Approach for refugees in Mozambique[10] by sequencing interventions through a combination of livelihood protections and livelihood promotions that would address the special situation of refugees, including a psychosocial component to improve participants' emotional health (Kuhle et al. 2017). The involvement of the host communities is a key factor.[11]

---

[8] Patrick Fine and Kristin M. Lord, "International Development's Awkward Stage," *ForeignPolicy* online, March 13, 2015.

[9] Fine and Lord, "International Development's Awkward Stage."

[10] Theresa Beltramo and Sandra Sequeria, "Compelling Evidence that the Graduation Approach Promotes Economic and Social Integration in Displacement Settings: The Case of Mozambique," *UNCHR Blogs*, March 9, 2022.

[11] Bobby Irven, "Using the Graduation Approach to Uplift Refugees in a Changing World: An Interview with UNCHR's Ziad Ayoubi," *brac blog*, June 19, 2020.

The examples demonstrate the challenges that come with the commitment to Integral Human Development. A commitment to considering "the development of the whole person" may run up against the obstacle of having to challenge cultural norms in order to overcome discursive or operational taboos. It may have to struggle with the complexity of designing a holistic approach that is obviously more costly, more complex, and more time consuming than less ambitious programs. Integral Human Development may be an aspirational concept, but it is not impossible to find projects and initiatives that are substantially in line with the approach. The commitment to "the development of the whole person" can be translated into a commitment to holistic approaches that consider the human person in all her dimensions. This claim, as we have seen in the previous chapter, points to the relevance of both a material and an immaterial dimension. The person needs bread but does not live on bread alone. For the design and implementation of development projects and initiatives, this means a commitment to honoring the complexity of human life and the person in her multidimensionality.

The "whole person" has many facets that deserve our attention. A holistic approach to the challenge of homelessness has been pursued, for instance, in a project in the Bratislava region in Slovakia. Streetworkers identify people without a home and organize medical support, food support, housing support, and connections to services including counseling services and day care centers. There is also a work integration program and a policy advocacy program attached to the initiative.[12] Proper consideration of the multifaceted person can slow processes down and can make then more demanding. In this sense, Integral Human Development is not a simplification strategy.

The holistic anthropology of integral human development emerges from a particular tradition. The challenges that necessitate deliberate and demanding processes can be even greater when special consideration is given to the most disadvantaged, the most vulnerable, the most difficult to reach. In the tradition that has coined the term "Integral Human Development," the Catholic Social Tradition, a key phrase that has emerged to express this concern is "the preferential option for the poor" (Gutiérrez 1993). This option is a nonexclusive option that pays special attention to those suffering from deprivations of different kinds. Even though the language has its limitations, the ideas and values are clear: pay special attention to the least privileged, to those who are normally not at the center of the stage. In his encyclical *Sollicitudo Rei Socialis*, Pope John Paul II has called the preferential option for the poor "a special form of primacy in

---

[12] "From the Street to a Home," *SozialMarie: Prize for Social Innovation* online, 2022.

the exercise of Christian charity." This fundamental attitude affects the life of each Christian, "but it applies equally to our social responsibilities and hence to our manner of living, and to the logical decisions to be made concerning the ownership and use of goods" (*Sollicitudo Rei Socialis* 42). The option for the poor affects individuals' major life decisions as well as institutions at the structural level of society. Based on the universal nature of human dignity, one could and should argue that the preferential option for the poor is in the realm of the discourse on and practice of charity and in the realm of justice, since respecting the dignity of a person (and thus doing justice to a person) requires more intentional efforts with regard to the situation of disadvantaged people. "John Paul proposed that distribution of wealth and engrained, structural injustice require the Church's spirited advocacy for—and in defense of—the rights of the poor" (Twomey 2006, 327–28). The idea of a preferential option for the poor expresses the commitment to build inclusive communities and can be found in liberation theology as well as in an organization like "Partner in Health" (Farmer and Gutiérrez 2013). Pope Francis has called the preferential option for the poor an "option for those who are least, those whom society discards" (*Evangelii Gaudium* 195). He has also exhorted the church to go out to "the peripheries" (*Evangelii Gaudium* 20). Even though the language of "peripheries" is contested, the concern with leaving our comfort zones and journeying on the road less traveled expresses the noble intention to care about "each person."

This principle of a preferential option for the poor could also be called *reverse privileging*. It is directed to counteract the temptation of the "Matthew effect." Coined by Robert Merton, the "Matthew effect" describes the phenomenon when "eminent scientists get disproportionately great credit for their contributions to science while relatively unknown scientists get disproportionately little credit for comparable contributions" (Merton 1968, 57). The term is based on the Gospel of Matthew, where we read, "For to all those who have, more will be given, and they will have an abundance; but from those who have nothing, even what they have will be taken away" (Matthew 25:29 NRSVCE). Said differently, the dynamic of advantage begetting further advantage (Rigney 2010) corresponds to the dynamic of cumulative disadvantage: one advantage in one field leading to further advantages in other fields (Wolff and De-Shalit 2007). If you have a disadvantage in the area of health, for instance, the probability that you will also have a disadvantage in the area of education increases. This disadvantage, in turn, increases the likelihood of disadvantages in the area of employment and work. The cruel dynamics of downward spirals correspond to the unjust dynamic of privileging the privileged.

The Matthew principle can be experienced on the ground. For example, a development worker collaborated on an investment strategy for the National Agency on the Development of Tourism. She recommended one particular, though not very popular, region in the North of the country, perceiving tourism to be

> *an opportunity to change lives and experiences of those who worked in the tourism industry and the tourists themselves. The investment could create job opportunities, bring life and motion to the region, possibly protect some underfunded cultural heritage sites, and influence people's standard of living, education, and health in the long run.*

The recommendations were ignored. One particular southern site was chosen *since it had the biggest potential success rate, along with the lowest potential failure rate.* The decision is understandable, but an IHD approach would at least pause and reconsider the priorities.

Another development worker observed that the NGO she had worked with

> *Tended to prioritize successful students over those less fortunate. Many times, the nonprofit recognized the accolades of their scholarship students specifically to have them serve as poster boards for the organization, hoping to attract more donors and media attention.*

This is an example of the Matthew principle.

Similarly, an English teacher who worked abroad admitted that

> *Much of my work was skewed to benefiting those who already had a strong level of English or desired to learn it. I was unconsciously biased in my instruction to work more with those who participated more in my classes and clubs, and neglected those who remained quiet.*

And another teacher explained:

> *I think there are some natural limitations to IHD. I've been reflecting on this evolutionary thing within humanity, that, in order to survive, we naturally work with or focus on the most capable people. So that's kind of like a natural Matthew Principle thing. Even in group work in class, you want to work with the people you perceive to be smart go-getters. Or working with students in Ukraine in the Peace Corps—I was naturally inclined to work with the kids that were better English speakers. I could have helped the students at the lower end of the class, though. And IHD has made me reflect on that.*

Another voice from the field said,

> *In our grant-assessment criteria, I had focused on the concept of the "multiplier"—how far the dollar could go in terms of the people impacted, and nodes of leverage. This often meant looking at programs and individuals in terms of the "most potential" economically, socially and academically.*

These examples illustrate that countering the Matthew effect has to be intentional. Integral Human Development challenges "natural inclinations" and comfort zones, where the dynamic of the effect has a tendency to kick in. The means of resisting the Matthew effect is the effort of reverse privileging, of privileging "the last over the first." For each person to have access to a dignified life, reverse privileging is morally justified as long as some have in abundance while many are deprived of basic goods. Dignity language, then, is not harmless. It is a ground to challenge disparities and the dynamics of privileges and disadvantages.

Integral Human Development may be an aspirational concept, but it does offer a sense of direction, especially through two main commitments: a commitment to a dignified (rich and deep) life in accordance with a person's dignity and to integral ecology ("the development of the whole person"), and a commitment to special attention to the most disadvantaged and reverse privileging ("the development of each person"). On a more foundational level, these two commitments lead to a third commitment on the operational level of project design and project implementation: subsidiarity and inclusive participation. Respecting human dignity means respecting the agency of people and avoiding the three traps of infantilization, instrumentalization, and humiliation.

The idea of subsidiarity, rooted in Catholic Social Tradition, expresses this respect for local agency. The principle of subsidiarity means that, in a complex social structure with different levels and a hierarchy of power, a maximum of freedom and a maximum of responsibility is to be given at the lowest possible level. Subsidiarity is a principle that strengthens the agency of individuals and communities. Pope Pius XI offered the following understanding in his 1931 encyclical *Quadragesimo Anno* (79): "Just as it is gravely wrong to take from individuals what they can accomplish by their own initiative and industry and give it to the community, so also it is an injustice and at the same time a grave evil and disturbance of right order to assign to a greater and higher association what lesser and subordinate organizations can do." The principle emphasizes freedom, power, and responsibility. Respecting the dignity of a person means respecting and promoting the person's freedom. Respecting the dignity of each person means making sure that each person can appropriately participate in decision-making processes. The agency-promoting principle of subsidiarity cannot be separated from the idea of inclusion.

The commitment to deep inclusion in the effort to consider each person and honor each person's dignity, especially the dignity of those easily neglected, leads to an imperative of inclusive participation. The commitment to deep inclusion is a commitment to pursue an inclusive approach, even in the face of structural and cultural obstacles. Inclusive kindergartens in Hungary, for example, intentionally include children from the Roma community to fight segregation and marginalization. These kindergartens involve the children, their families, and the teachers in a regular forum and are supported by a social worker.[13] This network makes participation possible. Designing projects in the spirit of Integral Human Development is an inclusive and participatory process.

For Integral Human Development, there are multiple levels of participation: recognition of presence, listening, co-deciding, and decision making, the latter including the handing over of decision-making powers. These four levels evoke different ways of showing respect for a person. Subsidiarity encourages the highest possible level of participation, accepting the risk that comes with co-deciding or the handing over of decision-making powers. In his 2021 Christmas Message to the Roman Curia, Pope Francis inspirationally described participation that

> ought to be expressed through a style of co-responsibility. Certainly, in the diversity of our roles and ministries, responsibilities will differ, yet it is important that everyone feel involved, co-responsible for the work, without having the depersonalizing experience of implementing a programme devised by someone else.... This occurs especially where room is made and space found for everyone, even those who appear, hierarchically, to occupy a marginal place.

In other words, participation is a process of building co-ownership.

This gives us three major commitments based on Integral Human Development: dignified life and integral ecology; special attention to the most disadvantaged and reverse privileging; subsidiarity and inclusive participation. These three commitments are interlinked, as we have seen—respecting the dignity of each person leads to a commitment to subsidiarity and inclusive participation.

---

[13] *Inclusive Kindergartens*, 2022 SozialMarie Prize for Social Innovation.

Figure 2: The Three Commitments of IHD

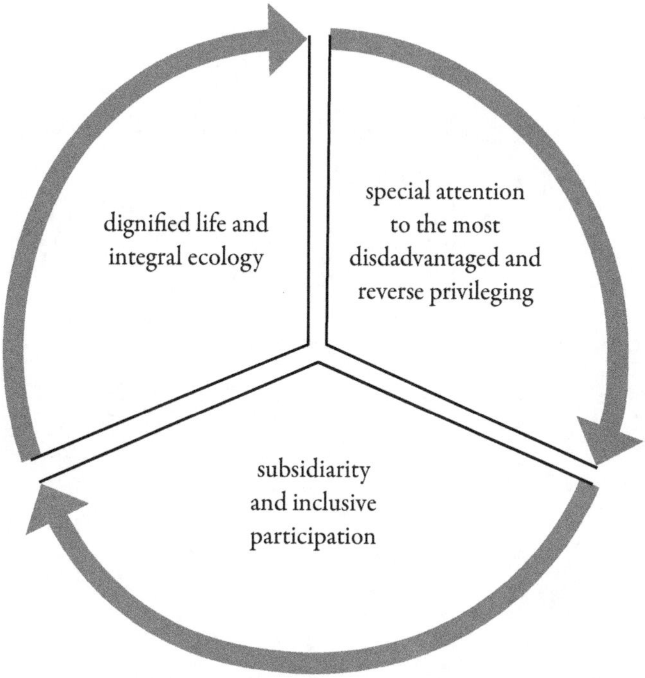

With regard to development projects, these three commitments lead to the following questions, among others: Is the project sensitive to the dignity of all stakeholders, and does it honor their sense of values? Does the project consider the idea of integral ecology? Does the project reflect a special commitment to the most disadvantaged? Does the project counteract the Matthew effect? Has the project been designed and implemented in a participatory manner, that is, with the inclusion of all relevant stakeholders? Has an effort been made to include those hardest and most difficult to include? Has a maximum of power (freedom) and responsibility been given to the lowest possible level?

5

Transforming Lives: Development Projects and the Challenges of Dignity-Centered Change

Integral Human Development approaches social change and political transformation by placing dignity and the respect for the dignity of each person at the center of the conversation. Rooted in Pope Paul VI's encyclical *Populorum Progressio*, it constructs a close link between dignity and development. The encyclical commends the efforts "to remove every obstacle which offends man's dignity" (*Populorum Progressio* 6). In paragraph 21, the encyclical addresses the plight of "less than human conditions," understood in material terms as the "material poverty of those who lack the bare necessities of life," in moral terms as "the moral poverty of those who are crushed under the weight of their own self-love," and in political terms as the "oppressive political structures resulting from the abuse of ownership or the improper exercise of power." In the same paragraph, awareness of dignity, common good, and peace form three pillars for the humanization of a person's life context and serve as key drivers of human development.

The encyclical links dignity to three further motifs: desire, enhancement, equality. By recognizing the connection between the language of dignity and the language of desire, the encyclical encourages us to establish a desire for dignity in order to create a culture of dignity.[1] Development emerges as a concept connected to well-ordered desires. Janusz Korczak, a Polish pediatrician, who ran an orphanage in the Warsaw ghetto under increasingly difficult conditions, told his children (since he was left in a space where he could not offer much material comfort and safety to them), "I can give you one thing only: a longing for a better life, a life of truth and justice" (Efron 2008, 43). For Integral Human Development,

---

[1] *Populorum Progressio* 32: The encyclical urges people with resources to "be responsive to men's longings and faithful to the Holy Spirit, because 'the ferment of the Gospel, too, has aroused and continues to arouse in man's heart the irresistible requirements of his dignity.'"

the invitation to social change is based on a promise of a better world and the experience of imperfection; people are motivated to move if there is a sense of something lacking. Both the promise of a better life and the experience of deficits contain value statements. A longing for a better world, a dignity-based world, can indeed be seen as a central driver of development efforts—both as a source of orientation and as a source of motivation.

The encyclical also uses the language of "enhancement," which is familiar from the capabilities approach, with its emphasis on the enhancement of freedoms (Nussbaum 2013, 17–45). Properly "planned programs do more than promote economic and social progress. They give force and meaning to the work undertaken, put due order into human life, and thus enhance man's dignity and his capabilities" (*Populorum Progressio* 50). Paragraph 71 uses the same language of enhancement in connection with experts and their motivations: "The people of a country soon discover whether their new helpers are motivated by good will or not, whether they want to enhance human dignity or merely try out their special techniques." Development projects aim to enhance the conditions of a dignified life. "Dignity-enhancement" can be understood as a more and more comprehensive response to dignity needs and the desire for a dignity-affirming culture, where people respect each other and where institutions respect people's dignity. Thirdly, dignity is connected to equality: "what is needed is mutual cooperation among nations, freely undertaken, where each enjoys equal dignity and can help to shape a world community truly worthy of man" (*Populorum Progressio* 54). This is, of course, clearly in line with the Universal Declaration of Human Rights. The idea of the fundamental dignity-equality of human beings establishes grounds for political demands to translate this commitment to equality into policies and institutional practices.

Populorum Progressio underlines the moral dimension of development and the immaterial dimension of the human person (and thus of development), notably regarding an inner life, to dignity, and to a certain understanding of self-respect (with the idea that a person is responsible for her self-fulfillment [*Populorum Progressio* 150]). This can be understood as another way of saying that the human person has a duty to do something with her life, that "human self-fulfillment may be said to sum up our obligations" (*Populorum Progressio* 16).[2] The highest goal of human self-fulfillment is "a new fullness of life" (*Populorum Progressio* 16). The notion of "fullness of life" is not a term used to

---

[2] Ronald Dworkin has expressed this duty to self-realization from a different angle in his *Justice for Hedgehogs* (Cambridge, MA: Harvard University Press, 2011). It is an expression of self-respect.

express developmental minimalism or a sufficientism; it is not enough to cover "basic needs"; it is not enough to ensure human survival. The goal of development that takes the dignity of each human person seriously is not modest. It is ambitious, for the ultimate goal of development is a full-bodied humanism (*Populorum Progressio* 41).[3] Robust concern for the other promotes genuine and inclusive development (Sedmak 2017, 24–25), and underdevelopment is judged to happen because of an erosion of "brotherly ties between individuals and nations" (*Populorum Progressio* 66). Additionally, *Populorum Progressio* makes two important connections—one between development and justice, and one between development and peace (Heidt 2017, 7).

Four pillars of proper development emerge from *Populorum Progressio*: dignity, common good, justice, and peace. Three aspects of enacting dignity can be identified as well: well-ordered desires, enhancement of capabilities, and equality of dignity status. This gives us reference points for a specific understanding of development and an initial vocabulary to talk about development. This vocabulary is part of the "background theory" of integral human development, but it is clearly not the only way to talk about development. Different languages offer different insights into understanding development. Thinking about the landscape of terms and concepts with their respective ideas and values is a meaningful exercise.

Different Notions of Development

The German term *Entwicklung* points to the unfolding of something wrapped. For development, this points to something implicit that must be made explicit. This movement can also be associated with liberation, as a student from Burkina Faso pointed out from his mother tongue Mooré,

> We have the term "Yidigri" which etymologically means "the action of unknotting something or somebody." This concept harkens back to the image of something that is chained and that gradually unravels and blossoms. This term can be applied to people as well as to an entire country.

Here, the direction of development is a move toward freedom. In Swahili, a commonly used word for "development" is "*maendeleo*," which literally means development or progress. It is coined from the root word "*endelea*," which means

---

[3] A full-bodied humanism in the understanding of Paul VI is a humanism that points the way to God (*Populorum Progressio* 42). This conception of humanism is shaped by the thinking of Jacques Maritain; see De Torre (2001).

"continue" or "go on." Here, the term suggests a continuation. A student of mine from the Philippines offered an understanding that emphasized newness and disruption—she chose the word in "Pagbabago":

> The root word in pagbabago is "bago" which can be defined as "new" or "change." This word is mostly used during election campaigns with their promises of newness through the phrase "patungo sa pagbabago" meaning "towards change" and for the betterment of the lives of Filipinos. Furthermore, in Philippine society, people would use this word if they changed something in their lives, as in "Nagbago ako ng trabaho" (I changed my work) or "may bago akong kotse" (I have a new car).

Here, development is most closely associated with change. A student researched a term from Icibemba, one of more than sixty languages in Zambia. She was taught the word "*buyantanshi*," a word that was explained by her language teacher as follows: "Buya comes from the word ukuya which means 'to go.' Ntanashi comes from Kuntanshi which means 'forward or front.' So, the direct translation is to go forward." Here, development is about moving in one direction, making progress step by step, moving away from a point of departure. The Meru of Kenya use different words to describe development, including *Gukura*, a word that has its roots in "kura," which means "to grow, to progress, to mature." Here the idea of a connection between development and maturity is intriguing. In Farsi, توسعه (Tos-heh) means development, expansion, extension, enlargement, increase—with a clear sense of development as "expansion," as "more." An African student of mine reflected on a term in Asante Twi (Ghana): "Nkankorɔ, according to the world wide web, is one word for development that literally means ascension, however, I asked a Ghanian friend and she translated it as progressive. Both have more positive annotations. Though both indicate a process of moving towards something." Here, we see the idea of "ascent" that also played a role in Lebret's thinking. The student commented: "Ascent is a movement upwards, an act of rising to an important position or higher level. It reminded me of an almost religious movement towards God." Obviously, this idea is very close to the idea of an "integral humanism" that influenced the term "integral human development."

Understanding the way people see development in their own terms is valuable because of the way these understandings shape the imaginations and the landscapes of accepted values and plausible practices. The term "development" can work as an organizing frame because the term allows the linking of diverse social, economic, political and cultural phenomena to a single process of "development" (Ziai 2011). The term covers a heterogeneity of activities and aspects, including ecological projects, road building, resettlement, hydroenergy, technological innovations, food-for-work programs, fighting corruption, micro-credit initiatives. Indeed, the term "development" creates a semantic field that allows for associations and nuances and insinuations of implicit values.

In a remarkable article on the indigenous concept of development among the Yoruba of Ilesha (Nigeria), John David Peel (Peel 1978, 142–43) reports on answers he has gathered from this community when he asked about "changes for the better" (we have become healthier, we have become more enlightened, people travel, education has come, vehicles are on the road, better roads, trade is happening) and "changes for the worse" (children are more enlightened and because of that less obedient, no respect for elders as there used to be, immoral ways of life, people have moved away from traditional customs). The term *"olaju,"* used frequently to talk about development, can be translated with "enlighten-ment" (Peel 1978, 141). The case study illustrates the ambivalence of social change. Being enlightened can be a desirable state, but it can also be as a state with deplorable implications and consequences. However, there are other words that are being used, words that can be translated as "going forward," "rising to be an elder" ("growing up"), "remaking" ("improvement"). Again, which ideas of development (or progress) are being transported through linguistic devices is telling. Learning more about the history of the terms is interesting, for *"Olaju* was first definitely used ... to refer to the cultural package brought from outside by, above all, missionaries" (Peel 1978, 147); *Olaju* was first known by its fruit and "was closely linked with ... education and ... books, book-learning" (Peel 1978, 148). Here again, we see an emerging background theory for the "develop-ment imagination" in this particular context.

The "development imagination," that is, the semantic horizon of the term, has led a nongovernmental organization to change its name from "IDEX—International Development Exchange" to "Thousand Currents." The decision was based on the insights that "development" is a loaded term that cannot easily be separated from colonial history and the concentration of economic power.[4] Global inequity is part of the history of the term "development" and the surrounding practices. This is why it is important to be aware of both the local nuances of the "development imagination" and the power dynamics of processes of social change.

---

[4] Jennifer Lentfer, "'International Development' Is a Loaded Term. It's Time for a Rethink." *The Guardian* online, May 3, 2017.

The Dynamics of Social Change

A development project or program is an intentional movement from A to B. A is the status quo, the point of departure, the way things are; B is the destination, the alternative world, the way things could be and should be. For people to feel motivated to move from A to B, there has to be "a promise of a better world." In other words, B has to be more desirable than A, and there have to be reasons why this should be the case. This also means that there is an inevitable value dimension in development work.

Any project design, at least implicitly, contains normative assumptions about "the good life" and more or less desirable living conditions. Development depends on evaluation—as Amartya Sen has put it: "What is or is not regarded as a case of 'development' depends inescapably on the notion of what things are valuable to promote" (Sen 1988, 20). Some people might benefit from a particular social change; others might lose privileges. The idea that there are winners and losers counters the original optimism associated with the term of "development as progress." Aram Ziai identified two roots of development theory—nineteenth-century evolutionism and nineteenth-century social technology—that are themselves rooted in Enlightenment philosophy and designed to reconcile order and progress in the face of the problems caused by industrial capitalism (Ziai 2011). Evolutionism assumed that social change in societies proceeds according to a universal pattern (usually in historical stages), while social technology claimed that social interventions based on expert knowledge (possessed by a privileged group that acts as a trustee for the common good) are necessary to achieve positive social change.

The discourse on development works with assumptions. There is a practical assumption that development can be achieved, a normative assumption that development is a good thing, and a methodological assumption that different units can be compared according to their "development" (Ziai 2011). Change means that there must be something new that comes to be, something old that passes away, and something that stays the same throughout the change process. Change involves three types of aspects: (1) aspects that begin to exist, (2) aspects that cease to exist, and (3) aspects that are constants throughout the process. Change can be a gradual transformation or a disruption. The concept of "disruptive innovations" points to an understanding of interventions to end destructive practices, like the use of a chlorhexidine antiseptic gel in Nepal to reduce neonatal mortality thus replacing established cultural practices (such as treating the fresh umbilical stump with turmeric, mustard oil paste, ash, cow dung, or vermillion).[5]

---

[5] Alex Their, "Disruptive Innovations Bringing Nepal Closer to Ending Extreme Poverty," *USAID Blog*, January 9, 2015.

With its message of "remedies for past wrongs and ills," disruption is morally ambivalent. Interventions from the outside must fight the suspicion of technocracy and epistemic imperialism. Habitual practices and lack of trust in the new interventions and their "ambassadors of change" are barriers to social change. Trust-based dialogue, training, and education, as well as institutional protocols, can all help negotiate these challenges (Rana et al. 2019). We will come back to this point of community-based dialogue again and again. Dialogue changes the imagination, the sense of what is possible and necessary, the structure of what is culturally acceptable and epistemically plausible. It offers new ways of comanaging change.

Even though the unplanned aspects of a project are as important as the planned features, change can be managed and intentionally be brought about. If we follow some philosophical insights offered by Aristotle,[6] we could distinguish four main concerns regarding planned change: (1) the understanding of the potentiality and actuality of particular objects in a given situation, (2) the understanding of the overall order, (3) the understanding of motion that transforms A into B, and (4) the justification of choices according to reason and desires.

---

[6] In an Aristotelian reading, change means a transformation from potential into real; this transformation happens via movement (*Metaphysics* XI.9.1065b15f.). This movement or motion happens through something that actually exists, that is already realized. The transformative power of motion is brought about by a particular already existing force, by something that has the power of causing motion. "A thing is capable of causing motion because it *can* do this, it is a mover because it actually *does* it" (*Physics* III.3.201a15f.). The point here is that intentional change has to rely on resources and inputs that already exist, that are real, that are available. There is a clear distinction between the potential and the real. Change needs to consider the potentials and possibilities of things—if you want to transform cold water into hot water, water needs to have the capability of being heated. Motion involves the presence of things that are capable of that motion (*Physics* VIII.1.251a10ff.). This is Aristotle's example: There must be something capable of being burned before there can be a process of being burned, and something capable of burning before there can be a process of burning (*Physics* VIII.1.251a10ff.). In order for change to be brought about by us we need to know a lot about "what is real" and about possibilities and potentials. This seems trivial, but it is one of the key points of any project—do the proposed initiatives work with genuine possibilities and potentials? You cannot expect a change that is not "in the cards," "a change that is not covered by the nature of things. In Aristotle's language: "Change is always according to the categories of being" (*Metaphysics* XI.9. 1065b5–10). This thought can also be transferred to the cultural order. You cannot expect change to be sustainable or successful if it does not respect the cultural order and the local conditions. Change management requires a sense of what is possible, a concept of potency. "Potency" is a source of change (*Metaphysics* V.12 1019a15); potency can be seen as a capability in the sense that something may be capable of suffering or undergoing something. Probably the most important meaning for issues of change is "disposition," the potency of changing into something, for better or for worse.

First, proper change management has to work with a solid knowledge of what is possible; there has to be a sense of possibilities and potential. This is, once again, a matter of the imagination. Imagination is the capability of conceiving of alternatives to the way things are. The imagination can be nourished by examples that extend the sense of what is possible. Dialogue with others, encounters with difference, and education as well as a realistic sense of local potential emerge as key aspects in this regard. Second, understanding overall order refers to a knowledge of the local order, including the cultural order. Suggested change that runs against the established cultural order will be met with resistance. The phenomenon of vaccine hesitancy may come to mind (Volet et al. 2022). Third, "motion" concerns the appropriate process to bring about the change—how do you move a community from A to B? This is a matter of community organizing, of creating a shared desire for change. Fourth, justification is probably the most important concern, for, if you have a good sense of what is the case (what is real) and a good sense of what is possible, you will have a sense of options and choices. Once you are able to select from among different options, you will have to justify the choices made with reasons that people can recognize as reasons.

Social change requires a sense of what is missing, a sense of what is possible, and the resources to bridge the gap between what is missing and what is possible. Hence, the beginning of a social change initiative demands the realization of "nonrealities" and then of "possibilities." In other words, there needs to be the recognition of a gap, a lacuna, a chasm between what is and what ought to be, a sense of something not covered or taken care of, a "hole in the fabric of reality." A "nonreality" can then be translated into "possibilities," and this sense of possibilities leads to the identification of resources to realize a possibility.

Save the Children, founded by Eglantyne Jebb and her sister Dorothy Buxton in 1919, is a helpful example. The beginnings of the organization can be traced back to the experience of "something lacking": lack of proper information about the war situation, leading Dorothy to organize translation services of twenty-five foreign newspapers permitted to enter the country during WWI in order to provide balanced information (Mulley 2009). Weekly leaflets, "Notes from the Foreign Press," were intended to influence public opinion and discourse as well as politicians. Eglantyne Jebb became part of this operation in 1917 and, together with dozens of volunteers, helped in the translations of news from Europe. The reports from non-British newspapers made it very clear that a humanitarian crisis had hit continental Europe, something about which the British had no idea since the information was "lacking" from their own home papers.

The translation project continued after the Great War, gathering momentum in its sense of urgency:

Armed with their knowledge of conditions in Europe gleaned from the press translations, and inspired by a sense of life and death urgency, at the end of 1918 Eglantyne and Dorothy quickly joined like-minded contacts from the Women's International League to form a new single-issue political pressure group: the "Fight the Famine Council." (Mulley 2009, 227)

They aimed to provide accurate information, country by country, drew up a list of potential supporters, and held a public inaugural meeting on New Year's Day 1919 at Central Hall, Westminster. The aim of the Council was to end the blockade that paralyzed Europe—this accurate information had to be lobbied in Parliament since the British government was reluctant to disclose to the public the human costs of the economic blockade policy. Eglantyne Jebb was convinced that conditions on the continent were so terrible that something had to be done about it by changing public opinion. She had to bridge the gap between "indifference" and "concern," as well as the gap between "ignorance" and "knowledge."[7] She understood the importance of facts and statistics ("We must have figures.... It is the only way to combat political influences" [Mulley 2009, 236]) and managed to organize a research mission to Vienna, conducted by the highly regarded Dr. Hector Munro. He could provide the Famine Council with statistics and first-hand narrative evidence. The Save the Children Fund was launched during a "Famine Meeting" at the Royal Albert Hall on May 19, 1919, where the journalist Henry Noel Brailsford provided a shocking eyewitness account of the situation in Berlin and Vienna. Munro and Brailsford served as "bridges" to the public. Pope Benedict XV was a further important bridge to move people's conscience, publishing two encyclicals on behalf of the children of Eastern Europe: the document *Paterno Iam Diu* (November 24, 1919) and the letter *Annus Iam Plenus* (December 1, 1920). He pleaded for help and pledged to contribute out of his own funds as well.

In other words, Eglantyne Jebb and her sister had—based (1) on their sense of a gap between ideal and reality and (2) on their sense of the possibility to bridge this gap—systematically built bridges to move people from indifference to action. The bridge of knowledge of the situation on the ground in continental Europe was the basis for this "motion to move." Eglantyne and Dorothy also felt

---

[7] This challenge to move people was particularly tough in postwar times: "Some people resented giving space to the sufferings of the enemy while there was so much loss at home" (Mulley 2009, 222); "the British people had been taxed beyond endurance by the horrors of the war and were now preoccupied with their own sorrows and plans, and still intensely hostile to the countries that had taken the lives of so many young men" (Mulley 2009, 229–30).

obliged to bridge a gap that was not being dealt with by anyone else. They identified and targeted something that was lacking: "Save the Children was the first charity specifically set up for non-domicile children, and coincidentally the first to be founded by women" (Mulley 2009, 248; cf. Mahood 2009).

Because of the importance of a sense of what is missing and a sense of what is possible, the question of beginnings of social change is clearly relevant. Let us call the reflection on beginnings of development initiatives "development protology."

Development Protology

Projects are responsive; they respond to challenges. These challenges are often experienced on a visceral level. The motivation to change the world and to change one's life has to be nourished. The "development imagination" must be stretched and cultivated. Giwa-Tubosun founded *LifeBank*, a digital medical distribution company that has facilitated the delivery of essential medical products like blood, oxygen, plasma, and vaccines to hospitals in Nigeria since 2016. She was inspired to start this initiative during an internship as a public administration student, when she witnessed a young pregnant woman fight for her life after a difficult labor, including suffering heavy blood loss.[8] The beginning of the social transformation that she initiated can be found in her experience.

There are many similar examples of "founding stories" of initiatives. Vikram Akula, an American-born son of an Indian doctor, went back to India and helped with a microfinance initiative.

> Then, one day, a woman walked into our regional office. Barefoot, emaciated, and wearing a faded purple sari; she was obviously poor and from a lower caste. But she'd found her way to our office because she'd heard about our program and wanted to learn more. This was no small achievement, as she'd either paid to take a bus or had walked quite a distance to find us.

He listens to her and then consults with his boss to find out that there are no funds left. He travels to the village to give her the bad news. "The woman looked me in the eye, and with great dignity, she spoke the words that would change my life. 'Am I not poor, too?'" She was simply asking for an opportunity. These simple words "Am I not poor, too?" changed Akula's life and his perspective. This

---

[8] Kingsley Ighobor, "Temie Giwa-Tubosun: The Nigerian Entrepreneur Delivering Blood to Patients," *Africa Renewal—UN.org*, September 29, 2020.

was a defining moment that gave him a new mission (Akula 2011, 3–4).[9] Here we have a first point: "personal commitment" and "defining moment."

Wangari Maathai is credited with founding the *Green Belt Movement* in Kenya. She grew up in a rural area, where her family's daily life depended on the health of the environment. As a US-trained biologist, she had proper expertise in environmental issues. She had not lost the connection with her origins or with the rural areas she knew; her academic work put her in truly eye-opening situations where she obtained "knowledge by acquaintance" of soil degradation:

> While I was in the rural areas outside of Nairobi collecting the ticks, I noticed that the rivers would rush down the hillsides and along paths and roads when it rained, and that they were muddy with silt. This was very different from when I was growing up. "That is soil erosion," I remember thinking to myself. "We must do something about that." (Maathai 2007, 121)

During a home visit in Nyeri, she saw with her own eyes what happened to the land and the rivers once plantations of commercial trees (tea, coffee) had replaced indigenous forest. She made connections between this experience and the biology behind it. These sources of knowledge, together with the solution-oriented motivation to help, made her realize a way forward:

> It just came to me: "Why not plant trees?" The trees would provide a supply of wood that would enable women to cook nutritious foods. They would also have wood for fencing and fodder for cattle and goats. The trees would offer shade for humans and animals, protect watersheds and bind the soil, and, if they were fruit trees, provide food. They would also heal the land by bringing back birds and small animals and regenerate the vitality of the earth. (Maathai 2007, 125)

This was the defining moment of the movement that she started.

Adam Braun, founder of *Pencils of Promise*, recounts a significant encounter in India, when visiting Agra Fort, close to the Taj Mahal. He approached a begging child and asked the boy what he would want to have if he could have

---

[9] He had experienced such a defining moment years earlier when he was in India for a wedding, and saw how two boys ate all the waste, the food left ove by the wedding guests. "That was the moment I knew, beyond doubt, what I would do when I got older: I wanted to come back to India and help people like those boys to get out of poverty. Why should I have an easy, comfortable life while others, by the luck of the draw, had to struggle hard to survive?" (Akula 2011, 11).

anything in the world. The child answered, "a pencil" (Braun 2014, 35). Braun handed him a pencil, and the child "looked at it as if it were a diamond." The pencil was the key to unlock a door of possibilities. Braun experienced this moment as a defining moment with a vision of distributing pencils to kids, and it became the founding story of his organization.

Any project begins somewhere—beginnings are telling. "Mother died today. Or, maybe, yesterday; I can't be sure" ("*Aujourd'hui, maman est morte. Ou peut-être hier, je ne sais pas*") are the famous first lines of Camus's *L'Etranger*. The beginning of the text sets the tone and the stage. These first words negotiate both the expectations and the framing of the work to follow. Camus managed to bring his existentialist sense of the absurd into the very beginning of the novel; a sense of "being a stranger in the world." According to Israeli author Amos Oz, the beginning of any text establishes a direct contract between author and reader, an agreement is concluded from the outset about what can be expected from the text to come (Oz 1999). However, a beginning is not an absolute beginning. There are beginnings before the beginning—in any piece of writing it takes an effort, sometimes a huge effort, to construct the first sentence. In any case, the *first* sentence will and must reflect the background story, the story before and the experience of the author. Just as a lot has happened before the first sentence is written down, a lot must happen before a project is designed.

How does a development project begin? We can learn from theology. The reflection on first things is called *protology*. The famous theologian Karl Rahner uses the term in his *Theological Investigations* to establish a connection between *first things* and *last things* through divine intentionality ("purpose of creation"). God has the end of creation in mind even before God begins. Rahner confirms Amos Oz's point about "beginnings before beginnings."

Turning to theology gives us two main points about protology: you cannot properly speak about "first things" (beginnings, points of departure, starting points) without speaking about "last things" (ends, purposes, ultimate visions) as well; and you cannot properly speak about "first things" (and their connection to "last things") without first looking into the foundations before the foundations, that is, the background leading up to the (choice of) first things.[10] The connection

---

[10] Rahner emphasized "the way in which the truth and richness of content both of a 'protology' as well as of an eschatology essentially depend on its becoming clear that man and his environment and his history are from the first devised with a view to Christ, and that the man Christ at the end of all history still retains his fundamental significance" (Rahner 1961, 199). In other words, the first things and the last things form a union because of "the beginnings before the beginnings," that is, divine intentionality. We have to see, as he sees in a later volume, "protology and eschatology within a single conspectus" (Rahner 1973, 378).

between "first things" and "last things" ensures that the key questions are being asked. In light of this connection between "first things" and "last things," we can reflect on some "risk points" of development projects. There are three simple points: (1) wrong beginnings can lead to wrong ends; (2) wrong ends can lead to wrong beginnings; and (3) wrong readings of "beginnings before beginnings" can lead to wrong beginnings and wrong ends.

The first situation ("wrong beginnings") is the case if a development project gets off to a bad start, maybe without involving all the stakeholders. Martin Kämpchen describes a sanitary project in a North Indian village that went wrong because of not considering the needs and potentials of the villagers from the beginning (Kämpchen 2011, 118–19). A similar example in a similar context was made by Vikram Akula, mentioned above. He learned some bitter lessons in humility after he failed to respect local knowledge. He realized the importance of proper beginnings in an especially painful way when, in having requested permission to open a new branch of the Decan Development Society in a remote area, he arrived to find out that he, who had come to help the poor, was himself in need of help. He started off "on the wrong foot." "As I quickly learned, I pretty much didn't know how to do anything I needed to do" (Akula 2011, 37). He had his share of embarrassing learning moments, too, for example, how to protect his accommodation from local wild animals, how to cook rice, how to use the bathroom village style. It is like solving a math problem: if you get it wrong at the beginning, all the rest will be wrong, too.

The second situation ("wrong ends") can be found in the failure of projects that have been started for the wrong reasons—Mao's Great Leap Forward, based on his vanity to overtake Great Britain economically, was an expression of megalomania that cost the lives of close to forty million people (Dikötter 2010; Jisheng 2012). Self-serving projects that calm the conscience of the donors are another example as they will not be sustainable and may even do more harm than good. Stacey Edgar struggled with development initiatives based on wrong ends such as selling African crafts; projects that do not make the producer grow and that do not go beyond appealing to persons' goodwill and bad conscience serve wrong ends:

We arrive at the beginnings from this revelation-based "beginnings before the beginnings," that is, with a theological sense of God's personhood: "all protology, and so too the doctrine of original sin, is ipso facto theology, albeit a theology worked out in the writings of the New Testament (and the Old) themselves, and thereby guaranteed, so far as we are concerned, to be valid. In other words, all protology comes to us as explicated and deduced from a more original source, from a primary revelation" (Rahner 1974, 249). The main point is that we can only understand the first things if we understand what brought these first things about.

I call the problem the Carved Giraffe Theory. I don't know anyone with a carved giraffe at the top of her birthday wish list, and carved giraffes are rarely the "go-to" gift for Mother's Day or any other holiday. Even I, with a keen interest in all things African, have never felt a longing for a carved giraffe. My beef is not with wooden giraffes specifically. My problem is with not teaching artisans in the developing world what mainstream consumers are buying so that the artisans can increase their business and therefore reduce poverty in their lives and communities. Because fund-raising is a nonprofit's real income, non-profit fair-trade organizations did not require their artisans to grow and change with the market. And so artisans made more giraffes, which sat in church basements across the nation until next year's sale. (Edgar 2011, 42)

Wrong ends are real, and they lead to real failures. In addition to "wrong ends," "unclear ends" are a significant challenge to project development.[11]

The third situation ("wrong readings of beginnings before beginnings") is the case if stakeholders are not honest in their intentions. Jacqueline Novogratz experienced this dynamic of strategically hiding real intentions in donor-driven development projects in Africa: "The real problem with the money from such donors was that it usually came with strings attached—they wanted us to carry out *their* projects and typically wanted the money spent within a year" (Novogratz 2009, 59). Women in need of money, for example, would be tempted to say yes to money if it came their way, no matter how ridiculous the enterprise seemed, just to play the game of pleasing the donors and getting money to survive. In Novogratz's experience, many projects like this fail because of a lack of "honesty to reality," and lack of attention to real intentions and real needs. Paying attention to "the beginnings before the beginnings" is an absolute must.

These (negative) examples illustrate the relevance of considerations of "development protology." International development work as social change work negotiates processes of social transformation and, by doing so, inevitably, questions

---

[11] N. F. Matta and R. N. Ashkenas discuss this challenge for complex and large-scale projects in the September 2003 issue of the *Harvard Business Review*: "The problem is, the traditional approach to project management shifts the project teams' focus away from the end result toward developing recommendations, new technologies, and partial solutions. The intent, of course, is to piece these together into a blueprint that will achieve the ultimate goal, but when a project involves many people working over an extended period of time, it's very hard for managers planning it to predict all the activities and work streams that will be needed. Unless the end product is very well understood, as it is in highly technical engineering projects such as building an airplane, it's almost inevitable that some things will be left off the plan" (Matta and Ashkenas 2003).

to do with newness and beginnings. For issues of development protology, Integral Human Development considers "first things," "last things," and "the beginnings before the beginnings." Beginnings are ethically relevant, for they suggest and express preferences in human agency. Any sentence could be picked as the first sentence; many an act could be chosen as the first act of a project. Philosophers have argued that the specificity of the human condition, even human dignity, can be linked to a person's ability to begin something new.[12] Let us now move to more systematic considerations of the ethics of development projects.

---

[12] Margalit (1996); cf. Mahlmann (2012, 378n.51).

6

Ethical Aspects of Project Management

Development projects begin "somewhere," and they bring about new beginnings. That is, they initiate change. Development projects are morally relevant because of potential benefits and harms. Development measures *can* be harmful for a number of reasons: (1) the dynamics of opportunity costs, (2) the challenge of the "second agenda" of development agents, (3) the reality of social and epistemic discontinuity of care, (4) misleading structure of promises, and (5) the ambivalence of progress.

There are *opportunity costs and trade-offs* for any measure. Owen Barder has analyzed the trade-offs between tackling current and future poverty, between helping as many poor people as possible and focusing on those in chronic poverty, and between measures that tackle the causes of poverty and those that deal with the symptoms (Barder 2009). There are trade-offs between investing in poverty prevention or in poverty alleviation, between alleviating child poverty or poverty in later life. Given scarce resources, any measure comes with opportunity costs. Developing pilot villages will prevent the developing of other areas given scarcity of resources. Bruno Crépon, Esther Duflo, Marc Gurgand, Roland Rathelot, and Philippe Zamora, for example, examined the short- and long-run impacts of job counseling among those who were, and were not, offered the program. They identified a displacement effect (Crépon et al. 2013). Many measures have similar "screening processes" that are put in place to ensure that the success rates of the intervention can be increased, leading to the paradox that those who need support most are "screened out" (or "outqualified" by others). In other words, successful measures require appropriate agents, and prioritizing the success of the intervention over the capacity-building of the most disadvantaged will come with the price tag of the Matthew effect, giving to those who already have and, by doing so (because of the transformation of relative social positions), weakening those who have least.

Development agents are defined by their commitment to development and by their commitment to their respective agency. There is a *second or even hidden agenda*. Social and cultural capital are at stake. Reputations must be safeguarded. Long-term agency must be protected. Governments, for instance, may give development aid because of the commitment to improve the lives of people in developing countries. They may also be interested in their own reputation and cultural capital, in protecting their citizens, in supporting their own suppliers, and in increasing the supply of global public goods. This can be said, *mutatis mutandis*, about organizations with their interests in donor intent satisfaction as well. Of course, the above-mentioned aims are not mutually exclusive, but a potential dynamic of divided loyalties is in place. An agency with a contract at point T is interested in acting to increase the probability of securing further contracts at point T+1. This requires proper negotiation of relationships, probably not primarily with those living in poverty. Robert Chambers's well-known observation about "project bias" and "report bias" in developing projects (Chambers 2013, chap. 3) can be extended to an "agency bias," that is, to a preferential consideration of maintaining and expanding agency. Austrian Africanist Walter Schicho has discussed the second agenda of poverty alleviation agencies by embracing strategies to show higher professional competence than competitors and to increase the urgency and relevance of their mission and the difficulties in dealing with it (Schicho 2007a In other words, it is not clear whether poverty eradication can be a reasonable aim of agents of poverty alleviation. Development interventions can be damaging because of the second agenda—China's "great leap forward" was primarily a prestige project, leading to a famine that killed 36 to 42 million people. Hence, a good question to ask is simply, what is really at stake?

One of the well-documented challenges in medical care is the phenomenon of *social discontinuity of care*, the phenomenon whereby patients are repeatedly faced with changing partners in the diagnostic and curative process (Zerubavel 1979; Moore et al. 2003; Dekker 2007; Sharman et al. 2008). This phenomenon leads to transmission and transition losses and to frustrated needs of support and safety. This same challenge can be identified in the context of development measures. Development thinking in "projects" rather than "programs" constitutes fiduciary risks in the sense that trust carefully built over time is lost if a project-related practice comes to an abrupt end. A project is, by definition, an organized set of activity with a limited time line. Nongovernmental organizations (NGOs) change, personnel fluctuate, programs are limited, and any new program needs to have a proper element of "innovation," which puts additional pressure on discontinuity and heightens risk of losing lasting relationships and gains.

Development measures invariably involve or are even based on *promises for a better future*. How else could people be motivated to participate in often wide-reaching change processes rather than coerced? Promises are acts rather than announcements of acts. They are useful for the addressee and present some "good" ("bonum"). Their binding force can be intensified by publicity.[1] The introduction of development measures often comes with the public announcement of social transformation processes, and, if a local community or constituency is involved, as is usually the case, development interventions will have to create some kind of public good. Promises create expectations, but raising expectations and then failing to come up with the goods promised and so eagerly awaited can lead to deep frustration. Ted Gurr goes even further in considering failed outcomes by suggesting that frustrated expectations lead to aggression (and even widespread violence), which may well be the case in socially unstable situations in various parts of South Africa (Gurr 2011).[2] Development measures can create expectations that build horizons anticipating a particular version and vision of the future. If this "thick description" of this particular future does not manifest itself, frustrations cannot be avoided. There is a conundrum here: the thicker the promise of a better future, the more powerful the incentive to become involved; however, the higher the motivation, the deeper the commitment; the deeper the commitment, the more severe the potential frustration. Yet, at the same time, the thicker the promise, the higher the probability of disappointment and frustration.

Progress is ambivalent. With the contributions of Critical Theory and postcolonial discourse, there has been widespread recognition of the ambivalence of progress and "the dialectics of Enlightenment." Gone are the days of linear "theories of stages" in the tradition of Auguste Comte or James Frazer. New developments may mean new solutions, but they will also generate new problems. Microloans for women can increase domestic violence (Christian 2015). Development processes can lead to new forms of competitiveness, as Kyle Jaros has observed for the politics of spatial development in different provinces competing with each other in China (Jaros 2019) The introduction of new technologies can lead to new entry points for social exclusion, for example, a "digital divide." Changes are ambivalent. Gaining element A can come at the expense of element B. If B was treasured, the loss of B can be felt as a significant loss (even greater than the gain of A), but it could also mean "loss of skills," "loss of imagination," or "loss of relationship and interactions." And all this could mean loss of subjective well-being and quality of life.

Development projects are morally relevant and development ethics becomes a justified discipline because of these aspects and potential harms. The ethics of

---

[1] See the analysis of promises through Aquinas in his STh II-II, q. 88.

[2] Gurr (2011); see also Abell and Jenkins (1971), Alexander (2010), and Scrimgeour (2012).

development projects, one can argue, must pursue the defensive task of minimizing the harm of development measures. The defensive task of development ethics focuses on the minimization of harm by asking questions such as "who are (potential and significant) losers and victims of a particular measure?"; "which undesired consequences can occur owing to the measure?"; "which are the nonprimary agendas driving the measure?" This idea echoes Karl Popper's version of negative utilitarianism (Popper 1971), inviting ethicists and change makers to minimize harm rather than to maximize pleasure, to eliminate suffering rather than to optimize well-being, to minimize hell on earth rather than to introduce heaven. In short, minimize damage and harm. Popper's key point is that it is easier to reach ("negative") consensus on what constitutes pain and harm than ("positive") consensus about pleasure or happiness.

However, it seems impossible to tackle the defensive task without acknowledging the constructive task as well. Every rejection contains, at least implicitly, commitment. There are situations where negative utilitarianism supports wicked moral positions. Roderick Ninian Smart had criticized Karl Popper along those lines, citing the examples of painless destruction of the human race or painless murder (Smart 1958). In such cases, a "minimizing pain" argument can be used to support the course of action, but, surely, there are additional moral considerations that have to be taken into account. One cannot endeavor to minimize damages to integrity without a concept of integrity. One cannot isolate the imperative to minimize pain from other relevant moral considerations. Hence, in addition to the defensive task, the other task of the ethics of development projects is a constructive one—how to bring about desired change.

Dignity-Centered Project Management

The key question regarding change in the light of Integral Human Development (or IHD) is simple: What does a dignity-sensitive approach to social change look like? The ethics of development projects based on integral human development can offer some positive guidance. We have identified three core normative reference points for development projects in the spirit of Integral Human Development: dignified life and integral ecology, special attention to the most disadvantaged and reverse privileging, subsidiarity and inclusive participation.

Any project offers specific entry points for ethical consideration: the design of the project, the implementation, and the system of monitoring and evaluation. In the design stage, we can specifically look at the participation criterion and the planning process in terms of "procedural justice." Does the design of the planning process satisfy the criteria of a just process? Is it an inclusive process that is designed to be conducted in a participatory manner? Who are the stakeholders? And are the stakeholders properly considered? Robert Chambers titled one of his books *Whose Reality Counts?* This question is particularly relevant in the design stage of a project. A development worker, involved in the design of projects and programs, reflects on a real challenge:

> *One of our key roles in the program design phase was to "put our donor cap on" and envisage how the donor might want the program to look, or what points and questions they might consider and ask. One of the key consider-ations was whether the program reached enough beneficiaries or whether it would meet their agenda. A calculation we always had to make was the cost per beneficiary, regardless of log frame outcomes. This often meant that psychosocial programs were often much harder to receive funding.*

From the perspective of Integral Human Development, we see the challenge again to be open to the hidden dimensions of human life and to be willing to support less "donor-attractive" initiatives. In terms of the content of the project, the commitment to reverse privileging will ask for the project's impact on the distribution of and access to privileges—does the project benefit the most disad-vantaged? In the project management and implementation stage, we will be concerned with a dignity-based approach to management.

Projects have to be properly managed. Management can be defined as the coordination of processes and practices to achieve explicit and specific goals. Processes are regulated ways of transforming situations. Practices are complex forms of socially established cooperative human activities with the goal of bringing about certain results and reaching certain goals. Dignity-based management is the coordination of integrity-respecting processes and integ-rity-enhancing practices to achieve explicit and specific goals that strengthen conditions of dignified lives, especially for the most disadvantaged people.

The approach of integral human development takes "the whole person" and "each person" seriously, which means that the uniqueness of the person is an important category aspect of development ethics. Given the uniqueness of each person, the freedom of the person, and the dignity of the person, management techniques must be careful with regard to three in-built aspects of management: standardization, regulation, and instrumentalization. "Standardization" is the attempt to create coherent and replicable processes and can conflict with respect for the uniqueness of the person. At the same time, it is part of a commitment to accountability and a commitment to professional culture to establish standards. "Regulation" is the establishment of rules and policies as standard management tools and may conflict with the idea of freedom. Again, the coordination of different roles and tasks requires a rule-based approach, which is also an expression of "good governance." "Instrumentalization" is an important management aspect of assigning roles and using employees for particular tasks, but it has been identified as incompatible with the dignity of the person in the first chapter. Again, every employee or project worker has certain responsibilities, inhabits certain roles, and fulfills certain functions that have to be properly managed in the sense that the person is "a means to an end" (since any project is defined by "ends"). Dignity-based management will obviously not shy away from standardization, regulation, and a certain kind of instrumentalization, but it will be particularly sensitive to the modes and the costs. Dignity-based management in the spirit of integral human development will counter the potentially negative effects of standardization, regulation, and a certain kind of instrumentalization. The establishment of a culture of professional subsidiarity will mitigate potentially negative effects of standardization, a model of "leadership by reasoning" (providing transparent reasons and justifications for decisions and allowing for dialogue about choices) will counteract potential harm through regulation, and a culture of recognition, as indicated in the first chapter, will make sure that the effects of a certain kind of instrumentalization are not humiliating and dehumanizing.

A management model that can be offered as an example of dignity-based management to deal with the above-mentioned challenges is Dan Honig's approach in *Navigating by Judgment* (2018). At the beginning of his book, Honig offers an example from a project in East Timor.

A foreign aid agency wanted to help East Timorese farmers improve their agricultural practices by training government agricultural extension workers so that they could deliver appropriate support to farmers. However, as the project went on, something unexpected happened: basically, every government extension worker who had received the training left government employment in order to pursue higher-paying jobs elsewhere (most even outside of the agricultural sector). In other words, the project was designed to improve the living and working conditions of farmers but ended up increasing the portfolio of marketable skills of government employees. People on the ground implementing the project felt the need for a change of the project's strategy (for good reasons). The idea was obvious—offer the training directly to the farmers. They presented the proposal to the aid agency's representatives. The response was hesitant: the success metric of the project was the number of successfully trained government extension workers. In this sense the project was clearly successful. Changing the project strategy would require high-level approval with the cost of disclosing unintended and undesired consequences of the project. Result: no change happened.

In addition to clear issues with agency and judgment, there were also issues with trust and fear; rigid hierarchies and mandates; a misleading incentive structure; cultural complexity; and, possibly, a theory of change that did not center on the target population. This example points to management-related agency problems, more specifically to principal agent problems whereby the principal asks the agent to perform work on behalf of the principal. However, the agent, who is "on site," knows more about the local dynamics on the ground. The principle of subsidiarity has an important role to play here. Dan Honig argues for agent freedom and makes the point that top-down control may preclude useful action by agents. Agents on the local level should be given space to be able to "navigate by judgment." Honig's conclusion is very much in line with the thoughts of Onora O'Neill, who explored another management challenge, namely, the culture of accountability in the National Health Service of the United Kingdom. She argued that the strict standardization that the culture of accountability brings is detrimental to the quality of decisions and behavior as well as overall trust levels; space for judgment has to be reserved for the agents (O'Neill 2002; 2004). Allocating freedoms and judgment spaces is not only an expression of subsidiarity and of respect for the person with her specific local knowledge. Rigid project designs are a major source of project failures (Mishra 2016).

A culture of respect is indeed a key aspect of dignity-centered project management. Projects that are especially at risk of undermining dignity needs are those with explicit dependence structures and asymmetries, as in the distribution of aid. A colleague of mine said in an interview: *When I first got into development and I went to Tijuana, Mexico, there was a huge organization handing things to people there. Although people needed them, I felt bad for them because people were begging. It was a terrible approach.*

A dignity-centered distribution of aid will counter the stigma associated with receiving aid in culturally resonant ways and will see the stakeholders involved not primarily as needy and vulnerable recipients of aid but as agents whose psychological and sociocultural realities have to be taken seriously (Thomas et al. 2020). If people need support—say, child support grants—there is stigma attached to that and to the experience of dependence that can be aggravated by bureaucratic procedures and a humiliating application process (Wright et al. 2015). At the same time, proper bureaucratic mechanisms can be helpful in combating the moral and practical challenge of regional favoritism, a recognized challenge in the distribution of aid, especially in countries with weak governance and a lack of robust bureaucracy and administration (Bommer et al. 2022). Two major dignity-affirming factors in humanitarian aid, identified in research carried out by the Humanitarian Policy Group Report from the Overseas Development

Institute, are respect and self-reliance (Mosel and Holloway 2019). One initiative suggested direct cash transfers as a dignity-enhancing measure in order to increase choice (ID Insight, Dignity and Cash 2022).[3] There is evidence that direct cash transfers can have wide-ranging impacts, including education and empowerment (Bastagli et al. 2016). Strengthening a person's agency is a key to the affirmation of dignity. Working with internally displaced people in Ukraine who had to flee their homes after the Russian invasion in February 2022, a Ukrainian Caritas worker talked about a program, very much in the spirit of Integral Human Development, that involves psychologists, entertainers, and social pedagogues to help the refugees—both children and adults—assimilate into their new environment. It is "important to help people regain confidence in their own abilities, not to remain in the role of the victim for long, which prevents them from being proactive and moving forward."[4] This approach offers a sense of agency and control over one's life. A sense of control can also be strengthened through proper distribution of information about available aid to reduce a chronic sense of insecurity (Shea 2022). Even though these points may seem obvious, explicitly considering dignity aspects in the project management makes a difference.

The art and skill of listening emerges as a major virtue for dignity-based management. Listening is a pathway toward coexistence, willing to give up the controlling aspect of talking. This requires discipline and a moment of self-effacement, a moment of emptiness even. Listening creates a space for meaning to be discovered, for meaning not yet revealed. In this sense, listening includes an openness to disruption. Gemma Corradi Fiumara (1990, 73) characterized listening as "the capacity of paying heed to a story that allows the unfolding of its meaning." She also argued that listening is a constitutive part of rationality, of making proper judgments. Appropriate speech depends on adequate listening. During a class visit, a diplomat told the students, *you cannot be accused of listening too much.*

Listening is one of the cardinal virtues of Integral Human Development. If you want to take the whole person seriously and if you consider each person, you have to take the time to listen. This is resource-intensive and slows processes down. As one colleague observed, *integral human development cannot be rushed. It takes time, it takes time to listen.* The willingness to listen is one of the most effective ways of showing respect for a person. Project management in the spirit of integral human development is based on two main virtues: "seeing" (the

---

[3] Christine Kahura, Rico Bergemann, Tom Wein, Caroline Teti, and Miriam Laker-Oketta, "Operationalizing Dignity in Humanitarian Aid," *IDinsight Blog*, November 10, 2022.

[4] Svitlana Dukhovych, "Dignity and Hope: Caritas Ukraine's Aid to Displaced People," *Vatican News* online, August 20, 2022.

person as a person) and "listening" (to all people involved). We could call these "the virtues of inclusive perception." These virtues, in between attitudes and acts, imply the humility to be corrected by the other, to be corrected by the encounter. The category of "encounter" can be offered as an IHD-relevant lens. The openness to encounter includes an attitude that has been called "magnanimity," a kind of intellectual "gentleness" and cognitive flexibility that allows someone to accommodate a wide spectrum of ideas or insights.

In order to create the conditions for the experience of dignity, Irina Mosel and Kerrie Holloway, based on their interviews with refugees and displaced people in six different countries, recommend face-to-face communication and investing time and resources in listening to the affected population from the start.

> A theme emerging from all the case studies is that people want to be listened to—properly listened to. Many of those interviewed lamented that humanitarians still mostly engage in tokenistic listening, structured around needs assessment tools that only look for things that have been preidentified as important.... Another theme coming out of this research is the importance of face-to-face communication. Across the six case studies, respondents highlighted how important this was in terms of feeling respected and dignified. (Mosel and Holloway 2019, 17)

Elinor Ostrom has shown that face-to-face communication increases the ability of a community to properly manage a common resource pool (Ostrom 1998, 9–10).

Lack of listening and lack of knowledge of the local history and culture threaten the success of projects and threaten peace. US diplomats reflecting on the genocide in Rwanda commented that rigid identity categories and a lack of a deep understanding of history had led to the unsuccessfulness of the Arusha Peace. "Using our own experience with contemporary democracy as a reference point," Western diplomats failed to understand the local context (Baker and Leader 2020, 295). "We failed to realize or accept that neither democracy nor peace was a panacea for resolving deep-seated conflicts" (Baker and Leader 2020, 9). "The international community underestimated the deep-seated complexities in Rwandan culture and the force of antagonism fueled by Rwanda's history" (Rawson 2018, 241). The mediators focused on standard instruments without realizing the historical complexity of the situation, without taking the time to listen.[5] There can be a high price for not listening enough.

---

[5] "Mediators, facilitators, and Observers involved in the international intervention did not fully comprehend the context of the crisis.... We glossed over the emotional roots of the conflict, which in the Rwandan case, were fear and loathing—fear that the 'other,' once empowered, would be a perpetual oppressor, and the loathing that comes from devaluing one's

Humility, understood as an openness to reality and the willingness to learn and accept contextual authority, becomes as much a part of a dignity-centered project management approach as patience and the willingness to invest time without imposing the pace. In this context, Pope Francis has mentioned a fundamental idea: "time is greater than space" (*Evangelii Gaudium* 222). He observes that "we are always more effective when we generate processes rather than holding on to positions of power" (*Laudato Si'* 178). This principle motivates patience without the obsession with immediate results. "Giving priority to time means being concerned about initiating processes rather than possessing spaces" (*Evangelii Gaudium* 123). Dignity-centered project management acknowledges the importance of processes and the time it takes to build inclusive processes for results that can be accepted by the stake holders.

This is all deceptively simple; as simple as the one imperative of respecting people, mentioned in part I. Dignity-centered project management is more a matter of the willingness to take the time to strive for inclusive perception than it is a complicated design problem. Another aspect of project management in the spirit of integral human development is similarly simple: a culture of integrity.

A Culture of Integrity

Integrity is a way of being in the world that can be characterized through three dimensions: sincerity and honesty, earnestness and robust concern, and the commitment to integrate the different aspects of a complex situation. Consequently, integrity is undermined by dishonesty and deceptiveness, carelessness and thoughtlessness, and fragmentation and disintegration. Corruption is a prime example of integrity erosion.

Corruption betrays an attitude that instrumentalizes projects and interactions for one's own advantage at the expense of the common good. This is not the place to enter into an in-depth discussion on corruption, but there can be no doubt that corruption is a social and political matter that arises in social situations that involve more than one player. Whether it be caused by need or greed, cultural, economic, social, or political factors (Hellsten 2019), corruption cannot be separated from the quality of relationships and the quality of

---

neighbor. The contenders were caught in an emotional recreation of self-images generated by diminution and demonization of the other side.... We underestimated the will to power.... The mediators were focused on democratic practice and power sharing; the negotiating parties were contesting for power. Diplomats proposed classic peacemaking devices for bringing the parties together; the parties negotiated out of deeply rooted cultural dispositions" (Rawson 2018, 15).

communication. On the project level, corruption can best be reduced through high quality communication, that is, communication that is conveyed through open and easily accessible communication channels, which is accurate, honest, swift, precise, and based on benevolence and trust.

Muurlink and Macht reconstruct the history of the NGO Co-operation in Development in a case study about corruption. Active in the Bangladesh delta, this organization was founded by the Australian businessman Fred Hyde, who established a simple steel school on Bhola Island in 1990 (Muurlink and Macht 2020). The idea was simple and practical:

> That first school set a formula that was to largely hold to the present day: around 6 *ghondas* (around half an acre) of donated land, community support to building up the school site (around 80 by 30 feet) to above the normal wet-season water level, and a concrete-pole and steel construction held together with nails, bolts and fencing wire in a formula that was sufficiently strong that in the 30 years since, not a single school suffered significant wind damage despite the exposure of the island to the brunt of bad weather in the Bay of Bengal. (Muurlink and Macht 2020, 1020)

Each standard school had a staff of four. After the retirement of the founder in 2015, Olav Muurlink took over as head of country (or HOC), Bangladesh—an operation of about fifty schools and a dozen kindergartens. On one of his trips to the country, he took an independent interpreter with him, making the local staff uncomfortable. Unannounced visits to school sites created an additional level of stress for the local staff since Muurlink decided to hire his own transport. The impression formed that the organization had something to hide. "The unwillingness of the local head office staff to welcome a bilingual outsider meant that when the HOC returned, in his new role as head of country, signalled there was some 'insider' information that they wanted to protect" (Muurlink and Macht 2020, 1021). Muurlink established a direct communication line with the frontline staff, outside of the local head office. He sensed panic and fear.

Two entry points for corruption could be identified: the communication structure and the payment system. First, the schools were widely separated with little social contact among them. The Australian head office was out of reach, giving a lot of power to the local head office that previously had also organized and controlled the translations. Second, wages had been distributed in cash, at the local head office, to the local heads of school, who then distributed to the school staff. The new head of country established his own communication channel and changed the payment system to individual bank accounts. Systemic corruption emerged in a hierarchical system. Invoice padding and the use of inferior building materials were just two ways of rechanneling funds to those in power.

> Considering the founder's success in building the school network, and decades-long exposure to the culture, the question arises as to how corruption was able to spread despite his presence and surveillance. The key was the flow of information. The "leadership group" because of their relative mastery of English, and the founder's lack of significant fluency in the Bangla language, held dual roles as administrators and interpreters/translators. The founder was of the view that everything had to be run on an absolute shoestring, and employing professional interpreters was a waste of donor funds. The "insiders" given this additional power were able to control the flow of information to the founder tightly. (Muurlink and Macht 2020, 1024)

Information flow and communication management emerged as the major factors of the project's problems.

Corruption cannot be separated from the question of communication. An Indian expatriate physics professor has invented a creative way to change the communication pattern between people in order to fight corruption. "As a way to fight corruption by shaming the officials who ask for bribes, the professor created a fake currency bill: the zero-rupee note."[6] This breaks a pattern of institutionalized practices, challenging ways of perception and relationships. Integral human development, with its relational understanding of the person, will pay special attention to relationality and the quality of interactions and communication. The quality of relationships and communication is also crucial in the management of failures and mistakes. Honesty is a constitutive aspect of integrity. A culture of honesty, however, is easy in the days of sunshine and more difficult in the days of rain.

Integral human development can be seen to be "integral" also in the way that this approach is motivated to integrate failures. Some projects simply fail. Everyone who has spent time working with projects or listening to development workers can give examples of failed projects.

A person bought an expensive water filter for a local NGO, and the device (since it was expensive) was put into a locked closet and never used. An NGO gives a few cows to a community to strengthen the village's asset basis with the result that girls were taken out of school to look after the cows. A project installed

---

[6] Alice Lloyd, "How a Professor Started a Campaign to Fight Everyday Corruption in India," *World Bank Blogs*, December 2, 2015.

computer kiosks in rural areas to find out that connectivity and electricity supply were major issues. A project intended to support masons established a start-up subsidy that created community resistance due to the perceived lack of fairness. An organization built a water purification system that was never used since it was built on sacred ground, a factor that was not revealed by the local interlocutors who were only interested in the generated cash flow. A project built a road to increase the market access for local farmers with the result that competitors moved in.

These are obviously matters of unintended and undesired consequences. There are, of course, well-documented cases of failures. A major well project, designed to provide landless people with wells so that they could sell the water to the farmers for irrigation purposes, failed because of a lack of insight into the power structures (MacMillan 2022, 191–92). The Chad-Cameroon Pipeline project, the largest private investment in the history of Sub-Saharan Africa, was a major failure (Clausen and Attaran 2011) and an example of infrastructural violence (Enns and Sneyd 2020).

Social change, as we have observed previously, is ambivalent. The influx of resources always changes an entire landscape of power, assets, and values:

> Aid intended for the social and economic sectors in order to generate improvements in welfare may simply substitute the funds that governments would have spent on these sectors anyway. Thus, instead of increasing funds directed at growth and welfare improvements, aid may free funds for other purposes not intended by donors—and which are unlikely to benefit the majority of the population—such as military, personal appropriation of funds etc. (Jensen Newby 2010, 9)

There are many reasons why projects fail. Some people fall into the "one size fits all trap" and import standard responses to predetermined problems (Ika 2012, 33). This phenomenon is connected to a naïve and decontextualized way of handling "best practices" with the risk of "institutional monocropping." Some projects fail because of poor governance and poor risk management (Ikediashi et al. 2014) or a lack of good governance capacity (Pritchett et al. 2010). Some projects fail because they are not properly owned, or the cultural context is not properly understood or considered. Some projects fail because of the "capacity trap" and "premature load bearing" (asking too much too soon). In other failures, there may be issues with the capacity to absorb imported resources, also through "donor proliferation" (Jensen Newby 2010, 14). Projects fail because of a distorted incentive structure or because of a bureaucracy trap and an unhelpful focus on reports. Some projects fail because of a lack of patience and a short-term perspective. Projects fail because of a lack of accountability and internal power asymmetries.

There are many entry points for mistakes and failures. Mistakes can happen in the planning or in the execution; there are human failures, technical failures, structural failures; and there are failures that reflect the "division of labor" between individuals and institutions. Moss et al. (2006) point to an "aid-institutions paradox": projects need a structural environment of well-functioning public institutions while, at the same time, the influx of massive aid undermines the motivation and capacity of institution-building. Projects are implemented within a particular culture and within a particular structural context. Both can create entry points for failures.

Projects can fail because of structural reasons on a macrolevel, institutional reasons, project management reasons, cultural reasons, and personal mistakes. Conversely, we can distinguish structural, institutional, and managerial success conditions for development projects (Ika and Donnelly 2017). One of the most important factors is lack of integrity in communication. Projects fail because of a lack of listening and open communication. Jacqueline Novogratz makes the point about the often-distorted communication between "donors" and "beneficiaries":

> The donors would visit, say, a group of a dozen women who had built a chicken coop for a couple of hundred chicks. The women would proudly present eggs that had recently been laid and talk about how they planned to sell them to the community. They would serve the donors Fantas and, often cookies, and sometimes sing and dance, as well. The donors would leave feeling satisfied, happy that they were making such a difference.... In reality, most donors were doing little to change lives. (Novogratz 2009, 95)

Novogratz's example touches upon listening and integrity, on the willingness to have open communication. Trust-based communication is a major project success factor (Diallo and Thuillier 2005).

A commitment to integral human development includes a commitment to "the whole picture," including the less pleasant aspects. Project failures can offer learning opportunities. Sadly, we do not like to think about failures too much, for we do not like to dwell on mistakes. Failure analysis is often shortchanged "because examining our failures in depth is emotionally unpleasant and can chip away at our self-esteem. Left to our own devices, most of us will speed through or avoid failure analysis altogether. Another reason is that analyzing organizational failures requires inquiry and openness, patience, and a tolerance for causal ambiguity" (Edmondson 2011). There is so much to learn from mistakes. An honest discussion about mistakes and failures can invite fruitful questions, questions of a fundamental nature. A Peace Corps Volunteer tells a story about a carefully designed bread-baking project in Benin. He had talked to a group of four women about the bread supply in the local village. The only bread available was of poor quality and had to be brought in by motorcycle from a city twenty-five kilometers away. They did some market research and confirmed the business opportunity. The Peace Corps Volunteer taught the women a system of accounting, and they established rules and a work schedule. He assisted in the financing and construction of the clay oven. The bread production began successfully, and the American volunteer was asked to control the money box, which he did. Gradually, he handed over responsibility to the women. One day, there was no bread. The women had come together the night before and had distributed all the cash among themselves, not leaving any resources to buy new supplies. The project was over. Had it failed? If so, why?

Discussing the experience with students, the responses brought many important aspects of development projects to the fore. There was a question about success criteria—what constitutes success or failure? Some students did not consider the project a failure. The women had more cash than before, and they had obtained new skills and gained work experience. Maybe their social standing in the community had been improved as well. There was a question about expectation management and clear communication of intentions and hopes.

Obviously, the available information was limited and left much to speculation. Did the women trust each other? Were they not comfortable working in a group and as a team? Were they put under external pressure (e.g., by their husbands)? What did they buy with the cash they had liquidated? Did they have to respond to an emergency?

There may have been a lack of sustainable pedagogy and insufficient accompaniment and "premature loading." There could have been a lack of inbuilt capacities to continue with the financial management and accounting once the process was handed over to the women. There may have been a lack of experience and depth on the part of the volunteer. As one student commented, "The culture of failure here represents the culture of having the poor as a playground for development experiments. This has nothing to do with the ethics of the volunteer whose intentions are clearly good. It has to do with the structures that allow programs to send inexperienced people to help."

There may have been the nonsupportive context: "The underlying issue is not that the people can't sustain a business, it is that the system or situation they're asked to operate within is not conducive to sustaining a business." Low-income entrepreneurs are often forced into being more reactive than proactive, following short-term thinking driven by a necessity to fulfill immediate needs.

We do need conversations about success criteria. Context matters. Each community has its own dynamics. Open communication is crucial. Accountability structures must be established. Similar to the case study on corruption in Bangladesh, a commitment to integrity entails a commitment to honest conversations. These lessons, in turn, invite a different set of conversations when planning the next project.

7

Doing Justice to a Context

Development projects are realized in particular contexts, with their specific dynamics and history. Integral human development, with its invitation to understand the person in her complexity, will invite an effort to try to understand a particular context. There are obvious data points, and there may be more subtle sources of understanding such as the role of literature. Fiction can be a seismograph, a window into a culture, and the unfinished agenda of a culture. Martina Kopf has shown how fruitful the analysis of fiction can be for a contextual understanding of "development" (Kopf 2019). The idea of reverse privileging will also affect the selection of sources and the intentional labor to consider diverse conversation partners. The well-known "danger of the single story" (Adichie 2009) is another facet of the Matthew effect. It is also an expression of the dangers of construing identity not on the basis of a plurality of aspects (Sen 2006). The reading of any local context calls for this diversity and pluralism. Respecting local knowledge in all its forms is an important aspect of respect.

Pope Francis has made this point in *Laudato Si'*:

> There is a need to respect the rights of peoples and cultures, and to appreciate that the development of a social group presupposes an historical process which takes place within a cultural context and demands the constant and active involvement of local people from within their proper culture. Nor can the notion of the quality of life be imposed from without, for quality of life must be understood within the world of symbols and customs proper to each human group. (*Laudato Si'* 144)

Taking the trouble to get a deeper sense of local knowledge has a moral dimension as well as a pragmatic dimension—an understanding of the particular context improves the quality of actions and interactions; it reduces transaction costs and leads to a more complete reading of a context. Doing justice to a local context can be called a project of striving for "local epistemic justice."

Local Epistemic Justice

Respecting a person means respecting her knowledge. Doing justice to a local context requires the proper consideration of types of local knowledge that have been characterized by terms like "indigenous knowledge," "traditional knowledge," "folk knowledge," or "informal knowledge." Ignoring local knowledge is a matter of epistemic injustice, that is, a matter of systematically underestimating a person's or group's contribution to knowledge and insight. There is a power asymmetry at work here, and recognizing knowledge claims matters to development theory and development practices: "There *is* an epistemology of development based on a certain epistemology embedded within a particular social imaginary that excludes other epistemologies, such as those from poorer countries or of those living in less-advantaged situations" (Malavisi 2019, 44). Epistemic injustice has been linked to colonialism and postcolonialism overwriting local knowledge with its claims to truth (Bhargava 2013; Gentile 2013).[1] Rebecca Tsosie (2012) has argued that indigenous people have been mistreated in the name of "knowledge" and "discovery." Even seemingly neutral science has been used to disadvantage indigenous people who are predominantly seen as "objects" of epistemic agency rather than epistemic agents.

A politics of recognition is at stake when discussing local knowledge. Knowledge claims are generally expected to be backed up by appropriate justification. The very idea of "justification" and "bringing forth reasons" can be identified as a potential source of epistemic injustice. Ian Werkheiser has pointed out that the question of "good reasons" can be used as a mechanism of exclusion:

> Asking for reasons privileges people who are able to come up with reasons over people who actually have a lot of knowledge. Some people will be able to provide reasons and thus maintain knowledge when others in the same situation would lose knowledge; this is not because of epistemic differences but differences in rhetorical ability. It is perhaps no great revelation to say that people who are able to sound convincing are more likely to have what they say taken up by an audience, and that people who are good at rationalizing things are more likely to be able to convince themselves of things as well. What is perhaps less often considered is that when we ask for someone's reasons, people who are better able to produce convincing-sounding reasons *whether or not they are the actual causes of their belief* will be able to maintain their knowledge, while people who are less able to do this will lose their knowledge. (Werkheiser 2014, 185)

---

[1] For the link between epistemic injustice and recognition, see also McConkey (2004).

Asking for reasons from people who are not trusted is also a power issue. Hence, different levels of justification apply to different epistemic agents. "This means that people who are from marginalized groups in our society and who are therefore not trusted to know things will be epistemically oppressed by the increased demand to provide reasons, and their knowledge will in fact have less uptake in the community" (Werkheiser 2014, 185). Werkheiser calls for special attention to the marginalized, to a conscious effort to listen to underheard voices (Werkheiser 2014, 187). Determining which person is given which kind of attention is a matter of individual goodwill and a matter of institutional arrangements and cultural practices. Epistemic justice needs to be linked, then, both to individuals and to institutions (Anderson 2012).

The idea of epistemic injustice has been significantly shaped by Miranda Fricker who discussed recognition of credibility as a key issue in the debate. Certain people's claims are assigned privileged status, and other people's claims are not taken seriously (Fricker 1999; 2007; 2012). Some people are ignored and made silent. One way of silencing is a kind of "testimonial quieting" that occurs when a speaker is not recognized as an epistemic agent and feels compelled to adjust her message to the receptive expectations of a powerful hearer (Dotson 2011).[2]

There is a growing sense that local knowledge matters and that the relationship between local knowledge and other types of knowledge can be reconstructed in integral rather than competitive terms. For example, in a study on forestry management in Mexico, D. J. Klooster has shown that both scientific and local forest knowledge are limited in their respective ways and can complement each other (Klooster 2002). This seems to be a promising approach, moving us into a direction of epistemic justice. Local knowledge is an important element to bring about sustainable change that is accepted and culturally acceptable (Diekens 2007, 14–15). Jason Corburn has identified local knowledge (understood as "firsthand experience") as a key issue in proper environmental planning. It can contribute to the planning process epistemologically and procedurally in terms of effectiveness and regarding distributive justice (Corburn 2003). At the same time, epistemic justice may call for a recognition of the limits of any type of knowledge, including local knowledge. John Briggs opens a study on the use of indigenous knowledge in development work with a statement from a Tanzanian small-scale farmer: "If indigenous knowledge is so good, why is my farm so poor?" (Briggs 1999, 99).

---

[2] In another paper Dotson describes another incidence of epistemic injustice when an interlocutor is willfully ignorant of the hermeneutical resources used by the speaker resulting in a diminishment of the speaker's ability to contribute to the discourse (Dotson 2012); this very point about willful hermeneutical ignorance has also been made by Gaile Pohlhaus (Pohlhaus 2012).

Knowledge claims are limited. The, maybe idyllic, idea that projects can be designed in a participatory manner that includes "the local community" is equally limited. Local communities are usually not homogeneous entities. Accordingly,

> Local knowledge is scattered and institutionally dispersed; it is located at the individual and household level as well as collectively through community stewards and other key social actors (e.g., shamans, elders, local religious and political leaders, and healing artists). As such, one can distinguish between common (or everyday or public) knowledge (i.e., held by the whole community) and specialist knowledge (i.e., retained by a few local experts, e.g., healers with specific medical expertise and knowledge of local curative plants; knowledge of local plants known only by women; or knowledge of crops known only by men). (Diekens 2007, 24)

Different types of local knowledge are generated by different local players, and gender differences come heavily into play. Hilary Warburton and Adrienne Martin quote an example from the Mbeere people of central Kenya:

> Generally, the best information about the small annual herbs is obtained from older women; herd boys, being always hungry and also experimental, are experts on the range of wild edible fruits; honey collectors show the most detailed knowledge of flowering sequences, and indeed know most differential characteristics of their local plants. Yet even within a group, one individual will stand out because of keen powers of observation, prodigious memory, curiosity and intellect. (Warburton and Martin 1999, 2)

Local knowledge is unevenly distributed, a matter of power as well as of initiative.

Local epistemic justice, then, means to "see" the epistemic agents involved, to see the different and diverse local people as "knowers" and "knowledge claim holders," and to respect this status by taking the claims made and the resources used seriously. This does not mean to wholeheartedly accept whatever is claimed, but it definitely means to subscribe to "principles of charity" in the hermeneutics of approaching a particular situation. Child patients who are not always taken seriously in their claims about their health situations illustrate this approach (Carel and Györffy 2014). Proper consideration of the epistemic agents involved requires "epistemic vigilance" (Sperber et al. 2010), a sense of attention and openness that can also be linked to the concept of "prudence." Local epistemic justice means secondly to make an effort to understand the local context in both its particularity and its historicity. Local epistemic justice is connected to a culture of remembering the local stories and histories, to an experience of communicative memory. Within the power questions that characterize an ethics of remembering (Medina 2011), there may even be grounds to consider "epistemic disobedience," following the example of the Argentinian mothers of the Plaza de Mayo, who refused to accept forgetting.

Understanding the knowledge necessary to navigate a local context may give rise to higher levels of respect for local realities. I mentioned Vikram Akula's "village" experience above; he had to obtain "knowledge by description," allowing him to gain a thick understanding of a local context. Knowledge by description is different from knowledge by acquaintance in the dynamics of the personalization of knowledge (Russell 2009). Knowledge by acquaintance can more easily become "personal knowledge," integrated into a person's form of life and personality. There is an undeniable link between one's form of life and one's understanding and knowing since the former shapes the kinds of examples and the thickness of possible descriptions. Akula's encounter with local realities, however difficult it was, instilled in him a new sense of respect for local knowledge and for those everyday—literally "every day"—life burdens carried by poor villagers. "Anyone who thinks poor people are lazy should spend a week living as they do. With none of the conveniences the developed world takes for granted, every chore takes inordinate amounts of time and energy" (Akula 2011, 38). Akula came to see the villagers as teachers, very much in the sense that Pope Francis sees "the poor" as teachers[3] and local practices as sources of wisdom.[4]

Respecting the local context implies a hesitation to believe that processes of social change that have worked in context A can simply be reproduced in context B. Such an implication brings us to the requirement for and the limits of planning.

The Necessity and Fragility of Planning

While working in Bhutan in the mid-1990s, I explored some of the social changes brought about by an integral forest management project. One change occurred in gender relations as a direct consequence of the project in the province of Bumthang. The project, focused fundamentally on exploring possibilities of setting up ecologically responsible and economically viable fir tree management, generated jobs mainly for men, which made them cash earners rather than "employees" on their wives' farms. This consequence meant that men could make more money than their wives in an otherwise subsistence economy and gained asset independence as a direct result of the innovative possibilities triggered by a

---

[3] "They [the poor] have much to teach us" (*Evangelii Gaudium* 198).
[4] "Expressions of popular piety have much to teach us." (*Evangelii Gaudium* 126).

newly built cash economy. These dynamics changed the gender-power relations in a context where, "in most cases, women own and inherit land and assets" (Crins 2004, 581) and where "women do not surrender their property to the man when they marry," which enables them "to be financially independent" (Pommaret 1999, 18–19). The project, as one may well envisage, was carefully planned, and these consequences were neither intended nor desired. In a number of instances, women felt aggravation and annoyance; in other words, the project translated into unplanned frustrations.

As we have seen above, certain aspects of a project can be planned and certain aspects cannot be planned. We have seen that some projects simply fail because of unforeseen (and sometimes unforeseeable) developments. An approach that honors the complexity of the whole person will be less tempted to overestimate the range of what can be planned. There are limits to planning and limits to what can be managed. Because of the complexity and interdependence of our social lives, any social transformation will imply different kinds of change: planned change and unplanned change (intended and unintended consequences), desired and desirable change, and less desired and less desirable change.

Hannah Arendt, writing about the fragility of our social lives, observed that "action and speech are surrounded by and in constant contact with the acts and the words of other men [persons]" (Arendt 1998, 188). A young development worker captured her sentiment:

> *It is important to keep in mind that there is no air-tight plan or project if it involves people. We are not perfect and life is in a state of flux. We don't have the full knowledge of the whole picture nor do we have full control of everything. We might all have our best intentions and great well thought out plans but still one small decision or indecision will affect the project.*

We know of many examples of unintended and undesired consequences, including price effects, behavioral effects, migration effects, conflict effects, or governance effects (Koch et al. 2021, 6). Some unintended effects may manifest themselves in the short term, others in the long term. Here is the testimony of a colleague who worked as a consultant to the educational system in Punjab:

> *From my experience of working with the Punjab Education System through a large-scale development project, I will demonstrate an example of how a solution that seemed to be producing positive results simultaneously caused problems for people on the ground. I was involved in design and imple-mentation of a large-scale tablet-based assessment system to test public primary school children. Since public schools lacked a reliable assessment*

system, this innovation provided valuable insights to policy makers about student learning scores. Within a year, the continuous process of testing children, sharing scores and supporting interventions improved the learning outcomes by 10%. This was celebrated and documented, and the testing system became an essential part of the Punjab Education System. After two years, I met a government school teacher and inquired about the usefulness of the testing system. He revealed that the policy makers had started punishing teachers with low assessment scores. Salaries of teachers were halted and teachers were demoted. Further, teachers vented their frustrations by punishing students with low scores in test. This was not intended when the system was designed.

Unintended consequences are common and unavoidable. Even still, the concept of integral human development offers important background encouragement for planning tools. Thomas Aquinas, an important voice in the Catholic tradition, hailed prudence as the ability to have a long-term perspective and a "circumspect view."[5] The logic of change framework is one prominent organizing tool for designing coherent projects. Originating in the 1990s, in the field of community-based social change initiatives in the United States, the tool was initially designed to make pathways of change explicit, leading to specific long-term goals and showing the connections between activities, outputs, and outcomes that occur in the course of a particular project. As useful as these logic models are, they tend to offer a rather linear view of reality, built on the belief that the world is a place of clear causal relationships. They tend to be expert driven and donor driven, and these models are rarely sensitive to undesirable outcomes.

Given the above-mentioned importance of the "development imagination," logic models restrict rather than expand thinking about solutions, working with "checklists." They offer a particular way of looking at complex realities with the risks of becoming too rigid, too output or outcome focused, and too simplistic in assuming causal relations. Nonetheless, the simple categories of these models, such as "context/baseline," "inputs," "activities," "outputs," and "outcomes," are helpful.

From an Integral Human Development perspective, one of the most important aspects of planning is the assessment of the status quo, the reconstruction of baseline and point of departure. When I did my postgraduate development studies program in Zurich, we were asked to explore a conflict between a farmer, a neighbor, and the city of Zurich. We were told to carry out an interview with each stakeholder in which we should ask how the conflict started. Learning that the three parties had very different views on the history of the conflict and,

---

[5] Cf. Aquinas, STh II-II, qq 46–55.

consequently, on the status quo was eye-opening. These different interpretations were the source of further conflicts.

Any change is a move from A to B. In designing a change process, energy and time must be invested to understand how people see the question of "where we are." Taking the time to listen and find out what is seen as problematic and in need of change is worthwhile. We find an example of the price of nonlistening in the well-known account *Three Cups of Tea*, reconstructing the beginnings of Greg Mortenson's work in Pakistan.

Mortenson was indebted to the inhabitants of Korphe, a small Pakistani village, since they nursed him back to life after a failed attempt to climb the K2. After his recuperation, Mortenson was shocked to find out that they did not have a school. "He was appalled to see eighty-two children, seventy-eight boys, and the four girls who had the pluck to join them, kneeling on the frosty ground, in the open ... most scratched in the dirt with sticks they'd brought for that purpose ... there was a fierceness in their desire to learn" (Mortenson and Relin 2007, 31–32). The village could not afford a teacher of its own, so they shared a teacher with the neighboring village, which resulted in the children being without supervision three days a week. Mortenson decided to build a school. He returned to the United States to get the funds necessary for the construction of a school building. He worked hard, made sacrifices, and came back to Korphe, ready to build a school. To his surprise, the villagers told him that they needed a bridge first, not a school. Mortenson "felt angry at himself for not planning better. He decided to stay in Korphe until he understood everything else he had to do to bring the school to life" (Mortenson and Relin 2007, 103). Patience and flexibility, the ability to listen, and the ability to wait became key factors in Mortenson's journey. When planning, investing time in an integrated view of the status quo, including the survey of hopes, desires, and priorities, is a good investment in the long run.

8

The Moral Biography of Projects

A commitment to integral human development will be interested in "the whole person" and in the "whole project." The moral stakes are higher with an Integral Human Development (or IHD) approach (with the risk, mentioned in the introduction, that IHD-defenders see themselves on a moral high horse). A commitment to "leaving no one behind" is a moral claim that makes the moral dimension of development work particularly interesting and relevant. Below, I introduce an approach that pays special attention to the moral side of development projects, their value basis, and the moral challenges that emerge: moral biographies of projects.

Biographies are descriptions of life histories. They can be done from a moral perspective, looking at a person's integrity and moral performance; at moral challenges encountered; and at moral dilemmas faced. A moral biography of a person or group will look into the choices, decisions, attitudes, and actions of a person. Furthermore, it will explore the conditions, structural frameworks, circumstances, relationships, and interactions from the point of view of ethics. "The term moral biography refers to the way individuals conscientiously combine two elements in daily life: personal capacity and moral compass" (Schervish 2016). Biographies of that kind are especially interested in agency and attitudes.

A moral biography is an exercise in writing moral history. A moral history can be written about a particular historical event, such as Harry S. Stout's *Upon the Altar of the Nation: A Moral History of the American Civil War*, or about an entire century, such as Jonathan Glover's *Humanity: A Moral History of the Twentieth Century*. Moral histories can be written about groups (Sierakowski 2019), texts (Sellers-García 2016),[1] monuments, cities, or even wealth (Schervish 2016).

---

[1] Sylvia Sellers-García (2016) has provided a stellar example of this approach in her article "The Biography of a Colonial Document: Creation, Mobility, Preservation, Politics, Research," exploring document creation, travel, and storage of colonial documents. Donald McKenzie's 1986 lecture *Bibliography and the Sociology of Texts* (McKenzie 1999) can be read as an eloquent plea to increased attention to the social aspects of document creation and use.

Moral histories explore the moral aspects of the genesis and development of their objects. We can also write a moral biography of development projects. We could be interested in the value basis and value claims of a project, in the moral challenges it faces, or in the moral growth it may bring.

Integral Human Development is an approach that is particularly sensitive to and interested in normative dimensions of social change. Development projects are the result of decisions and reflect human agency and moral attitudes in their design, their implementation, and their consequences and implications. Some moral biographies of projects may be quite bleak, like a moral biography of the so-called Grand Ethiopian Renaissance Dam in the western Benishangul-Gumuz region, or the moral biography of the oil for food program in Iraq. Phenomena like conflicts or corruption are obviously morally relevant, with a huge impact on project progress and success. Moral aspects enter a project, even in the planning stage (Locatelli et al. 2017). We have illustrated how project failures are shaped by moral aspects. The consequences and the impact of a project are equally morally relevant, as is experienced when development projects have an impact on civil conflict (Crost et al. 2014).

Proposing moral biographies of projects is an attempt to make the implicit moral dimension explicit. A moral biography of a project would explore morally relevant aspects of a project in a diachronic perspective (the history of the project) and a synchronic perspective (the status quo and current situation of a project); it would look at moral challenges in past and present (e.g., in conflict situations); it would attend to morally significant milestones (e.g., through decisions); it would account for widely and deeply debated "hot issues." Questions such as the following will be of interest: Which values and normative commitments were key in the design of the project/program? What were the moral challenges and moral conflicts in the implementation of the project/program? Which views on the moral aspects of the program/project are conflicting or, at least, contrasting?

Sketching a moral biography of the Bethany Land Institute (or BLI) can help demonstrate the value of moral biographies for projects. Following a short introduction, I will briefly reconstruct moral aspects of the story and history of the Bethany Land Institute. I am interested in the value basis of the project and in some of its moral challenges.

The Bethany Land Institute is an agricultural training center in Uganda. It is located in central Uganda—in the Kasana-Luweero Diocese, about eighty-five kilometers north of Kampala along the Gulu Highway. It is, in itself, an example of Integral Human Development, since it is based on an idea of integral ecology and is designed to connect human capabilities with aspects of spiritual growth. The initiative was founded in 2012 by three Ugandan Catholic priests: Fr. Emmanuel

Katongole, Fr. Cornelius Ssempala, and the late Fr. Anthony Rweza. They bought land to start an ecological initiative. Seven years later, the diocese of Kasana-Luweero gave more land (three hundred acres), and the BLI signed a lease for forty-nine years. The Bethany Land Institute runs a "Caretaker Program," an intensive two-year residential program that trains its students in farming, agro-business, and personal formation. In 2022, the first cohort of BLI students graduated from a two-year program.[2] Emmanuel Katongole serves as president of the Bethany Land Institute and is also professor of theology and peace studies at the University of Notre Dame.

The Value Basis

The beginnings of the project reflect the experience of changes in rural life. Emmanuel Katongole offered the following founding story:

> My own village, Malube, sixteen miles to the west of Kampala, off the Kampala–Fort Portal highway, paints the picture of the changes that are occurring. When I was growing up there in the 1960s, our lives and daily routines were shaped by and centered on the three-acre plot of land that my parents had bought when they migrated from Rwanda in the late 1940s. My parents would wake us up at dawn and send us to the garden, where we grew coffee, beans, maize, bananas, and other food crops. A couple of hours later, our morning work in the garden done, we would trek down the forest path to draw water from a spring.... To be sure, there was nothing romantic about growing up in Malube. Life was tough. But if ours was a simple and "primitive" lifestyle, it was marked by a deep sense of belonging—to the family, to the community, to the land (that supplied our food), and to the forest (where we collected fire-wood and drew water, and on whose outskirts we played). That was then. Now when I visit Malube, there are more people living in it, the forest that surrounded it has all disappeared, the spring has dried up, and where it used to run young men are burning bricks. There is an acute "water poverty" in the village.... The land looks dry, and the banana trees and other crops on it all look miserable. It is not surprising that little food is produced on the land. Where in the past we carried produce from the village to our relatives living in the city, now whenever I visit home I have to buy food and groceries in the city to bring to the village. (Katongole 2022b, 131–32)

---

[2] For more information on the Bethany Land Institute, see BethanyLandInstitute.org.

The founding story points to the experience of "slow violence," that remains largely and long undetected and untreated. "The effects of the slow violence of ecological degradation, especially on poor communities, are many: food insecurity, diminishing livelihoods, loss of water, and overall ongoing vulnerability to unpredictable climatic and weather conditions" (Katongole 2022b, 135). Interpreted in moral terms, the founding story already reveals a sense of challenges. The perception of a situation as a source of moral concern requires a normative framework. Emmanuel Katongole's perception of "the village life lost" is the story of developments that are labeled as morally problematic.

In an interview conducted in 1999, Emmanuel Katongole also talked about moral aspects of education and the low prestige of manual work in the seminary that he attended. We have seen in a previous chapter how the image or reputation of a profession (the example given was the profession of farmers) shapes the development imagination. Katongole and his fellow students were not motivated to do agricultural work, given their perceived elevated intellectual and spiritual status. This attitude was clearly nourished by his high school experience, where he does not remember a single lesson about millet, goats, beans, or bananas. He grew up with "a vision that excludes the majority of Africans."

Moral aspects of work have been part of the history of Christianity since the beginning. The recognition of manual labor was easier for the Christian tradition, recognizing that Jesus worked as a carpenter, than for Greek or Roman elitist philosophy. Deep theological and philosophical questions lay behind the Bethany Land Institute. With the struggle for education and values, the project has a clear connection to the founder's biography and his education. We can find a particular type of knowledge ("knowledge by acquaintance") and a particular experience at the beginning of the project, an experience of loss and decline. The twenty-fifth anniversary year (2012) of Emmanuel Katongole's priestly ordination became a critical year for the BLI. He was fifty-two years old at that time, a good moment to take stock and reflect on what matters most.

In our interview, Fr. Katongole talked about the historical and motivational beginnings: "2012 is a significant date. I was 25 years as priest. We were on a retreat to celebrate.... I talked to a classmate, another priest." Katongole told him about his idea of a forest like the one near where he had grown up, "running around and gathering wood. And now there is no forest. I am angry that there is no forest. Instead of being angry about what has been lost, I decided to plant a forest," he recalled. Possibilities opened up.

My friend knew of a place where they had land for a forest. We visited it and I bought 25 acres of land, he bought 23 acres of land. He said that part of the problem of cutting the forest is because the education system is messed up. There are no jobs and people cut down trees to gain income. I asked him why he bought the acres of land he bought, he said he wants to build a school. He said he's interested in education and ecological issues.... So, we started talking about these ideas. We started with the three E's: economics, ecology, education.... What if we built a farm that would be sustainable? We could teach people to take care of the land.

The vision of the project was based on the perception of educational, economic, and ecological challenges. These were identified as moral and spiritual problems, very much in line with the encyclical *Laudato Si'*, which offered, three years after the initial land acquisition, the normative framework for the project. "There was obviously a need for new educational programs that taught young people to care for creation, but also for new economic opportunities in the village where young people could earn a living while taking care of the land" (Katongole 2022a, 166).

The mission of the Bethany Land Institute exemplifies the idea of Integral Human Development: the formation of leaders who are committed and equipped to transform rural communities in Uganda through an integrated approach ("integral ecology") that fights poverty, cares for creation, and advances human dignity. Emmanuel Katongole distinguished different ecologies in the approach to an integral ecology: economic ecology, social ecology, cultural ecology, and the ecology of daily life (Katongole 2022a, 167–68). These are pillars on which the training program is built: "Caretaker trainees spend two and half years in the training program which revolves around BLI's three learning centers: Mary's Farm, Lazarus Trees and Martha's Market" (Katongole 2022a, 169). The core values, listed in the Strategic Plan 2020–2024, are human dignity, nobility in the care of creation, hard work, self-esteem, a sense of beauty, a spirit of service, gratitude, and tenderness.

These values are reflective of Pope Francis's pontificate and his encyclical *Laudato Si'*. Beauty is used as a countercategory to pragmatism: "By learning to see and appreciate beauty, we learn to reject self-interested pragmatism" (*Laudato Si'* 215). Furthermore, beauty becomes an important category to understand poverty and deprivation: "In some places, rural and urban alike, the privatization of certain spaces has restricted people's access to places of particular beauty" (*Laudato Si'* 45). Pope Francis regularly uses the category "tenderness" when speaking about God's tender love (for example, *Laudato Si'* 73, 77; *Evangelii Gaudium* 274) or in connection with ecology: "A sense of deep communion with the rest of nature cannot be real if our hearts lack tenderness, compassion and concern for our fellow human beings" (*Laudato Si'* 91). An ecological conversion "calls for a number of attitudes which together foster a spirit of generous care, full of tenderness" (*Laudato Si'* 220).

These categories may seem quite idealistic, but the project of the Bethany Land Institute also had a well-established and tangible role model. Emmanuel Katongole drew inspiration for his initiative from an existing project, St. Jude's Farm ("St. Jude Family Projects") near Masaka, in southern Uganda.[3] St. Jude's Farm is a community-based organization that began as a small organic farm on three acres owned by John and Josephine Kizza in the 1980s. They embarked on a journey to improve rural living conditions by introducing innovative methods (based on scientific research) for organic farming. In his imagination, Katongole did not start "*ex nihilo*" (out of nothing) but had a reference point. This illustrates a simple insight proposed by Nelson Goodman—we may be able to create new "worlds," but never *ex nihilo*. Whatever world we create is created out of existing worlds (Goodman 1991).

Katongole was also inspired by the biblical topos of "Bethany," described in the Gospels as the home of Mary, Martha, and Lazarus, friends of Jesus (Katongole 2013). There is a certain theological ethics behind the Bethany Land Institute, based on a theology of Bethany, a theology of the ecology (*Laudato Si'*), and a theology of the land. The category of "land" is theologically relevant (Cole 1990; Cunningham 2013; Williams 2018; Khiok-Khng, and Green 2021) and ethically important, with its identity-conferring and livelihood-enabling features, and its potential for conflict due to scarcity and the potential for deterioration. Theologically, Katongole works with a theology of creation that centers God as farmer, the human person as entrusted with tilling the earth, and a theology of conversion in the spirit of *Laudato Si'* 111, a passage that has become a guiding text for the project:

> Ecological culture cannot be reduced to a series of urgent and partial responses to the immediate problems of pollution, environmental decay and the depletion of natural resources. There needs to be a distinctive way of looking at things, a way of thinking, policies, an educational programme, a lifestyle and a spirituality which together generate resistance to the assault of the technocratic paradigm.

The text calls for the holistic approach that integral human development is all about. The Bethany Land Institute is modeled with an innovative spirit, finding a new way of looking at things through an educational program that

---

[3] For more information on St. Jude's Farm and other projects, see StJudeFamilyProjects.org.

connects questions of knowledge and practice with questions of spirituality and lifestyle. In an interview, Emmanuel Katongole mentioned the possibly counter-cultural witness of the BLI: *We committed ourselves to do sustainable agriculture. That is against the grain because modern agriculture has become so technical and scientific and based on pesticides, etc.*

Laudato Si' (201) also refers to the principle that "realities are more impor-tant than ideas," a principle that can also be found in Pope Francis's Apostolic Exhortation *Evangelii Gaudium* (231–33). Read within the wider context of *Evangelii Gaudium*, this principle resists misleading idealism, puritanism, perfec-tionism, and positionalism; and it is meant to challenge closed ideas, safe ideas, and static ideas. Deforestation, food insecurity, and poverty, the three major chal-lenges in rural Uganda that the BLI aims to tackle, are a clear demonstration of the thesis of *Laudato Si'* that "we are faced not with two separate crises, one envi-ronmental and the other social, but rather with one complex crisis which is both social and environmental" (*Laudato Si'* 139). The region faces mass deforestation and resulting topsoil cover depletion as a direct consequence of unsustainable rural practices—such as the cutting of trees for firewood or digging up of marshes for brick making. A rapidly growing population and continuously changing rain patterns due to climate change only exacerbate the issue, making the land increas-ingly arid and unproductive, triggering a food insecurity crisis across the country. Families often resort to extending their property boundaries to compensate for the land's sterility. This, in turn, has ignited widespread land disputes between neighbors. "Land" emerges as a dominant category in disputes.

In fact, because of a land title fight, the plans to start the BLI at the originally purchased site could not be realized. I mentioned above that the local bishop of Kasana-Luweero was open to a contract that allowed the BLI to be built on diocesan territory with agricultural and forest land. The project management had to show resilience, flexibility, and ingenuity in this process. It helped that Emmanuel Katongole's brother serves as a priest in the diocese and that the local bishop at the time had the vision of building a "*Laudato Si'* diocese."

These reference points to the background story show the value of landscape to the initiative. It is based on a model of "bridge-building." The project is built on bridges, and it builds bridges between the United States and Uganda (in the person of Emmanuel Katongole and in the fact that there are two boards, one in the United States and one in Uganda). This bridge-building can also be challenging because of the long-distance management and a "divided loyalty chal-lenge" between the new project and the founders' employer. There are bridges between disciplines (theology and agriculture), bridges between the tangible and the intangible, bridges between the religious and the secular. There are further bridges between the new project and an existing structure, the diocese of Kasana-Luweero. There are bridges between modern technologies and traditional African wisdom, since the project intends to learn from "African native practices and wisdom concerning care of creation and for the land" (Katongole 2022a, 173). The project itself is a bridge between the theology of integral human development and institutional practices. Even amid all of the bridges, some significant moral challenges exist.

Moral Challenges

A moral biography of a project will be particularly interested in the moral aspects that have emerged in the course of the project design and implementation. These observations should not diminish the fact that the story of the Bethany Land Institute shows an impressive and inspiring effort to enact integral human development. And these observations should also not insinuate that the moral challenges are not identified and managed. The moral and spiritual sensitivities of the founder are important resources to navigate these challenges. It is, however, worthwhile to reflect on some areas of concern. There is the obvious challenge of "means and ends." As with any other ecological project, there is the fundamental question of the additional burdens on the environment created through the project with its local, national, and international traffic of visitors, and the need to transport goods and persons. The simple question "What emission-causing travels would not have happened without the project?" may sound naïve, but it is, nonetheless, morally relevant.

Four specific areas of moral concern can be identified with regard to the BLI. An initial moral challenge of all new initiatives is the question of opportunity costs and displacement effects. Instead of supporting existing initiatives, the founders decided to start a new project. This is, of course, legitimate, and the new project attracts new resources and generates new energy, but it points to the above-mentioned moral issue of opportunity costs. The new project binds energy and resources that could be used elsewhere. The project needs to make investments in project visibility; name recognition; reputation management; organizational development; administrative infrastructure; and, of course, the tangible infrastructure and running costs of the project itself. The project generates self-referential obligations in the sense that it has to be maintained and also in the sense that it faces pressures to increase the level of institutionalization. The founders of the Bethany Land Institute could have chosen to support an existing educational institution, for there is no shortage of educational institutions with financial needs in Uganda. They opted for a new project that inhabits a landscape of projects in an innovative and complementary way. The BLI created and inhabits a niche. Creating something will have its own ripple effects and will inevitably change the local context. The story of the Bethany Land Institute shows an impressive journey from a vision to a tangible infrastructure with activities. All this would not have happened without a small group of people pursuing the project. The project clearly inhabits its own "ecological niche" and has its own charism.

At the same time, there is a competitive aspect. The BLI is competing with other stakeholders for resources and market shares, and also for the best students. The competitive aspects can become risk factors for achieving the mission. A training institute that intends to have excellent students will compete with other institutions and is at risk of supporting the Matthew effect by selecting the best students who would have many options. These options would even increase due to the training program. Training caretakers to then transform villages and rural communities may face challenges that are similar to the unintended consequences Dan Honig has described in the training program in East Timor, a story told in chapter 6. The graduates will have to have robust commitments to serve the village communities after completing the training; they might have to resist the temptation to move away for further studies, for example. In response to this moral challenge, the training program does invest in "the inner lives" of the trainees and their moral and spiritual commitments.

Secondly, a land title conflict emerged with a family who claimed the legally purchased land as their ancestral land. The issue of land, in an African context, points to larger discourses and deeper roots, as mentioned above. The challenge was, however, very local and very concrete. As Katongole said in the interview,

> *As soon as we purchased the land, many people started claiming that it was their land, they brought bogus documents.... Part of the problem was the Ugandan government that passed an act that said if people were cultivating the land, the buyer must compensate them. But we knew that all these claims were fake. What to do?*

The above-mentioned bridge aspect of the project could also be interpreted as the possibility of bridges between "poor local villagers" and "resources from the Global North." "The more people we compensated, the more came forward" (Katongole 2022a, 172). This challenge also shows the permanent challenge of a "decolonized project" that is committed to local ownership and, nonetheless, dependent on resources (and expertise) from the Global North. Perceptions matter, as we have seen. The perception of the project as a bridge between Uganda and the United States has its drawbacks. This conflict continues to be taxing: "For the development of BLI, the land dispute was a major setback, and continues to be a stressful and distracting challenge" (Katongole 2022a, 172). At the same time, without the land title challenge, the lease of diocesan land would not have happened. Roadblocks can become sources of opportunity.

This moral challenge shows the fact that any project operates in a wider structural-political-legal context and that there are factors beyond the project's control that have a deep impact on the project itself. The project management decided to respond to this challenge by making use of the legal system of Uganda. Once again, this shows the moral vulnerability of a project that depends on macrostructures. The project's success is also dependent on a certain level of political and legal stability in the country.

Thirdly, the interactions with stakeholders have to be managed. There are some obvious moral aspects such as the management of interests and expectations from the different stakeholders—donors, board members, the local community; the bishop; the employees; the family. Donors from the United States may come with the expectation of seeing immediate results and being able to apply a US business model to the context of rural Uganda. The employees may expect a long-term perspective and a living wage that is constantly adjusted to inflation rates. Local board members may be suspicious of any trace of colonialism expressed through cash flows from the United States into the project. There is the usual pressure that comes from dependence on donations, pressure on marketing the project, and investing in reporting structures that are conducive to fundraising.

There may also be the temptation to instrumentalize relationships as social capital for the benefit of the project. The moral risk of "being greedy for a good cause" is present in many a development initiative. This risk is connected to concern for the sustainability of an initiative. It is well known that it is easier to obtain funds for an initial start-up, and it is more difficult to find sources to cover the running costs. The partnership with the diocese is promising in terms of the long-term stabilization of the project; however, the relationship with the diocese requires appropriate management, especially given the fact that bishops have limited terms. The management of relationships is also a special responsibility for the founding president of the BLI who emerged as "the face" of the project. An initiative like the Bethany Land Institute, which is closely linked to one central person, will change the web of relationships of the founder. New relationships emerge between Emmanuel Katongole as the president of the BLI and other people, and existing relationships are partially transformed because of this additional and identity-shaping commitment that adds to the "multiple identities" of the founder (Katongole 2022b, 178).

The management of relations also pertains to the local community. Previous land users and previous ways of using land had to be negotiated. The project created new mechanisms for inclusion (hiring of staff, admitting students) and exclusion (removal of squatters, fencing off the property). In the interview, Emmanuel Katongole mentioned squatters, people who lived on the land. Obviously, if there is a piece of land without much management and exercised ownership, people will put it to use. In both sites, there were people staying on the land, squatters that had to be resettled. They would probably see themselves as losers in the social change initiated by the project. Building a fence to secure the property is a protective and, at the same time, excluding measure. The decision was made to compensate those who lived on the land, which is a generous gesture toward those who might see themselves as disadvantaged by the social change brought about by the project.

Part of the moral challenge of relationship management is also the ambivalent relationship with the village community. In addition to a fear of competition, there were hopes and expectations with regard to employment possibilities, economic opportunities, and reputational gain. Obviously, the local community is not completely homogeneous, and different stakeholders positioned themselves differently vis-à-vis the new project. Managing stakeholders is a moral challenge in any project. In the case of the BLI, its international profile made for layers of complexity that also have to be navigated.

Fourth, balancing vision and leadership with management and decision making is an important challenge. The project set out from an idealistic vision of integral ecology. The founding story, mentioned above, paints a contrast between realities on the ground and the vision of a responsible and sustainable way of caring for the earth. Emmanuel Katongole's language, providing the value basis for the project, is soft and narrative. Yet, project management has to deal with the question of recruitment, staff management, and the challenge of underperforming employees. The hard language of budgeting and planning has to meet the soft language of vision and mission. This moral challenge has a spiritual dimension. In our interview, Emmanuel Katongole expressed the concern in the following words:

> When you get so many challenges, how do you not lose heart? How do you keep the tenderness, the fragility? Working with vulnerable people almost makes you hard. That was a major worry. How do you keep a project that was born with the concern for the poor, for the weak, how do you keep the heart and the tenderness?

This is a question for any institution committed to integral human development. The Bethany Land Institute is both a project site with its own practices and dynamics and a source of insights into IHD. Emmanuel Katongole beautifully expresses these dynamics in a good final word for this chapter:

There is something about doing a program like the BLI that integrates economics, ecology, education, working on the land where everything is connected to everything else, where nothing goes to waste. This is exactly what we are talking about when we talk about IHD. It not just a set of principles. It's a form of engagement. It's a praxis. Not just an application of principle, it's a journey. But it becomes also a spirituality. Because we are involved totally, in the project and in other people. Not just the economics of other people, but their spirituality, their dignity. These are transcendental practices really. I am discovering more and more about the interconnectedness between the different kinds of knowledge. I am working now on a curriculum that incorporates this. For me, it has been about discovering IHD in the very praxis of BLI. In the farm, the market, the ecosystem. At the same time, it is an experiment. It's not a guarantee of success. The test of which will be, ten years from now, to see what they will be able to do in their communities. I am learning that it is never complete. Everything we do is always incomplete. I am an impatient person. I say to myself "it is taking too long; it is too small." It's tiny, fragile, fragmented, broken. When I think of IHD, I think of all that. It is in the context of doing, doing something. The process and the journey. IHD happens in the trying. This means that there might be setbacks, but it doesn't prevent us from moving on with it. Maybe that is life.

PART III

COMMON
GOOD-ORIENTED POLICIES

On October 16, 1979, Archbishop Óscar Romero noted in his diary that he wanted to invite political parties and popular political organizations

> To show true political maturity, flexibility and a capacity for dialogue. Only in this way can the people be sure that they are, in fact, motivated by what is truly good for the country. Fanaticism or idolatry of their own party or organization would be, today more than ever, a grave sin against the common good. The crisis that our country is trying to overcome cannot be resolved by one group alone; it has to be the work of all. (Romero 1993, 353)

The common good was the pole star that he used for his political analyses: the idea of a well-ordered and well-functioning community that allows for the flourishing of each of its members. Romero struggled with the political realities in his country and was disappointed by policy makers not willing to think in terms of "the whole."[1] He commented regularly on legislative proposals, policies, and laws during his three years as Archbishop of San Salvador, reminding the public of the common good as the main *raison d'être* of any government and any access to

---

[1] On November 3, 1979, he wrote in his journal after a meeting with two representatives of a political group: "It will be difficult to get these people to agree to dialogue about cooperation for the common good of the country; their only desire seems to be the triumph of the ideas of their organization" (Romero 1993, 373). A commitment to the common good calls for the ability to adopt a preferential option for the poor or a perspective that is not restricted by a partial search for the advantages of a particular group: "Everyone must give up their polarized attitudes and dedicate themselves to harmonizing different ways of thinking for the common good of the country" (Romero 1993, 462).

power.[2] On New Year's Day 1980, he had to deal with a crisis among the ministers and a conflict between civilians in the government and the military. "I try to understand and guide them and, above all, tell them that they must think of the people, for they must serve them" (Romero 1993, 430). Politics and policies have to serve "the people," the common good. In March 1980, less than two weeks before his assassination, in his Sunday homily, Archbishop Romero analyzed the government's reform proposals and the nationalization of the banks. He expressed satisfaction with the land reform, where land holdings greater than five hundred hectares were being taken over.

> This new law confronts the oligarchy.... This law takes possession of the land away from that minority, and they will be compensated for their land in bonds, as is just. The measure is not very drastic; it makes it clear that everything is being done according to a moderate capitalist schema.[3]

He was, however, worried about the process and the fact that the majority of the population that was hardest hit by these reforms had not been consulted and had no say in the political process. Romero concluded that there were some serious doubts about this process.

The process is an important aspect of the sphere of policies and laws, and the moral compass of the common good is relevant for both content and pathway. If we were to identify criteria for Integral Human Development (or IHD)–compatible policies, we would turn to the three criteria that were mentioned in the context of project design in the introduction to part II: dignified life and integral ecology, special attention to the most disadvantaged and reverse privileging, subsidiarity and inclusive participation. These three criteria are equally relevant for the chosen method of policy making and the substance of policies. Additionally, we need to consider the common good as a main criterion for policy making in the spirit of Integral Human Development.

The term "Integral Human Development" was introduced in the context of global ethics and an understanding of a "global common good." The historical reference point for global justice and the development of each person globally is the idea of a "universal destination of goods." In religious language, this could be said as "God created the earth for all." This idea has influenced the motif

---

    [2] This is a key idea in the Catholic tradition; Thomas Aquinas defines law as "an ordinance of reason for the common good, made by someone who has care of the community, and promulgated" (STh I-II, 90, 4). Justice directs the person to the common good (STh II-II, 58, 5).

    [3] Óscar Romero, "Conversion is Necessary for True Liberation According to God's Plan," The Archbishop Romero Trust online, Sermon, March 9, 1980.

of a preferential option for the poor. This lens can serve as an analytical lens for local and global policies. Global food system transformations, for example, can be analyzed through the lens of a preferential option for the poor, paying special attention to the livelihoods of poor rural people (Davis et al. 2022). The idea of the universal destination of goods is also normatively relevant regarding national positions and policies. Policies that exclusively express the interests of small groups or forms of nationalism deny this principle and are incompatible with IHD. Two examples of this IHD-incompatible nationalism would be US President Trump's June 2017 arguments to withdraw from the Paris Climate Accord based on an "America first" ideology and Brazilian President Bolsonaro's position, expressed in his conflict with French President Macron in August 2019, about the fires in the Amazon, arguing that this was solely a Brazilian matter and not an issue of global relevance. These examples point to a particularly challenging aspect of global ethics—the mismatch between the organization of the planet in nation-states and the nature of global challenges that do not respect borders and require concerted efforts beyond a "my nation first" approach.

Pope Francis laments the fact that "instances of a myopic, extremist, resentful and aggressive nationalism are on the rise" (*Fratelli Tutti* 11). Integral human development is committed to the idea of the common good, to the idea of a global common good. The COVID-19 pandemic has taught some sad lessons about forms of nationalism that are incompatible with IHD. Pope Francis's encyclical *Fratelli Tutti*, written during the pandemic, warns against narrow nationalism and reminds the world of the need to think in global terms and in terms of a global human family:

> The true worth of the different countries of our world is measured by their ability to think not simply as a country but also as part of the larger human family. This is seen especially in times of crisis. Narrow forms of nationalism are an extreme expression of an inability to grasp the meaning of this gratuitousness. (*Fratelli Tutti* 141)

Policies need to reflect this commitment to the common good.

Policies are sets of ideas, courses of action, or principles of action proposed or imposed by an authority. Policies are used as a basis for decision making and structure agency into the categories of "desirable/permissible" and "prohibited/discouraged." In many instances, policies are based on official processes or agreements. In all cases, policies talk about what people should do, regulating individual and institutional agency as normative devices that define ways people ought to behave or ought to be perceived. Moral aspects enter the process and content of policy making, the "How" and the "What."

Applying Integral Human Development to policies is a critical aspect of enacting IHD. In principle, we could distinguish a negative and a positive function of IHD regarding policies. In its defensive, critical, and negative function, IHD can serve as a lens and reference point to critically assess existing policies. In its constructive, generative, and positive function, the idea and concept of Integral Human Development can assist in guiding and designing policies. The idea of Integral Human Development can inform policies, and policies can be more or less "IHD compatible."

I once asked some of my esteemed colleagues for examples of IHD-conducive or dignity-affirming policies. I received several responses. Policies to increase the number of Black police officers (Pyo 2023) or policies to establish women's police stations (Córdova and Kras 2022) were mentioned as candidates for IHD-conducive policies in the context of law enforcement. In the context of educational policies, a colleague recommended to investigate the Kenyan policy of language of instruction: literacy is taught in the learners' first language to enable them to acquire skills in reading and writing, communicate with others and promote learning to learn.[4] One colleague mentioned the challenge of deaf education and the need for proper policies:

> *Deaf children are often not diagnosed or hidden away by parents who do now know any sign language or how to support their kids. The systems are under-developed to identify those with hearing impairment or there may be too few programs in schools. As a result, many hearing-impaired children do not make it into schools with instruction in sign language until quite late, and they essentially lack any language development or capacity until they get into a language-rich sign language environment. Based upon everything we know about cognitive and brain development, language and thought, this is just unbelievable and must have major enduring developmental implications, not to mention the issues related to the dignity of children in those situations prior to being exposed to environments that can begin to foster basic language development, not to mention the ongoing challenges thereafter.*

Another colleague, also in the field of educational policy, suggested a Recommendation of the Committee of Ministers to member states of the European Union

---

[4] Acquisition of skills in reading and writing will facilitate the learning of the other subjects—not only do children tend to learn better when they begin to learn in the language they speak most fluently (in full or in part), there are also several things the research suggests about cultural identity affirmation tied to language and influence on students' sense of self, sense of belonging, teacher-student relationships, home-school connections / parental engagement, etc.

on the inclusion of the history of Roma and Travellers in school curricula and teaching materials (Council of Europe 2020). The recommendation suggested revisiting school curricular with a special focus on the (re)presentation of Roma and Travellers. The recommendation was designed in a spirit of inclusion and was motivated by stereotypical and often negative presentations of these minority groups who are depicted as a separate group rather than an integral part of the respective national society. The recommendation was responding to the neglect of cultural richness and traditions and the little effort that was made to describe contemporary Roma communities. The ministers recommended revisiting current school curricula, textbooks, and other teaching material with the purpose of eliminating stereotyping related to Roma and/or Travellers.

Within the area of health policy, I was drawn to the World Health Organization recommendations for "Postnatal Care for Mothers and Newborns" (World Health Organization 2015). Three main policy recommendations are worth mentioning for an IHD approach: (1) provide postnatal care in the first twenty-four hours to all mothers and babies, regardless of where the birth occurs, including a full clinical examination to be done around one hour after birth; (2) ensure healthy women and newborns stay at a health facility at least twenty-four hours and are not discharged early; (3) all mothers and babies need at least four postnatal checkups in the first six weeks.

On the societal level, the idea of baby bonds was recommended as an example of an IHD-sensitive policy. This idea reflects an ambition for a higher level of equity. The federal government would start a fund for every child born in the United States and contribute to it every year until the child's eighteenth birthday. The state contributions would vary depending on the income of the child's family. This scheme should create more than $50,000 and enable college attendance, increasing entrepreneurship and homeownership as an asset-building strategy, for children.[5] Asset building is an eminent avenue out of poverty.

The Conditional Grants Scheme in Nigeria's Office of Millennium Development Goals is a macrolevel example. In this flexible finance mechanism, block grants in support of education, health, and water facilities were allocated to Nigeria's 36 states and 774 local government areas, representing a "pro poor policy" that was implemented under the leadership of Amina Mohammed. The scheme was designed to make financial grants available to governments on different levels in a conditional partnership agreement to provide necessary social infrastructures (Okere and Okezie Okeyika 2016). The poorest areas of the poorest parts of the country were given priority, and decisions were made with proper representation

---

[5] Kiara Taylor, "Can Baby Bonds Fix Intergenerational Wealth Inequality?" *Investopedia*, February 22, 2022.

of the different areas in a decentralized approach, with data-driven planning at the local level. An evaluation showed that an important factor in the success, particularly regarding sustainability risks, was the role of local elites (Yunusa and Hulme 2019). Also in this sense, the approach has to be "integral."

The examples show that the normative reference point of Integral Human Development can very well serve as a source of orientation. The four criteria for just policies based on IHD provide moral anchors. More specifically, in assessing policies and in making use of the four criteria that we mentioned, we could ask questions such as the following:

1. *Dignified life and integral ecology*: Does the policy offer the possibility to consider the uniqueness of the human person and particular circumstances? Does the policy ensure the nonhumiliation, noninstrumentalization, and noninfantilization of the human person? Is the policy well justified (respecting the dignity of a person can be understood to imply a "right to reason/s")? Does the policy promote conditions for a dignified life? Does the policy have the potential to lead to dehumanizing practices?

   Even though Integral Human Development as a concept is anthropocentric, this anthropocentrism can be mitigated and corrected by the discourse on integral ecology, recognizing the intrinsic dignity of the world and the interconnectedness between nature and humanity. This suggests questions like the following: Does the policy properly consider the context of human lives, human ecology? Does the policy reflect a commitment to sustainability, ecological integrity, and a long-term perspective? Does the policy consider future generations?

2. *Special attention to the most disadvantaged and reverse privileging*: How does the policy affect the most disadvantaged and most vulnerable? Who are the most vulnerable in this particular policy context? Who are the "winners" and "losers" of the policy? Does the policy consolidate structures of vulnerability or even create new forms of social exclusion and vulnerability?

   The question of excessiveness is an important aspect of reverse privileging to consider. Integral Human Development recognizes that there can be inappropriate development dynamics ("overdevelopment"). The concept of Integral Human Development is part of a tradition that recognizes "excessiveness" as morally problematic.[6] This will invite

---

[6] For example, a just wage, in this tradition, is not only about a bottom, it is also about a ceiling; see Himes (2017).

questions such as the following: How does the policy affect established structures of privilege? How does the policy relate to the dynamics of the Matthew principle" ("those who have will be given more")? How does the policy affect the most privileged and most advantaged? Does the policy enhance risks of "overdevelopment"? How does the policy affect the structure and distribution of privileges?

3. *Subsidiarity and inclusive participation*: Is there a maximum of responsibility and a maximum of freedom on the lowest possible level? Is the burden of proof properly recognized as lying on the respective higher level, that is, with those who centralize and not with those who argue for de-centralization? Is the individual person recognized in the policy? Does the policy properly protect and consider fundamental social units like families?

   Consideration of each human person underlines respect for the agency of each human person. The basic unit of IHD is the relational individual person and her agency, initiative, freedom, and responsibility. The agency of smaller communities (e.g., families) is to be protected on the same grounds. This is the idea of subsidiarity. Participation is the idea of intentionally involving groups and individuals with relevant interests, those who will be (most) affected by the policy. This will move us to questions like the following: Has the policy been designed in a participatory manner, including all relevant stakeholders, especially the less and least privileged stake holders? What was the process of generating the policy? Has the process of creating the policy involved epistemic injustice? Does the policy neglect relevant stake holders?

4. *The common good*: Does the policy consider the "environment" of its immediate context beyond the immediate interests of the key stakeholders? How does the policy affect this wider context? Does the policy have transcontextual implications? Does the policy have adverse indirect effects?

These are, of course, only examples of guiding questions, but they show that integral human development can serve as a source of orientation. The idea of Integral Human Development can give us four main normative reference points for designing and evaluating policies, which can be illustrated as follows:

Figure 3: Normative References for Designing and Evaluating Policy

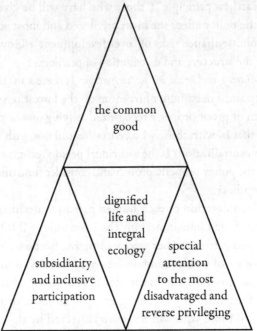

9

Moral Relevance of
Policies and Political Decisions

Reflecting on relevant criteria for morally justifiable policies shows the normative relevance of policies and political decisions. Furthermore, these reflections show how policies and political decisions require a proper moral compass to be evaluated. Policies open avenues for agency and create opportunities for action. They design pathways to development and change. Change always comes with morally relevant implications.

Social change impacts both the *relative* situation of social players and the *absolute* situation of stakeholders. Usually, there are losers and winners. Louis Joseph Lebret, one of the founders of the discourse on integral human development, was appalled by the poverty of fishermen on the coast of Brittany. As mentioned in the introduction, they no longer stood a chance of making a decent living against large-scale commercial fishing. In other contexts, planning studies "legitimated creating parks for rich tourists at the cost of removing the livelihoods of poor local residents on the basis of projections of future numbers of tourists that were never plausible" (Gasper 2012, 118). In such cases, we can identify moral failure in both the planning process as well as in the implementation.

Usually, most development measures will make a difference to people's lives and living. The gains of some are directly linked to the suffering of others, as is often the case in resettlement projects, which are regularly conducted without adequate compensation for the population who lose out and have their livelihoods removed (McDowell 1996; Scudder 2006; Cernea and Mathur 2008). Several measures, such as expropriation, can be justified "in the name of development." There are countless examples of that kind. Robert Aiken and Colin Leigh have analyzed the struggle of Malaysia's indigenous peoples to keep control over their land rather than being "assimilated" into modernized mainstream society, including the effect of incorporation of land into the sphere of national asset markets (Aiken and Leigh 2011). Noam Schimmel has analyzed abusive use of development rhetoric to justify the violation of human rights of indigenous people in Botswana, resulting in evictions and forced resettlement (Schimmel 2009).

The People's Republic of China's One Child Policy had dramatic impacts though it was designed as a development measure to lift the People's Republic of China out of extreme poverty. The policy was intended to ease pressure on the use of natural resources in China, to reduce unemployment, and to increase the quality of health care. These are noble intentions. The implementation of this policy came with morally costly consequences. The policy created social situations and forms of life of a particular kind, for example, situations where two adults would have to support four elderly parents and one child, or, conversely, a situation where an unmarried single child would have to support two elderly parents (and maybe even grandparents as well). Some of the consequences were dramatic and tragic. Mei Fong describes the connection between the policy and the 2008 Sichuan earthquake, which impacted heavily on Shifang, a test area for the one-child policy. "In Shifang, where over two-thirds of families are single-child families, the quake was said to have wiped out a generation in some villages" (Fong 2016, 3).

From a more systematic perspective, negative consequences of the one-child policy include (1) the progressive aging of Chinese society, with the corresponding care competition: "people living longer, fewer being born. The former has nothing to do with the one-child-policy; the latter everything" (Fong 2016, 139); (2) gender disparities, with certain implications such as the neglect of baby girls, a rise in human trafficking, including children sold into adoption, forced prostitution, or concerns about increases in crimes of a sexual nature (Edlund et al. 2007; Ebenstein 2008; Attané 2009; Attané et al. 2013; Edlund 2013); (3) violations of the bodily integrity of women through forced abortions and forced sterilizations; (4) destruction of traditional family models based on seniority by raising what has been called little emperors in an atmosphere of overprotectiveness, with side effects on character formation, social skills, and employability;[1] (5) toxic stress for children with the pressure to meet expectations, based on the loss of distribution of family roles among several siblings and the loss of "division of expectation-guided labor," in a context of deepening disparities between urban and rural areas (the latter being contexts characterized by poor health care standards and the pressure on the one child to drop out of school and work for

---

[1] It has been observed that only children had less behavioral control, a higher demand for instant gratification, and reduced abilities of self-care (Jiao et al. 1986; Wan et al. 1994). Educational patterns change significantly with grandparents and parents sharing pedagogical responsibility (Goh 2006).

the family); and (6) stress on marriage, sexuality, and kinship structure (Attané et al. 2013). These moral concerns point to the far-reaching consequences of a policy that violated, at least, articles 12, 16.1, and 16.3, and 25 of the Universal Declaration of Human Rights from the outset. The policy was characterized by radical means and quick results, over and against a gradual approach, through a rather simplistic calculation of demographic development and ideas of human relationships. These characteristics are concerning. "The one-child policy regulated births on the assumption that all this procreation was going on between married couples. There was little leeway for underage pregnancy, or unmarried mothers, or women who'd simply gotten pregnant before the official waiting period elapsed" (Fong 2016, 25). The complexity of "the whole person" was not considered.

Policies matter, and the justifications of policies matter. Debating and designing policies is a matter of value judgments. The 1862 American Homestead Act in the United States presents a useful case study to illustrate the moral relevance of policies in design, justification, implementation, and (intended and unintended) consequences.

A Case Study

The American Homestead Act was a well-justified development measure. President Abraham Lincoln signed the act on May 20, 1862, and it became law on January 1, 1863. The Homestead Act gave 160 acres of land to settlers—twenty-one years of age or older and usually American citizens—who were willing to cultivate the land for at least five years. The Log Cabin Bill of 1840, allowing settlers who had claimed land by simply living on it, that is, squatting, to buy 160 acres of land at $1.25 an acre, and the land Donation Acts passed between 1842 and 1850, providing incentives to pioneers to settle in unpopulated areas, including Oregon and Florida, had preceded the Homestead Act and provided milestones in asset management efforts. There was heated debate leading up to the legislation, including a May 10, 1860, veto by President Buchanan, who rejected the suggested homestead bill on the grounds of justice. He saw it as unfair to old settlers who had paid for the land, unfair to veterans who had received land as service compensation, and unfair to nonfarmers. Furthermore, President Buchanan was worried about the spread of demoralization, a sharp rise in land speculation, and a decrease of government revenue (Anderson 2011). Nevertheless, the law was signed by Abraham Lincoln two years later.

This measure was a well-planned development initiative, generating real and concrete opportunities. Core planning challenges included persuading those resisting the idea, like industrialists worried about cheap labor or Southern state representatives concerned about the future of the plantation system, to accept it and administrative hurdles, such as access conditions and terms of appropriation. "The homesteader was required to pay a ten dollar filing fee and live on and cultivate the homestead for five years. Another option," Anderson notes, "was to pay $1.25 per acre and live on the homestead for six months. Those who had fought against the U.S. government were restricted from filing a claim" (Anderson 2011, 120).

The consequences of the Homestead Act were mixed. It was definitely a major asset-building policy in American history. It has been argued that about a quarter of the US population in 2000 are descendants from homesteaders, profiting from the Homestead Act (Williams Shanks 2005, 3). It contributed to democracy and state-building, encouraged migration with new agricultural techniques,[2] promoted a long-term perspective, supported small farmers, added to economic growth, ensured an adequate food supply, encouraged the cultivation (and protection) of unpopulated land, and the building of tangible infrastructures such as roads and railroads.

However, in some less fertile areas, 160 acres turned out to be insufficient to sustain a livelihood (Libecap and Hansen 2002). Overproduction and preservation of the land became significant challenges due to issues like overgrazing. There was also some misuse with speculation and the challenge of distinguishing between bona fide settlers and those with speculative interests. Most importantly, the American Homestead Act contributed to the dispossession of Indian lands, furthering exploitation of Native Americans. Some of these consequences could have been anticipated, others would have been more difficult to estimate in the planning process. Paul Gates mentions explicitly "the old evils of careless drafting of land legislation, weak and inefficient administrations (inadequately staffed) and the anxiety of interests to take advantage of loopholes in the laws" (Gates 1996, 52).

Four years after the American Homestead Act, Congress passed the Southern Homestead Act in July 1866, distributing land in Alabama, Arkansas, Florida, Louisiana, and Mississippi to all Americans, Black and White (Hoffnagle 1970; Lanza 1990). The basic idea, enabling former slaves to appropriate income-generating assets that would allow them to build an existence, was honorable. Legal freedom without material freedom remains a legal fiction. Asset-building policies such as the Southern Homestead Act are among the most powerful strategies for creating opportunities and for reducing wealth inequality. However, the conditions of the Southern Homestead Act were less than a level playing field, leading

---

[2] Even though the debate here is full of nuances (see Dovring 1962).

to what has been described as "asset discrimination," disadvantaging African Americans (Bailey 2010, 87–98).

The Southern Homestead Act differed from the American Homestead Act in that it permitted land to be used exclusively for agricultural homesteading during a five-year waiting period. However, most of the forty-six million acres offered to settlers through the Southern Homestead Act needed the removal of stands of pines in order to make them "farmable" and productive; thus, the actual physical state of land made available was problematic. The Southern Homestead Act led to planned frustrations since

> none of the provisions took into account the ravages of war and nature, the depressed economic condition of the freedmen, the quality of the public land, the condition of land offices in the Southern states, and the slow working of the government bureaucracy. Furthermore, any provisions intended for the exclusive benefit of blacks and loyal whites aggravated the existing racial and political tensions. (Oubre 1976, 144)

Chaotic conditions prevailed in the land offices, and there were a number of racism-related incidents. In some cases, Black land ownership was not legally protected, and their titles to the land were inaccurately recorded. In some instances, public land was illegally devalued by excessive timber cutting. Quite often, "living on the land for five years proved difficult when the Black homesteaders had few financial resources and sometimes had to work other people's land to support their families" (Williams Shanks 2003, 9). The mechanisms of land appropriation were different for Whites and Blacks. Black Americans had to go through a government agency to acquire land. This agency, "The Freedmen's Bureau," cooperated closely with the Freedmen's Savings and Trust Company, also known as "the Freedman's Bank," which collapsed in 1874 mainly because of "questionable no-interest loans from the bank to white companies" (Sherraden 1991, 133). This was a major contribution to the patterns of asset discrimination. "Of the 1.5 million families which received land under the Homestead Act and Southern Homestead Act, only 5,500 of the new homesteads were owned by black families" (Bailey 2010, 94).

We gain several insights by looking at the Homestead Acts from the perspective of an ethics of planning. Trina R. Williams Shanks (2003, 12) suggests the following lessons: create a simple asset-building opportunity that is enduring and open to all, design incentives that are particularly attractive to the nonwealthy, allow some flexibility to complement local conditions, resist racist or other structural impediments that exclude particular groups from full participation, and consider the intergenerational benefits for participants and their families by allowing families to pass the land on to descendants. Let us look at some of the ethical points at stake.

First, the Homestead Acts were well-justified development measures that followed the logic of "developing people through developing land" or "creating asset-building opportunities as a driver of development." Land, especially in the nineteenth-century context, is a key asset, and assets are foundations of freedom. This has been identified for twenty-first-century development ambitions as well.[3] Land is crucial—the choice of adopting this asset as the focus of a development measure is well justified.

Second, we can see that a morally well-justified measure does not abrogate the moral perceptions of people. In other words, you cannot automatically change attitudes or a culture by top-down policy making. You cannot change racist attitudes by law. In fact, there may be a "civic counterreaction" to state-imposed moral expectations however well justified they may be.

Third, as in any other development measure, we see a concern of abuse. In the case of the Homestead Acts, there were specific worries about fraud and speculation. This concern could justify an ethical version of Ockham's razor, that is, an argument for a "prudential moral minimalism" in planning, a commitment to a minimum of moral demands. In other words, do not expect people to act as if they were moral saints by demanding that they follow unrealistically high moral standards. Make it as easy as possible for people to abide by the law.

Fourth, a key issue in the implementation of any law is the culture of enactment. "Good governance" is both a matter of the quality of legislation and a matter of the quality of enforcement, of enabling people to "live up to" or "make use of" the law. In the 1930s, Fred Shannon rather pessimistically commented that "the trouble with the Homestead Act in operation ... was that Congress merely adopted the law and then did absolutely nothing in the way of helping the needy persons out to the land or extending them credit and guidance in the first heartbreaking years of occupancy" (Shannon 1936, 644). Laws are necessary but not sufficient to bring about social change. They need to be culturally plausible.

Laws, Culture, and Values

Integral human development is a concept that points to the subtle power of cultures. Laws are important, but laws can leave space for activities that are "awful, but lawful" (Búzás 2021). Legal mechanisms do not operate in a vacuum. They

---

[3] See, for instance, the Southern African Catholic Bishops Conference's statement: Catholic Church Vision for Land Reform in South Africa (Pretoria: Justice and Peace Department, 2012); for a Brazilian context with explicit reference to our case study, see Intrator (2011).

are culturally embedded and can also be approached from an anthropological perspective. Because we can observe fascinating dynamics of internal decision-making processes in legal institutions and complex interactions between legal and nonlegal norms (Sarfaty 2021), a law is not enough. Entitlements or legal provisions are necessary but not sufficient conditions for change. There have to be political, social, and cultural provisions as well.[4] In this way, a law is like a plan for defining (setting limits to) agency. Implementation of the law requires a different level of human agency and reasoning. A law cannot regulate its own application. The basis for the proper implementation of a law has been called a sense of justice, and laws require trust that this sense of justice is shared and respected within a community by individuals and institutions.

Fighting contemporary forms of slavery, for example, is a noble goal, but these efforts must take deep-rooted cultural traditions into account. Social and cultural factors, like the caste system in India, can cause or reinforce bondage. Even though the *Kamaiya* system of bonded labor in Nepal "was finally banned by the Nepali government in 2000 . . . this policy does not seem to have eliminated kamaiya practice, but rather altered the bonded arrangements from adults to children" (Giri 2009, 600). It is difficult to change culturally and socially established perceptions. The *Restavek* system in Haiti was initially built on the values of hospitality and solidarity. "When Haitian parents experienced financial difficulties, they would send their children to wealthier distant relatives to raise their children as their own" (de la Pena de Berrazueta 2019, 10). This has opened doors for abuse, exploitation, practices of child labor, and slavery. The practice dates back to the French colonial era, when children could be instrumentalized as slaves as long as basic needs were met and religious education was provided, and is embedded in the culture. "Haitian culture plays an important role in perpetuating the restavek system" (Breyer 2016, 153). This, of course, makes it difficult to change the system. The *Kafala* system in the United Arab Emirates is based on the idea of sponsorship: a migrant worker is required to have a sponsor (*kafil*) who functions as a "guarantor" and bears economic and legal responsibility for the worker. The system was motivated by economic needs to respond quickly to labor force demands and has offered many entry points for exploitation due to the legalized dependence of the worker on the sponsor. Policies and laws cannot easily change deep-seated patterns of practices and perceptions (Damir-Geilsdorf 2016). Reforming institutions is not enough. Social relations and perceptions, as well, must be transformed.

An Integral Human Development lens, with its commitment to the whole person, will pay special attention to the cultural environment of policies and

---

[4] See some aspects of the critique of an entitlement approach or "legal optimism": Devereux (2001); Davis and Trebilcock (2008); Chimni (2008).

to unintended consequences of policies. In his study on contemporary slavery, Siddharth Kara discusses the H-2A visa, which allows a foreign national to enter the United States as a guest worker for temporary or seasonal agricultural work. This visa was specifically established to give employers in the agricultural sector the chance to bring foreign farm workers legally into the United States. The visa was designed to protect workers' rights and to frame their labor through US labor laws. The workers

> are meant to be provided with free housing for the duration of their contracts, the same health and safety protections as U.S. citizens performing the same work, workers' compensation benefits for medical costs and time off work for medical reasons, free legal services relating to their employment under the visa program, and reimbursement of the full costs of their travel to the job site once they have completed 50 percent of their contract period. Despite these important protections stipulated in the H-2A visa program, I found that forced labor was often present among the guest workers in California's Central Valley. (Kara 2018, 87)

This is, of course, disappointing.

> The primary reason for coercing a guest worker into forced labor appears to be related to the cumbersome requirements on the employer for bringing in migrants under the program, which makes it desirable to keep the workers for more than one season rather than reapplying each year. (Kara 2018, 87)

The visa program could not prevent the abusive practices.

This points to an important aspect of any policy: policies intend to change people's behavior. People need to be motivated to commit or omit certain actions, which is a question of the incentive structure. Policies operate with a certain understanding of the person and her motivations. The above-mentioned one-child policy in China operated with both monetary and nonmonetary aspects in its reward system. Fong notes that doctors and birth planning officials would receive bonuses for abortions and sterilizations (Fong 2016, 25). David Howden describes nonpecuniary sanctions set in place, such as negative repercussions for an entire extended family, based on a guilt-by-association model, who were "disadvantaged in its search for political appointments" and would have to "suffer from obstacles and discrimination when dealing with administrative formalities" (Howden and Zhou 2014, 354). A Matthew effect can be observed here that would, as in so many cases, follow patterns and power dynamics of politics and culture.

Culture and values matter. Integral human development prioritizes closing protection gaps for the most vulnerable in policy making. We have discussed some aspects of the Matthew effect and the dynamics that "those who have will be given more." Counteracting the dynamics of the Matthew effect and protecting those who are most disadvantaged is a major task of dignity-affirming policies. Consider the following true story:

> *Minnie was only twelve years old when both of her parents passed away. She was passed on from one relative to another. In most cases, schooling is interrupted along with the challenging transition. Right after her parents died, she settled in with our grandmother and later with an aunt. She became pregnant three years later. As an orphan living in a relative's home, this would be the last thing you would want to deal with. At the time, she was a seventh-grader in primary school. She went to school one day but didn't come home again. Many efforts to locate her whereabouts were futile. Her sister later informed us that she had married. No one followed up, which is a sad reality about orphans: people rarely go the extra mile for them.*

The last sentence is telling: "people rarely go the extra mile for orphans." The statement is an indication of a protection gap. This is where policies and political decisions and institution-building come in. A moral division of labor is at stake, a division of labor between individuals and institutions. The "higher level" needs to support and complement the lower level. For example, a development worker and his nongovernmental organization developed policy recommendations for the government.

> *The response to our recommendations by the government was less than favorable, where we were told that the government "had to prioritize" certain groups due to resource constraints. This experience made me realize that, while civil society and grassroots organizations may operate with a dignity-centric approach, it is imperative to ensure that policies espoused from the top are designed with the same approach.*

Institutions and policies have to support the building of inclusive communities that do not leave people or peoples behind. Pope John XXIII pointed to the need for an appropriate division of labor in his 1963 encyclical *Pacem in Terris*.

Heads of States must make a positive contribution to the creation of an overall climate in which the individual can both safeguard his own rights and fulfill his duties, and can do so readily. For if there is one thing we have learned in the school of experience, it is surely this: that,

in the modern world especially, political, economic and cultural ineq-
uities among citizens become more and more widespread when public
authorities fail to take appropriate action in these spheres. And the
consequence is that human rights and duties are thus rendered totally
ineffective. (*Pacem in Terris* 63)

This statement has two important messages. First, integral human development
is about more than laws and policies. Integral human development is also about
an appropriate moral climate. Second, in the spirit of integral human development, policy makers and legislators need to be intentional about responding to
inequality and inequity. Otherwise, the dignity of each person cannot be upheld.

The moral climate mentioned in the first point can be interpreted as a shared
"sense of justice," an important aspect of forming a society. In the words of John
Rawls, a sense of justice "would appear to be a condition for human sociability"
(Rawls 1999, 433). Investing in an appropriate moral climate and common
good–attitudes can also be seen as a major responsibility of politics. Policies are
vehicles of this project.

Policies are meant to project human dignity as a core value. They are normatively relevant and define ways people ought to behave or ought to be perceived.
The latter can be a matter of categorization. Policy decisions can be used to label
people and behaviors. Introducing identity cards through the Belgian colonial administration of Rwanda in 1933 is a famous example of a policy-based
labeling. The policy introduced the main labels of "Tutsi" and "Hutu." The effect
was devastating: "Amorphous categories became exclusive, hardened identi-
fiers—matters of life and death." (Rawson 2018, 14). The decision to introduce
"identity cards that categorized all Rwandans as either Hutu or Tutsi ... ended
a precolonial custom of intergroup social mobility that allowed Hutu peasants
who accumulated enough cattle to accede to the Tutsi ruling class" (Baker and
Leader 2020, 3). The long-lasting impact of this policy was observed in many
accounts trying to explain the genocide from 1994.

Policies can indeed be a matter of life and death. As Abby Córdova and
Helen Kras argue, public policy implementation influences the general climate,
but also attitudes and opinions (Córdova and Kras 2022; see also Mettler 2019).
Policies influence "mass perceptions" (Campbell 2012). A colleague of mine, for
example, has worked on the effects of women's police stations on violence against
women. Policies establishing women's police stations have an effect on climate,
attitudes, and perception. Women's police stations

promote progressive attitudes toward VAW [violence against women]
among men, thereby addressing one of the underlying causes of gender-
based violence.... When there is a WPS [women's police station] in

town, men are more likely to perceive that calling the police to report VAW is worthwhile, thereby reinforcing bystander intervention attitudes ... as WPS criminalize VAW and increase survivors' access to specialized services, WPS promote progressive attitudes toward VAW among men, particularly if a WPS has been operating for a long time in the place of residence. (Córdova and Kras 2022, 2)

Policies respond to situations that are identified as problematic and can be seen as responses to questions. One way to assess policies is to simply ask the following: What is the question to which the policy responds? What is the moral status of the question? Recognizing a question as a response-deserving problem is an expression of a normative position, an expression of value beliefs. This recognition makes it necessary to reflect on an appropriate value basis. And this, in turn, will lead to some big questions that policy makers cannot easily avoid.

10

Big Questions:
The Point of Policies

In an interview about the concept of Integral Human Development (or IHD), a development expert said: "Integral Human Development is an important approach because it challenges us to think about the bigger picture." The big picture includes questions about "the beginning," "the point," and "the end" of social change processes. From the perspective of Integral Human Development, the "why" question counts. What is the point of policies and policy making? This is a matter of values and of the imagination. The imagination is the ability to consider alternatives to the status quo, to conceive of possibilities. When Václav Havel, the late president of the Czech Republic, reflected on the future of his country, he did that by way of "summer meditations" (Havel 1993). He imagined the future of flourishing communal life, including aspects of everyday life.

Havel reflected on the question: Where do we want to be thirty years from now? Which kinds of change should happen? The idea of desirable change necessarily involves value questions. Values can be understood to be conceptions of the desirable, to be aspirational orientations. Policies are designed to bring about social change. Social change has a "why" as well as a "where to" dimension. The relevance of a "sense of direction" points to the need to develop a specific understanding of human well-being (Dower 2008, 186). Development is intended and sets out to increase the well-being of people. In order to increase this human well-being, one needs to have a concept of "good life." Louis Joseph Lebret defines development as

> *le passage pour une population déterminée, d'une phase moins humaine (ou inférieure) à une phase plus humaine (ou supérieure), au rythme le plus rapide possible, au coût le moins élevé possible, compte tenu de la solidarité entre toutes les populations. (Lebret 1958, 47)*

Lebret offers a normative conception that presupposes indicators and a proper criteriology to justify the game of "superior/inferior" language that, in turn, presupposes a hierarchical model of life quality levels. Defining development by way of economic growth or by way of contributing to gross national happiness makes a difference. Both questions of "telos" and "values" shape the questions of incentives and motivations. The seemingly simple question "What is the point of economic practice?" can lead to further subtle questions, as discussed by approaches to "happiness economics" (Stutzer and Frey 2012) or the "Commission on the Measurement of Economic Performance and Social Progress," chaired by Joseph Stiglitz, advised by Amartya Sen, and coordinated by Jean-Paul Fitoussi. These discussions will have an influence on both direction and prioritization of development planning.

Where do we want to go? In an amusing book *The Curious Enlightenment of Professor Caritat*, Steven Lukes offers a fictional account of moral regimes. Professor Caritat travels to countries where a Kantian duty ethics or communitarianism is fully realized. *Utilitaria* is an especially attractive country, with its pervasive efficiency, prosperity, cleanliness, and order. He is told that Utilitarians have a deep affection for computers. "Indeed, calculating was the national obsession. All Utilitarians agreed with the principle that what counts is what can be counted" (Lukes 1995, 44). Professor Caritat also learns that, in Utilitaria, "there is no problem without a solution. The residents come with their problems and the experts calculate the answers" (Lukes 1995, 56). I asked students to reflect on the prompt: "After his visit to Utilitaria, Professor Caritat travelled to the IHD Republic. He wanted to visit his former teacher who was living in a nursing home."

One response:

> *Professor Caritat traveled to the IHD Republic by sail boat because there are no airports in the IHD republic; at the immigration he was warmly welcomed by a greeter who enjoyed what he was doing; he took an emission-free taxi (again driven by a person who enjoyed what she was doing) and went to a beautiful nursing home, a model of intergenerational living, surrounded by gardens where his former teacher was offering his wisdom in the nursing home university.*

We could ask ourselves the following: Too good to be true? Too boring to be good? Do we want to live in the IHD Republic?

One student expressed his belief that the IHD Republic would be an agrarian society, characterized by simple living and a lack of technology. Another response to the prompt was that Integral Human Development is about special attention to the most disadvantaged, reverse privileging, and decentering the center. The colleague reflected: *I believe that traveling to the IHD Republic as a person of privilege will move me out of my comfort zone—and so it should be. Living in the IHD Republic is uncomfortable.* This is a thoughtful response that leads us to the question: What are the key values?

Freedom or Dignity?

What are the key values? A few months ago, a colleague invited me to join a session of his class on the German *Grundgesetz*, the Basic Law for the Federal Republic of Germany from 1949. The class elaborated on the main differences between the US American Constitution and the German *Grundgesetz*. One takeaway was that the US American Constitution is a freedom-centered document, and the German *Grundgesetz* shows a dignity-centered approach to the foundations of a state. The dignity-centered nature of the German text is, of course, linked to Germany's dark history in the twentieth century, especially during the Nazi regime. A key value emerged in response to the atrocities, namely, dignity. The US American tradition, on the other hand, points to a colonial past and the commitment to freedom as the core value. This does not mean that the two normative traditions of the US and Germany are mutually exclusive. Freedom and dignity do not contradict each other, but they do create different nuances and different moral ecosystems.

The commitment to freedom is the main message of the prominent capability approach. While unable to discuss this approach in any depth, I want to focus on some nuances of freedom. *Development as Freedom* is the title of one of Amartya Sen's programmatic books. I have introduced the approach of integral human development as dignity centered. In a bold and simplifying move, I suggest that an IHD approach tends to be more dignity focused whereas the capability approach centers on freedom. As in the case of the two constitutions mentioned above, this does not mean incompatibility but different "moral ecologies."

Amartya Sen, one of the founders of the capability approach, sees his approach to be holistic in a similar way that the idea of integral human development can be seen as holistic. In *The Idea of Justice*, Sen argues that, while a measure like GDP focuses solely on the "culmination outcome" (the end result), the capabilities approach emphasizes a "comprehensive outcome," which includes the process by which that end result is reached (Sen 2009, 231–32). The organizing principle of the approach is, however, the concept of freedom (Robeyns 2017, 98–107). "Development as freedom" views "expansion of freedom ...

both as the primary end and as the principal means of development" (Sen 1999, xii). There is a clear link between freedom and quality of life (Sen 1999, 24). The capability approach translates development into "capability expansion" and positions "freedom" close to "capability," the latter to mean the set of life options from which a person can choose.[1] A person's capability set represents a person's freedom to achieve different "doings" and "beings." Capabilities are freedoms to achieve different lifestyles (Sen 1999, 75). They are also interpreted as entitlements where people must have the right and the opportunity to cultivate capabilities and access to capabilities (Nussbaum 2003).

The main point of development is to enhance people's freedom to choose the kind of life they value and have reasons to value. The ability to freely make moral choices is the key moral good. Development, one could say, is about "creating more opportunity of choice and substantive decisions for individuals who can then act responsibly on that basis" (Sen 1999, 284). The emphasis on capabilities has the strategic value of allowing for a deeper understanding of a person's life with her evaluations and commitments: "Being able to freely choose to lead a particular life may be a point of a richer description of the life we lead, including the choices we are able to make" (Sen 1999, 17). Choices are as much value statements as the statement about the option for choices and their maximization.

For many people on this planet, freedom is out of reach. Siddharth Kara quotes a young woman from Nepal at risk of labor trafficking. She told him,

> I do not want to leave my parents, but what are my options? I will not go to India for prostitution, and there is no work in Nepal. If I stay, I will have to marry, and then what kind of life will I have? I want to earn money so I can take my parents to a better home and we can live on our own terms. Most people in Nepal must live on terms they do not want. We are no different from anyone else. We want to live by our own determining. (Kara 2018, 192)

The capability approach recognizes the universality of the desire for freedom, autonomy, self-determination, and choices. Sen develops a notion of positive freedom, or freedom as capacity, rather than as only absence of active interference. For Sen,

---

[1] This closeness of concepts has been criticized; Bernard Williams remarks: "This ... idea of liberty as ability or capacity ... has an obvious disadvantage: we already have a concept of ability or capacity, and on this showing 'liberty' or 'freedom' turn out boringly just to be other names for it. More importantly, it misses the point of why we want these terms in the first place" (Williams 2001, 7–8).

Individual advantage is judged in the capability approach by a person's capability to do things he or she has reason to value. A person's advantage in terms of opportunities is judged to be lower than that of another if she has less capability—less real opportunity—to achieve those things that she has reason to value. (Sen 2009, 231)

The individual is at the center of the capability approach, for capabilities belong to individuals not groups (Sen 2009, 244–46). The individual as an agent is a basic block of analysis in the capability approach, a normative lens by which to judge structures. An agent is someone who "brings about change, and whose achievements can be judged in terms of her own values and objectives" (Sen 1999, 19). Poverty is consequently seen as a deprivation of agency, a deprivation of capabilities, and a deprivation of choices. To fight poverty means to offer access to capabilities, especially by way of education and by way of entitlements. This amounts to enlarging a person's capability set as the horizon of available choices, which includes an array of options and an understanding of the available possibilities.

However, the individual agent, whose agency is embedded in social traditions and political structures,[2] depends on the appropriate environment to be able to exercise freedoms. "Freedom is not a one-time event. It is not a box to be ticked or a moment to be congratulated. It is a fragile, precious condition that must be supported and protected for a full human life" (Kara 2018, 222). The freedom of former slaves after the American Civil War turned out to be a necessary but clearly not sufficient condition for a good life. Policy makers had not paid much attention to fundamental questions such as the following: Where would the former slaves live? What kind of labor would be open to them? How could they secure a place to stay, water to drink, food to eat, clothes to wear? Who would care for them in case of illness? Jim Downs describes, in his aptly titled book *Sick from Freedom*, how at least one-quarter of the four million former slaves got sick or died between 1862 and 1870. "The most significant factor that led to the widespread outbreak of disease was the massive dislocation that the war and emancipation caused. The failure to anticipate thousands of mobile people who congregated in places without an infrastructure to support them led to disease outbreaks and death" (Downs 2012, 41). Former slaves perished because of the outbreak of epidemics aggravated by their limited ability to cover their basic needs.

---

[2] See Emirbayer and Mische (1998) for an excellent analysis of the concept of agency.

Freedom, we could argue, needs to be embedded in a "dignity culture." It needs to consider relational aspects:

> The degree of economic and social autonomy achieved by the former slaves depended upon an elaborate series of power relationships, including the connection of the former slave society to the larger world economy and to outside, usually colonial, political authorities, the relative scarcity of land, and the degree to which, despite abolition, the planter class retained its local political hegemony. (Foner 1982, 92)

These observations invite a more relational understanding of agency, personhood, and, even, freedom. There are important reasons to put freedom at the center of development. The capability approach does not contradict the idea of integral human development, but the nuances are different. I suggest that there is a "discursive comfort zone" of the capability approach that is different from the discursive comfort zone of the idea of integral human development.

A discursive comfort zone is determined by the topics and motifs with which an approach is most prominently associated and by aspects of a discourse that fit without adjustment efforts into an approach. Whereas, for example, the capability approach is most comfortable with individual rational agents, other approaches may be more comfortable with the ideas of interdependence and community. Sen packages a lot in his concept of freedom, but even this approach is not able to easily subsume values such as justice, respect, friendship, or caring. Consequently, Des Gasper and Irene van Staveren talk about "the underdefinition and overextension of Sen's notion of freedom" (Gasper and van Staveren 2003, 149). There is a concern that the capabilities approach neglects interdependence and risks instrumentalizing relationships. Others may be valued only insofar as they foster the capabilities of the individual rather than being perceived as inherent goods (Hoffmann and Metz 2017). An even deeper critique concerns the implicit model of personal growth. To illustrate this point, Gerald Cohen criticized Amartya Sen's "athletic image of the person," the idea that the value of a person's life depends on choices and the realization of potential (Cohen 1993, 24–25). Sen's conception of growth is clearly influenced by Aristotle's understanding of the human person characterized by potentials and possibilities.

These concerns can be responded to, but they do point to the discursive comfort zone of the capability approach that needs to make adjustments to accommodate the interests of future generations, ecologically motivated restrictions of freedoms and choices, human suffering, and tragedy. The idea of integral human development seems to be more comfortable than the capabilities approach when addressing these issues. The idea of integral human development would nuance dignity over freedom. This nuance entails accentuating aspects like relationality, vulnerability, fundamental equality, and the idea of a dignified life that is characterized by agency freedom and by inner freedom and depth. Dignity language adds a dimension that goes beyond autonomy, especially in cases of limited agency or in cases where a person may be free to make choices but finds herself disrespected nonetheless.

There may also be cultural limits to a freedom-centered outlook on the individual that a more relational way of thinking could better accommodate. A development studies scholar shared with me a reflection on Saba Mahmood's *Politics of Piety*.

> *Mahmood conducted fieldwork in Egypt on the grassroots women's mosque movement, which was part of the broader piety movement at the time. A self-professed secular-liberal feminist, Mahmood sought to understand what motivated the comparatively conservative women who participated in the mosque movement—women whose actions seemed to go against Mahmood's vision of social change. A key conclusion from her fieldwork was that freedom cannot be assumed to be the desired end goal or motivating force for all people at all times. Members of the women's mosque movement, broadly speaking, did not aim to "maximize freedom," even in subtle or subversive ways within the constraints of their patriarchal society. Rather, they had a different and more communal conception of human flourishing which secular/liberal/Western persons, so deeply socialized as we are to be autonomous self-actualizing individuals, struggle greatly to understand because we essentially lack the language to articulate it.*

A dignity language can open spaces that a freedom language is less prepared to enter—and vice versa. We could also, as a matter of intellectual honesty, identify some areas where the idea of integral human development may be out of its discursive comfort zone; people have articulated concerns regarding communitarianism and approaches that emphasize the community rather than the individual, including the questions of how to deal with pluralism and diversity, how to decide "which community" and "whose community" is at stake, and which goods are considered to be part of "the common good" (Sedmak 2018).

No approach can be at home in all discursive zones, and this is rather a point in favor of the approach than a criticism, since this points to the distinctive profile of the approach. My modest claim is this: whereas the capability approach embraces freedom as the main organizing principle, integral human development is centered on the idea of dignity. Another big question in development theory and practice is the issue of equality and inequality.

Dignity and Inequality

The Sustainable Development Goals (or SDGs) are without any doubt an important source of global orientation and a major achievement. The process of designing the SDGs was intended to include many different stakeholders, and the goals reflect a sense of a global community, offering indicators and measurements that can inform policy decisions. There are, as one would expect, also fundamental criticisms. The Sustainable Development Goals fail to address root causes and do not identify larger issues within social and economic structures. They do not consider the intersectionality of the global challenges. They follow a growth-centric development model. They do not use strong human rights language. They face the challenges of diffuse responsibilities and of the question of how and what to prioritize. Some of these points are especially salient from a postcolonial and feminist perspective (Struckmann 2018).

In his address to the General Assembly of the United Nations in 2015, Pope Francis commented on the SDGs with the warning that

> We can rest content with the bureaucratic exercise of drawing up long lists of good proposals—goals, objectives and statistics—or we can think that a single theoretical and aprioristic solution will provide an answer to all the challenges. It must never be forgotten that political and economic activity is only effective when it is understood as a prudential activity, guided by a perennial concept of justice and constantly conscious of the fact that, above and beyond our plans and programmes, we are dealing with real men and women who live, struggle and suffer, and are often forced to live in great poverty, deprived of all rights.

Then, he referred explicitly to integral human development and the need for its implementation, without which there is the risk that

> The ideal of "saving succeeding generations from the scourge of war" (*Charter of the United Nations*, Preamble), and "promoting social progress and better standards of life in larger freedom" (*Charter of the UN*, Preamble), risks becoming an unattainable illusion, or, even worse, idle chatter which serves as a cover for all kinds of abuse and corruption, or for carrying out an ideological colonization by the imposition of anomalous models and lifestyles which are alien to people's identity and, in the end, irresponsible.

There is a simple question at stake: does integral human development call for a change of the global system? In a course I taught on integral human development, we looked at Sustainable Development Goal 10 ("Reduce inequality within and among countries"). My question was simple: What, if anything, is wrong with inequality?

In their response, students used terms like "unfair" and "unjust," but more and more students, especially when looking at the growing disparity between the poorest of the poor and the extremely rich, used the language of dignity and connected it to justice. The issue of inequality is not just that some people have no access to conditions of a dignified life while others have so much that they cannot spend it.

This is an indication that enacting human dignity is not harmless. Integral Human Development is not harmless. A commitment to human dignity, to the dignity of each person, cannot be disentangled from a commitment to the common good as the flourishing of a community in a way that each member of the community benefits. If the privilege of a few hampers the flourishing of the many, we are faced with an undeniable challenge. The UN secretary-general lamented the dynamics of the global financial system that privileges countries of the Global North and disadvantages countries from the Global South.[3] In light of the dignity-motivated concern with inequality, we can conclude that dignity language is neither necessarily lofty nor lame. Dignity language is politically powerful and relevant, especially if and when people cannot live dignified lives because of the agency, behavior, and choices of other human beings and institutions. This will require some uncomfortable conversations. Recounting a meeting he had to attend in Washington, DC, about global development, a colleague recalled one of the participants asking not to mention the "R-word." My colleague asked: "What do you mean: the R-word?" The person responded, "We do not want to talk about redistribution."

If we accept that human agency is instrumental in creating conditions of poverty, a dignity lens will not simply talk about poverty as if this was a natural condition. Poverty is based on choices and decisions, and these decisions and choices will have us talk about inequality. Nelson Mandela, in his 1998 address to the General Assembly of the United Nations, made this point about our responsibility for inequality central:

> The failure to achieve the vision contained in the Universal Declaration of Human Rights finds dramatic expression in the contrast between wealth and poverty which characterises the divide between the countries of the North and the countries of the South and within individual countries in all hemispheres.

---

[3] António Guterres, "Secretary-General's Remarks at the International Conference on a Climate Resilient Pakistan [as delivered]," *United Nations Secretary-General Statements* online, January 9, 2023.

It is made especially poignant and challenging by the fact that this coexistence of wealth and poverty, the perpetuation of the practice of the resolution of inter- and intra-state conflicts by war and the denial of the democratic right of many across the world, all result from the acts of commission and omission particularly by those who occupy positions of leadership in politics, in the economy and in other spheres of human activity.

What I am trying to say is that all these social ills which constitute an offence against the Universal Declaration of Human Rights are not a pre-ordained result of the forces of nature or the product of a curse of the deities.

They are the consequence of decisions which men and women take or refuse to take, all of whom will not hesitate to pledge their devoted support for the vision conveyed in the Universal Declaration of Human Rights.[4]

It is remarkable that Nelson Mandela uses the reference to the Universal Declaration of Human Rights to make the point about agency and failed agency. And this leads to an explicit concern with inequality. He continued:

Paradoxically, the challenge of poverty across the globe has been brought into sharp focus by the fact of the destructive "fast movements of currents" of wealth from one part of the world to the other.

Put starkly, we have a situation in which the further accumulation of wealth, rather than contributing to the improvement of the quality of life of all humanity, is generating poverty at a frighteningly accelerated pace.

The imperative to act on this urgent, life and death matter can no longer be ignored.

Inequality is not just a matter of relations between people. Inequality is a matter of the dignity of each person. Pope Francis explicitly connects a lack of proper human development with inequality: "Some economic rules have proved effective for growth, but not for integral human development.... Wealth has increased, but together with inequality, with the result that 'new forms of poverty are emerging'" (*Fratelli Tutti* 21). The lack of integral human development and the persistence of inequality put even peace at risk: "Those who work for tranquil social coexistence should never forget that inequality and lack of integral human development make peace impossible" (*Fratelli Tutti* 235). Pope Francis reflects on inequality in terms

---

[4] Nelson Mandela, "Address by President Nelson Mandela at 53rd United Nations General Assembly, New York—United States," September 21, 1998.

that are very similar to Nelson Mandela's line of thought. In his postsynodal exhortation *Querida Amazonia* (2020), he laments the fact that

> The original peoples often witnessed helplessly the destruction of the
> natural surroundings that enabled them to be nourished and kept
> healthy, to survive and to preserve a way of life in a culture which gave
> them identity and meaning. The imbalance of power is enormous; the
> weak have no means of defending themselves, while the winners take it
> all, and "the needy nations grow more destitute, while the rich nations
> become even richer." (*Querida Amazonia* 13)

The quotation at the end is taken from *Populorum Progressio* (57), the encyclical that laid the foundation for the concept of "Integral Human Development." Developed in the patristic era and reemphasized in modern times, the Christian Social Tradition is quite clear. Inequality cannot be justified as long as people do not have access to conditions for a dignified life.

In the twentieth century, Pope Paul VI quoted St Ambrose in *Populorum Progressio* 23, writing, "You are not making a gift of what is yours to the poor man, but you are giving him back what is his. You have been appropriating things that are meant to be for the common use of everyone. The earth belongs to everyone, not to the rich." In the twenty-first century, Pope Francis quotes John Chrysostom, "I encourage financial experts and political leaders to ponder the words of one of the sages of antiquity: 'Not to share one's wealth with the poor is to steal from them and to take away their livelihood. It is not our own goods which we hold, but theirs'" (*Evangelii Gaudium* 57). These are not harmless descriptive statements. They are powerful exhortations to talk about the "R-word," to make redistribution a moral necessity.[5] In short, dignity is not a harmless concept. Integral human development comes with major challenges to the existing global structures and the challenge of building more inclusive global systems.[6]

---

[5] In his Opening Address to the Third General Conference of the Latin American Episcopate in Puebla, Mexico, on January 28, 1979, Pope John Paul II also pointed to inequality as a major concern with regard to development: "When Paul VI declared that development is 'the new name of peace' (*Populorum Progressio* 76) he had in mind all the links of interdependence that exist not within the nations but also outside them, on the world level. He took into consideration the mechanisms that, because they happen to be imbued not with authentic humanism but with materialism, produce on the international level rich people ever more rich at the expense of poor people ever more poor. There is no economic rule capable of changing these mechanisms by itself. It is necessary, in international life, to call upon ethical principles, the demands of justice, the primary commandment which is that of love. Primacy must be given to what is moral, to what is spiritual, to what springs from the full truth concerning man."

[6] See Stiglitz (2021).

11

Epistemic Justice and Policy Making

Policy makers and policy advisors are typically among the elites, with the lifestyle of elites. These elites become privileged in their sources of information and their way of making judgments: "Political elites ... typically have more resources and support staff, which may enable more accurate judgments and decisions" (Vis 2019, 42). Yet, there exists the double challenge of social pressure and distance. Cohesive policy-making groups, like advisors to the president, can produce low quality decisions because of the ideological uniformity and the pressure to consent (Mintz and Wayne 2016). Pope Francis has been outspoken about the distance that comes with privilege.

> Indeed, when all is said and done, they frequently remain at the bottom of the pile. This is due partly to the fact that many professionals, opinion makers, communications media and centres of power, being located in affluent urban areas, are far removed from the poor, with little direct contact with their problems. They live and reason from the comfortable position of a high level of development and a quality of life well beyond the reach of the majority of the world's population. (*Laudato Si'* 49)

There is a distance between decision makers and those most affected by the decisions. As certain lifestyles lead to certain ways of knowing, certain life worlds will be represented while others will not. For example, in the Austrian National Assembly, there is currently no worker represented. Unlike in previous years, no member of the Parliament brings the background of a worker to the highest legislating body of the country. This may seem a minor point, but it influences the way the life realities of workers are being considered and represented. The "diet of examples" will be, accordingly, reduced.

Pope Francis exhorts a closeness to the most disadvantaged and does not accept the excuse of elites "that they cannot be close to the poor because their own lifestyle demands more attention to other areas." This is an excuse commonly heard in academic, business or professional, and even ecclesial circles" (*Evangelii Gaudium* 198). The creation of lifestyle bubbles creates comfort zones and distance from the life realities of the majority of the population. The form of life a person chooses will influence the examples she can draw from, the horizon of her "knowledge by acquaintance," and even her entire perception. Patterns of perception are shaped just like habits, by regular contact with certain realities. The idea of integral human development, with its call to the common good and the imperative of not leaving anyone behind, will consider these lifestyle questions.

Distance has been identified as a factor in failing to address local developments.[1] Raymond Apthorpe introduced the term "Aidland," describing the dynamics of aid workers inhabiting their own separate world with its own time, space, habits, beliefs, and economics. "Stepping into Aidland is like stepping off one planet into another, a virtual another, not that this means that it is any the less real to those who work in or depend on or are affected by it in other ways" (quoted after Harrison 2013, 263). Edited by David Mosse, the 2011 book *Adventures in Aidland* further discusses the construction and transmission of knowledge about global poverty and its reduction through development professionals who encounter each other in addition to, or more than, poverty (Mosse 2011). In a similar vein, Séverine Autesserre has reflected on "Peaceland," the bubble created and inhabited by international peace builders. Based on a year of ethnographic study in Congo and making use of close to three hundred in-depth interviews and hundreds of key documents, she is brutally honest about the dynamics that create a split between the international professionals and the local people. The former can claim high moral ground and have access to resources, global social capital, and specific knowledge.

> The international peace builders' daily routines, including their security procedures and their insistence on advertising their actions as well as the way that they value external expertise over local knowledge, further widen the split between them and local people.... The expatriates' daily routines publicize, perpetuate, and reinforce awareness of these advantages and construct an image of foreign peace builders as superior to local people." (Autesserre 2014, 13)

Next to the putative bubbles of "Aidland" and "Peaceland" there could be the bubble of "Human Rights Land." In the introduction to Part I, I discussed

---

[1] See Diamond 2005 (chaps. 1 and 14). Interestingly enough, "distance" was already one challenge Plato envisioned for this model of the philosopher-King—if the King is too far away from ordinary citizen, which understanding of the context of his reign would he be able to obtain? Plato, *Theaetetus* 173c–d, *Phaedrus* 249b–c.

Michael Ignatieff's attempt to describe how the moral universe of the human rights activist and the human rights intellectual, with its emphasis on abstract categories and on "the universal human being," differs from the concrete experiences and nongeneralizing accounts of "the nonelites" (Ignatieff 2017b). An intellectually honest discourse on human rights needs to be elaborate and refined, nuanced and well-versed in general terms and universal categories. But this discourse comes with a price tag —the costs of creating a discursive world of its own, and, beyond that, a social world of its own, "a life world," with conferences, papers, quotations, and resolutions.

The same can be said about the world of diplomats. Diplomats talk to each other and live in spaces protected by international law. Ambassadors usually interact with high-level officials, elites, and other ambassadors. Jérémie Cornut, a Canadian political scientist, has described the challenges and confusions embassies had to deal with during the political dynamics that ousted Egyptian president Hosni Mubarak during the Arab spring in late January and early February 2011 in Cairo (Cornut 2015). Diplomats who were interviewed at the time about their experience shared the difficulties of being able to "read the situation" given their social distance from "the people on the streets." Diplomats do not physically reside in the places where most Egyptians live. A diplomat commented: "We live in [upscale neighborhoods] Zamalek and Maadi, the person of the people is our cleaning lady, our driver, our gardener, but we have no contact with the working class" (Cornut 2015, 392). Cornut explicitly referenced the term "getting out of the bubble," by changing habits, changing clothes ("abandon the tie and the suit"), and changing the way of spending time in particular physical environments (Cornut 2015, 392).

Living in a bubble, with its own privileged comfort zone, creates a kind of distance that makes it challenging to understand the "realities outside." Leaving a bubble is both exciting and risky. In Michael Frayn's dystopia *A Very Private Life*, the British author describes the privileged life of a family who lives in an underground home after the planet has become uninhabitable. There is no need to leave the well-protected sphere and its constant temperature and entertainment programs. It is risky to leave this bubble, which is exactly what the protagonist, a girl named Uncumber, sets out to do. She is willing to take the risks of going outside for the sake of making "real experiences," of having "real encounters." Her parents, happy in their bubble, do not understand the girl. Pope Francis, with his insistence on the category of encounter, would have been a more understanding conversation partner for Uncumber, who was interested in leaving her comfort zone to "go out to the peripheries."

The Ethics of Policy Design

The question of how policies are being designed is morally relevant. The result and the process count. Integral human development is only integral if the necessary planning processes are properly designed and considered. Ethical questions (i.e., questions of concern from an Integral Human Development [or IHD] perspective) can enter the policy-making process on many different levels. Ethical concepts and values frequently come into play in the policy design process (Brall et al. 2019). In a simple model of policy making, we could identify five aspects that are all morally relevant and can be analyzed from the perspective of Integral Human Development: the perception of a problem, the deliberation process, the decision, communication and implementation, and evaluation.

Figure 4: Five Aspects of Policy Making

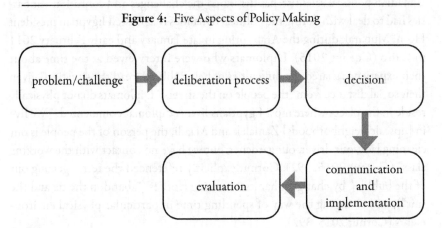

Problem: *Policy making starts with a challenge or a problem, and the perception of a situation as a problem already includes a normative element. A problem can be defined as a situation where important goals cannot be reached or a state of affairs where one's agency faces adversities and obstacles. An IHD perspective could already contribute to the reading of "problems." Whose perspective counts? Specifically considering most vulnerable people, we learn that the experiences of disadvantaged groups need to count more. Privileging usually nonprivileged perspectives will lead to a different perception of problems. The lack of public playgrounds may not be a problem for house owners with backyards, but it would be a problem for others. Problems are a matter of perspective. The lack of public restrooms in urban areas may be a problem for tourists and the homeless but not for those who work in downtown offices. So the question is, whose reality counts?*

Deliberation process: *The process of deliberation is a key question in policy making. The process will look at options, analyses, and arguments. Who is involved? Who is recognized as stakeholder? How is the deliberation process designed in terms of levels of participation? Whose voices are heard? "Who are the experts?" (Brock 2002, 14–15). When Austria's government, for example, considered a policy of mandatory COVID-19 vaccinations, they created an expert group with medical and legal experts but without social scientists, ethicists, teachers, or young parents. Who gets a place at the table? Which data points are being considered?*

Decision: *Policy makers have to arrive at a decision, and the decision has to be sufficiently simple and clear, otherwise it cannot be communicated or enforced. We may face a dilemma between the convenience of simple, broad, and crude categories and the higher level of complexity (in the spirit of "the whole person"). Regulations that allow for exceptions from the rules and insist on offering space to look into the uniqueness of cases (such as commission for cases of hardship) could and will slow down the process, but justifications for such decisions—which arguments are being used, which arguments count—are a crucially important aspect of the decision. From an IHD perspective, common good–related arguments or arguments based on the perspective of disprivileged groups have more weight than arguments using the challenges of privileged groups. The decision will have to be clear and will probably not be without trade-offs.*

Communication and implementation: *The decision has to be translated into a certain form. Policies are "wrapped" in a particular way, a literary genre. An IHD approach calls for clarity and simplicity in the language and plausibility in the presented justification. The project of a citizen-friendly language, with its inclusivity and low threshold, is very much in line with IHD.*[2] *The policy has to be communicated in a persuasive manner; again, arguments matter, but so do stories that help people see the plausibility of the new policy and the problem to which the policy responds. In the spirit of IHD, the implementation of the policy will be open to "exceptions from the rule."*

Evaluation: *Paul Perrin works on specific IHD approaches to evaluation, called "integral human evaluation" (Perrin 2022). Evaluating projects in an IHD frame requires honestly observing reality, even if the process is*

---

[2] "Designing a Regulatory Framework for Citizen-Friendly Data Communication by Public Actors," The Dutch Research Council (NWO) online, November 1, 2017–February 17, 2023.

*costly and uncomfortable. Because of the nuances of decisions and commu-
nication and implementation, IHD-focused evaluation will take time and
must be able to account for the experiences of and impacts on the whole
persons impacted by the project. During this evaluation, questions may
arise that seek to understand or uncover experiences of epistemic justice
or injustice. There is the obvious challenge of balancing standard processes
and the respect for the uniqueness of a situation and the particularity of a
context. IHD-sensitive evaluations will be especially sensitive to the criteria
for success. The defined criteria change the project dynamics as well as the
assessment of project activities. Metrics of success are powerful and drive
both (individual and collective) perceptions and behavior. Within an
IHD-framework, a reflection on the position and positionality of the evalu-
ator is as important as an analysis of the adopted process (taking the idea
of decolonizing power relations seriously). Guiding questions include the
following: Which data are we interested in? How do we collect, manage,
and use data? How do we translate data into narratives and narratives
into recommendations and decisions?*

All these steps and aspects point to the central concern with epistemic
justice. Epistemic justice is brought about by an appropriate way of considering
different perspectives. We can distinguish three different types of perspectives: a
first-person perspective, a second-person perspective, and a third-person perspective. Let us call these perspectives P1, P2, and P3, respectively.

P1 enables a person to make first-person statements. This view is irreducible,
for it cannot be replaced by "a view from nowhere." Microtheories, as sketched
in chapter 4, are a way to honor this perspective. P1 allows for statements such as
"My experience of poverty tells me," or "I have experienced poverty to mean" This
is a first-person statement that describes those kinds of experiential statements
with the proper authority of a personal experience. Proper authority means if the
interlocutor is recognized as being "reasonable," you cannot reject a first-person
statement expressing a first-person epistemic position as false. If a reasonable
person says, "I have been humiliated," I am not in a position to reject the claim
about the person's experience, only her choice of words or grounds of judgment.
Considering the experience of less-privileged persons will require intentional
efforts because of the reality of societal power dynamics. A young development
worker recounts a situation in which a farmer was asked his opinion of a problem
on the farm by a policy maker. The farmer replied, "Why would you ask what I
think when you are the one who will decide?"

P2 is a perspective constituted by the presence of a significant *Other*; the South African Truth and Reconciliation Commission, for instance, recognized "social truth" or "dialogical truth" as a category to talk about a type of truth that would only emerge in situations of dialogue, in situations of a genuine encounter and conversation (TRC 1998, §§ 39–42). Genuine conversations allow for correction and response. P2 follows a Gadamerian hermeneutics built on this model of genuine conversation. P2 has been identified as particularly relevant for ethics, since "second person accounts" generate specific responsibilities and moral demands. The presence of another person changes my personal moral situation (Darwall 2006). P2 changes the rules of the game. Gerald Cohen developed what he called the "interpersonal test" asking "whether the argument could serve as a justification of a mooted policy when uttered by any member of society to any other member" (Cohen 2008, 42). Which of the statements made in a P3-context would still be acceptable in a P2 situation?

P3 is an objectifying outsider perspective characterized by a certain distance to the object of inquiry. With P3, there is an epistemic advantage of easier access to ordering and systematization, but this advantage comes with the moral challenge of hegemony (Krumer-Nevo 2010).[3] Connected to policy making, P3 can mean that elite perceptions, particularly elite perceptions of poverty, are different from other perceptions since policy views on poverty change with wealth (Page et al. 2013). Both visible and invisible privileges change a person's perception and can lead to particularly reductionist accounts of social issues. The question "What would I do if I were in this situation?" can be unhelpful if the distance between the privileged person asking this question and the life realities of the people one would like to understand is too big. Gene Marks's "well-meant" article "If I Were a Poor Black Kid" in *Forbes Magazine* (December 12, 2011) illustrates this very point. The phenomenon of P3-related reductionisms can be observed in the development discourse as well:

> Social planners are prey to the same temptations which have beset other intellectuals at all times: to adopt roles which are personally gratifying but which fall short of their obligation to a new humanity in gestation.... Classically, these roles have been: counselor to the prince; the pure specialist in pursuit of apolitical goals; the faithful servant of a

---

[3] Krumer-Nevo (2010) underlines the importance of "counternarratives," as we know them from the works of Gayatri Spivak (1988). Atalia Omer, to name another example, has offered "subaltern visons of peace" in the context of Israel and Palestine (Omer 2013, 183–270).

committed cause; and the free-lancer with varying degrees of sympathy for some political party or movement.... Planners and other intellectuals find it so difficult to create a true professional ethic because they are crafters of words, ideas, and models. Consequently, they are timid about plunging into the heartland reality of ethics as existential power, and not as moral verbalism or conceptualism. (Goulet 1976, 40–41)

"The heartland reality of ethics" is the key phrase for procedural justice. In order to promote epistemic justice in the design of social change, a proper context has to be provided that does not encourage perspectival hegemony. The epistemic quality of judgments increases if P1, P2, and P3 are considered in a nonexclusive way. The best way of getting P1 and P2 to sit at the same table is, indeed, a table. That is, gathering space allows P2 to take the lead. Special attention will have to be paid to a culture of dialogue and encounter both for epistemological and ethical reasons. Including people in processes and respecting people's knowledge and opinions are actually hard work.

The reality of migration is a helpful example. It is one thing to think about migration in the abstract and suggest "limiting the numbers of migrants entering a country." It is another matter to be exposed to the dramatic reality and the proximity of human tragedy and to move beyond abstractions (Albahari 2016). Emma Jane Kirby, in her novel *The Optician of Lampedusa*, accounts for such dramatic realities. She tells of a citizen from Lampedusa who lives a quiet life as an optician in this Italian island town and is, all of a sudden, confronted with the reality of migrants drowning in the sea while on a boat trip with friends. He is surrounded by desperate persons: "Everywhere he looked, there were more of them! They seemed to multiply in the water, hands breeding hands" (Kirby 2016, 35). He took as many people as he possibly could, on his boat, the *Galata*. "He knew it was too many. From his vantage point, he did a rapid head count. One, two, twenty ... forty-six men and one woman. Plus eight crew. That meant there were fifty-five of them. Fifty-five on a boat built for a maximum of ten." (Kirby 2016, 38) And still, there were more and more people fighting for their lives. "There are too many of them. Too many of them and I don't know how to do this"(Kirby 2016, 3). There is drama, trauma, exasperation, and despair. What does it mean to design policies with knowledge by acquaintance of these situations in mind? What does it mean to consider, for example, the deadly and dangerous border of the Mediterranean Sea and the dismal conditions of migrants trying to reach Europe? What does it mean to recognize "the crimes of peace" occurring on a regular basis, not as a result of a few individual failures, but rather as a consequence of global and institutional arrangements (Albahari

2015)? What does it mean to analyze the encounters with immigration officials in terms of "humiliation" (Villegas 2015)?

This is not a plea for the emotionalization of policies, though, as Farhana Sultana recognizes in understanding water policy, emotions should matter (Sultana 2011). This is a plea for "realism" in the sense that decision makers are willing to be exposed to the realities of matters. Policy making in the spirit and light of integral human development will not shy away from seeing the whole person (including the tragic aspects) and each person (including the desperate) in a "thick way." What would, for example, migration policies look like if they were codesigned with the most vulnerable and the most wounded?

The Enduring Need for Judgment

I have suggested four main criteria for the design, implementation, and assessment of policies. These criteria are like reference points and should help with proper judgments. However, these four criteria will not easily lead to moral clarity with many policies. Let me provide an example: I asked students to look at a particular policy through the lens of Integral Human Development. Their charge was the assessment of the decision of the president of the University of Notre Dame, Fr. John Jenkins CSC, to reopen the campus in the academic year 2020/2021. The class was provided the message of the president that outlined this decision. The question asked was simple: President John Jenkins CSC communicated the decision to reopen campus and to have an "in person academic year 2020/2021" at the University of Notre Dame. Is this decision justified on the grounds of Integral Human Development?

The class was split about this question. Even though each student used the same criteria, they arrived at different conclusions. About half of the group voted for "Yes, Notre Dame's COVID-19 policy is an expression of Integral Human Development." The main arguments were the following: The decision to reopen campus reflects a holistic view of the person in the spirit of "the whole person" to be taken seriously, considering mental and social aspects of health in the decision;[4] the decision also reflects a holistic view of education and an emphasis on the quality of education, which has been identified as a key driver of human flourishing; the decision to invite students back to campus fosters inclusion and creates equity in terms of the enabling learning environment (since study conditions

---

[4] Interestingly enough, a critical comment observed the opposite: "this decision belittles a person's humaneness and treats her as a mechanized being who is supposed to get back to work as long as they are keeping up well physically."

for students in their respective homes vary vastly)[5]; the decision is in the spirit of Integral Human Development; President Jenkins offers reasons and a clear set of arguments for the decision and pursues an evidence-based approach.

However, there were also counterarguments: the policy would create new entry points for social exclusion since international students might not have the mobility to travel to the United States, given travel and visa restrictions; the policy would have negative effects on the environment, with the many disposable materials needed to ensure campus safety; some voiced concerns about the restrictions the policy would impose on members of the university community since this was not an "opt-in" approach and since vaccination was made mandatory[6] and the policy encouraged limited off-campus mobility, including the decision not to have a fall break, but rather an early end of the fall semester since the risk of having thousands of students leave campus and return was considered too big. There was also a reservation regarding the criterion of excessiveness with students articulating their worries about excessive workload for students (whose fall break was taken away), teaching faculty, and cleaning staff.

The class was split on three criteria: reverse privileging and special consideration of the most vulnerable/disadvantaged, the criteria of participation and subsidiarity, and the criterion of the wider common good. For some students, the fact that the university policy ensured inclusion of all students and offered pathways toward exceptions and accommodations of special risk groups was a sufficient expression of the criterion of the special consideration and protection of the most vulnerable.[7] For others, the consideration of immune-compromised or anxious people was inadequate. "Those with health conditions threatened by COVID will either be socially and structurally pressured to return to campus

---

[5] To quote one statement, "What resonated with me was the idea of letting everybody enter campus all at once because the educational experience should be consistent and accessible to all. In my opinion, it is a very bold decision because it requires taking more risks; however, it is compatible with IHD in terms of participation and leaving no one behind." Another student was more critical about these risks: "Reopening campus and expecting students, faculty, and staff to return increases everyone's risk of catching and spreading the virus, even if the most secure measures are put in place to limit the spread. Everyone staying home and social distancing would of course be a better way to curb the disease than bringing everyone together. In this way, bodily integrity is compromised as Notre Dame community members are being asked to increase their health risk for the 'common good' of education and an improved learning environment which is a trade-off that some people may not feel comfortable making."

[6] "The decision disrespects the agency of individuals who may not want to get vaccinated." Another colleague even used terms like "humiliation" and "infantilization" in this context.

[7] "The fact that the University was willing to make alternative accommodations for those who could not attend classes in-person also supports this IHD-based decision."

or rely on the kindness of their professors," one student stated. The critics also commented on the higher risks for cleaning crews and maintenance staff on campus. In terms of participation and subsidiarity, President Jenkins made it clear that he had consulted with experts as well as numerous groups on campus. Here again, critics missed consensus or observed that "the plan should have included more inputs from personnel who will be working at the frontline." In terms of the criterion of the common good, supporters of the policy quoted the appeal to the common good of the campus community to follow the safety protocols in order to protect the most vulnerable for the sake of the common good. Opponents worried about the risks, including the risks to the community of South Bend, Indiana, where the University of Notre Dame has its main campus.

In the students' reflections, there was a lot of "on the one hand, on the other hand" arguing.

> Based on how socially and emotionally difficult the pandemic and isolation was, bringing the campus community back together could be seen as upholding the IHD principle of intangibility as it allows people to invest in their mental, social, economic, and spiritual growth and development in ways that remote work/education often hinders. However, increased interconnectedness in the midst of the pandemic could have negative impacts for some in terms of increasing anxiety or stress.

Here again, the epistemological dynamics of enacting Integral Human Development are on full display. We have a set of general principles or criteria, but there has to be the assessment to which extent a particular criterion is being met.

From an IHD perspective, the "ability to afford IHD" is an additional aspect. One student commented, "The decision to reopen campus also demonstrates an enormous amount of privilege that the university had the resources to invest in extra measures and processes to create a safe learning environment in the middle of the pandemic," including purchasing hotels for students to quarantine in.

To close this chapter, I draw four conclusions from this exercise, which is one of many that confirm similar results:

1. Integral Human Development is an analytical lens. It is way of looking at matters, a perceptual mode.
2. The idea of Integral Human Development is a source of questions and a driver of a particular discourse. It draws the attention to certain aspects and to "ways of asking questions."
3. Using the analytical lens of Integral Human Development is not a mechanical process. There is no guarantee for a kind of "intersubjectivity"

that would make sure that two epistemic subjects using this lens will necessarily arrive at the same conclusion. There is a necessity to make judgments and to weigh aspects and criteria. Hence, there is an irreducible subjective element in the enactment of Integral Human Development.

4. In contested cases, the analytical lens of Integral Human Development will, in all likelihood, not lead to moral clarity but will reveal persistent ambiguities about its application and the result of this application.

In a way, this is disappointing news for those who had hoped to see IHD as a hammer that shatters ambiguity and ambivalence, offering the kind of clarity René Descartes talks about in his *Discours de la Methode*. But it points to the enduring need for making judgments, for bringing some general insights into IHD together with the specific dynamics of a situation. This is a personal as well as an ongoing task given the continuing changes and disruptions we face.

12

Institutionalizing Integral
Human Development

Integral Human Development (or IHD) is an aspirational concept. Some may call it unrealistic, but it offers a sense of direction and some criteria to decide whether that direction has been honored or not. We have identified four important criteria for social change processes and policies in the spirit of integral human development: dignified life and integral ecology, special attention to the most disadvantaged and reverse privileging, subsidiarity and inclusive participation, and the wider common good. Institutions that take these commitments seriously are good candidates for examples of how integral human development can be institutionalized and translated into organizational practices.

The story of BRAC, the largest nongovernmental organization (NGO) in the world, could be read as an attempt to institutionalize integral human development. As in cases mentioned in our reflections on "development protology," the story of BRAC begins with a visceral experience. After cyclone Bhola had hit present-day Bangladesh on November 12, 1970, Fazle Hasan Abed, who worked as a corporate manager at the time, flew to Manpura Island in the northern Bay of Bengal, at the mouth of the Meghna River. From the helicopter, he

> Saw an image that would haunt him for the rest of his life. In the shallow waters of the bay surrounding the island lay countless bodies of adults, children and livestock.... Abed's conscience felt a jolt from which it never fully recovered. He understood now, on a visceral level, the reason for their massive death toll. The dead had lived in thatched huts, doing what little they could for their family. Most were illiterate; many suffered frequent illness and daily hunger. They never had the means to build solid roofs to protect themselves or their families. There were

no doors to be blown from their hinges. Their circumstances had killed them, not the cyclone itself. They were born poor and died poor, and they died because they were poor. (MacMillan 2022, 15–16)

We have seen the power of founding experiences and founding stories before. In this case, Abed was shaken by what he saw and began to coordinate a response that grew, with an interruption from the Bangladesh Liberation War and Abed's exile in the United Kingdom, into an organization that was very much built on principles of "integral human development."

BRAC works with an integrated approach that addresses "the whole person." It is an organization enacting integral human development. The "graduation program," mentioned before, combines

> Adult education, agriculture, fisheries, vocational training for women, health and family planning.... Where a critic might see a hodge-podge of activities, Abed saw a holistic set of solutions that, delivered together, would give people the boost they needed to emancipate themselves from millennia of suffering and exploitation. (MacMillan 2022, 69)

An accompaniment model that would, for example, give a goat, a stipend, and personal coaching can ensure a multidimensional response to the multidimensional reality of poverty. This holistic approach works, nonetheless, with priorities, namely, an emphasis on literacy and numeracy to reduce the vulnerability of the poor. Education is a metacapability that opens the access to many capabilities.

The commitment to the ultrapoor set BRAC apart from other organizations. As early as November 1970, Abed and his friends discussed the question of how to reach those living on remote islands. The IHD-idea of "the development of each person" calls for the special consideration of the most disadvantaged. This "preferential option" or intentional prioritization often comes with a gender dimension.

> The ultra-poor ... were almost always women, often widowed or abandoned. They lived barefoot and in rags at the margins of the villages, in dwellings of sticks and thatch. They would beg or do menial labor for a pittance when able, and if no work was available, they might not eat for days. Some were reduced to foraging for bits of corn that rats had hoarded in their holes. For others, a meal might consist of the water left over from the neighbor's boiled rice. (MacMillan 2022, 203)

The choice to prioritize women was well justified.

> Abed would often observe that women were the "managers of poverty," bearing the responsibility, fairly or unfairly, for allocating the household's scant resources. They performed this role remarkably well given the circumstances. He came to believe that if they were the managers of poverty they should also be the managers of development. (MacMillan 2022, 116)

BRAC's commitment to truth and learning through science, research, and data became an important aspect of its commitment to the idea of integral human development. The organization had failures, as well as successes, and was willing to report the failures and learn from mistakes.

> When Abed first arrived in Sulla, he had the idea of redesigning, in a more orderly and efficient manner, two villages the Pakistan Army had razed. He even brought architects from Dhaka to help him. "Nothing existed, so we thought we might as well build the houses in a straight line and run a road through the center," he recalled. "The people were not interested and built their houses right where they previously had been." ... This was an obvious early lesson in the folly of paternalism. (MacMillan 2022, 67)

They had to deal with local power dynamics, underperforming local staff, and sinister laws, under which the exploited could become exploiters.

> In trying to empower exploited groups, however, Abed found they were often simply enabling the exploitation of others down the line. Fishermen's cooperatives, for instance, had existed long before BRAC arrived, but they were financed and controlled by money lenders, who charged usurious rates of interest and often acted in concert with the landowners, who charged exorbitant fees for fishing rights. The fishermen, in turn, would take advantage of the women in the community by paying them a pittance for endless hours of net making and fish drying. "Exploitation by an exploited group cannot be condoned," Abed wrote in his 1974 interim report. (MacMillan 2022, 108)

As Abed built the organization, structures of accountability and honest reporting lines were crucial for its identity as a learning organization.

BRAC has an impressive history and can tell us a lot about integral human development. There are some important challenges worth mentioning, though, which point to some general issues with the institutionalization of integral human development. I will mention three:

1. *Managing the disruptive force of BRAC*: The organization challenged power dynamics and had to deal with the resistance. The explicit plan to put moneylenders out of business and to disrupt their patterns was obviously not the best way to make friends with this group that is not without power (MacMillan 2022, 131). The work of BRAC affects social relationships among the poor and the relationships between the poor and more affluent social groups. They had to learn to bring the elites on board (MacMillan 2022, 211–12).

2. *Scaling up*: Several factors have been identified as contributing to BRAC's success in scaling up, including listening to the people, visioning, piloting, training, down-to-earth management, evaluation and adaptation, and advocacy (Ahmed and French 2006). Yet, scaling up has its risks. Abed pursued ambitious goals and one project, the establishment of community centers, failed because of pressure and haste—"the field staff had rushed to meet the construction targets Abed had set, and, as a result, they selected many sites without regard for the daily lives of the villagers" (MacMillan 2022, 71). BRAC began to expand globally, which meant operating in politically unfamiliar territory (Hossain and Sengupta 2009), and some people voiced concerns with accountability as BRAC became so big (Ahmed et al. 2022). With regard to integral human development, considering the concern that scaling up is only partially compatible with an integrated approach is important.

    In Manikganj and Sulla, BRAC had pursued "integrated development" with a wide swath of antipoverty programming, including group organization, solidarity building, adult education, health, family planning, and myriad forms of economic support. The philosophy was that because poverty did not have a single cause, it could never have a single solution, so it was necessary to work in all these areas. By now, however, Abed understood that integrated programming while ideal for an experimentation zone had practical limitations. It was harder to scale up complex programs than simpler ones. "If you want to do a national program an integrated program becomes more difficult," he said (MacMillan 2022, 136).

A question for worthwhile reflection emerges. Are there limits of IHD with regard to size and scale?

3. *Buying into the neo-liberal paradigm*: BRAC is sometimes criticized for working within an intrinsically problematic system. The organization moved from a more "revolutionary" organization to a major NGO that worked with the government. "Abed was acting like a canny serial entrepreneur on the lookout for moneymaking opportunities everywhere, as long as they would serve the poor while reducing BRAC's donor dependence" (MacMillan 2022, 135). Generating enterprises opened the room for innovation and experiments (Jonker 2009). Abed identified and pursued cash-generating activities such as the establishment of cold storage facilities for potatoes; milk collectors; and, especially, microfinance, which emerged as a major income stream. There is a concern that BRAC is a hybrid and no longer a nonprofit organization since it is operating business enterprises; there is also a concern that it diminishes state power through public service delivery (Bhandari 2017). The question of "the price for growth" is also interesting. Growth has major effects on organizations. When informal organizations become more and more formalized, they undergo changes. Activists who become "employees" have been observed to become more accountable to the organization and its donors than to its original constituencies (Scheepers and Lakhani 2020).

The story of BRAC can teach us a lot about integral human development in practice. There is a clear commitment to the most disadvantaged, an integrated approach, and a vision of the common good of Bangladesh, but there are also concerns about the limits of an integrated approach and the degree of institutionalization. In other words, building dignity-centered institutions is an ongoing challenge.

Building Dignity-Sensitive Institutions

Institution-building is a major aspect of sustainability. In his landmark book on the common good, David Hollenbach identified institutions as drivers of change: "the 'subject' of social justice, therefore, is the major institutions that enhance or impede people's participation in creating and benefiting from the common good" (Hollenbach 2002, 201). The ethics of institutions is an important aspect of integral human development since they play a major role in social change processes. Institutions, even though commonly understood to be the more enduring features of social life, are morally fragile and subject to abuse. State institutions, for example, can be abused by rebel groups as tools to pass resources to global markets (Sweet 2021). It takes institutions to monitor institutions, with all the limits that come with this trivial insight. There is an extensive body of literature on the role of institutions in development. Acemoglu and Robinson's widely discussed 2012 book *Why Nations Fail* has identified institutions as the decisive factor in the agenda of national development. Institutions establish structures that frame collaborative action situations, and the successful incentivization and management of collaborative action situations are key to integral human development's commitment to the development of the entire community, that is, all persons.

The Sustainable Development Goals include a commitment (goal 16) to building strong institutions. Institutions can be analyzed from a dignity or human rights perspective. Galit Sarfaty, for example, has discussed the marginality of human rights at the World Bank and attributed this lack of centrality with the culture of the institution (Sarfaty 2009). The idea of integral human development offers lenses through which to approach the assessment of institutions.

"Good governance," in an IHD framework, is based on integrity. Integral Human Development is a dignity-sensitive approach. Organizations, like Catholic Relief Services, that are explicitly built on the commitment to integral human development have to pursue an approach that is explicit and intentional in its efforts to respect the people with whom it deals. Building dignity-sensitive organizations is challenging when each organization operates within a larger context and depends on other institutions. This is the testimony of a young development worker:

> *We sometimes had to deal with local authorities, which tend to work in a very slow pace and take their time to respond to our requests. It is important to know that these are people too, and maybe their protocols are different than ours. More importantly, it is vital to remember why we are dealing with them. The ultimate goal was to help people in those rural communities to achieve a better quality of life, to have more decent wages, and to have a sustained business plan. With this in mind, it was easier to deal with governmental offices and go through the ups and downs we had to go through with them. We were there for the people, and the people is what inspired us to keep going.*

Institutions face the challenge of "interinstitutional dependence" and have to rely on collaborations in the wider framework. Institutions are embedded in larger frameworks, including larger historical frameworks. We need to consider, for example, the long shadow of colonialism in the shaping of and access to institutions. Lakshmi Iyer has shown, for the context of India, that areas that experienced direct colonial rule have significantly lower levels of access to schools, health centers, and roads in the postcolonial period (Iyer 2010). The reality of the moral vulnerability of institutions may not be enabled or empowered to realize their own moral ideas because of disynchronic and diachronic interconnectedness. Moral stress does not only exist on the personal level of individual employees, for it can be found on the levels of institutions. A gentle and inclusive Catholic school in South Bend, Indiana, that has had to implement standardized testing procedures against their own moral and pedagogical beliefs is an apt example. Dignity-centered approaches must be structurally supported. A development worker recounts her experience teaching science and math to primary grade students in a densely populated slum in the city of Pune:

A major issue I recognized in my classroom when I started was the wide differences in learning paces among the students. The assessments, then, were one-dimensional and essentially indicators of performance only for students already doing well in class. Moreover, preceding pedagogies too were shaped only to be relevant to the well-performing students in class. The rest, "fell through the cracks." The consequences of neglecting students in the context we taught in were higher—students did not have financial support in case of failure; families in the community depended heavily on their children to allow them upward mobility in society.... The classroom wasn't insulated from the domestic/community environment of the students. The learning gaps weren't necessarily a function of cognitive abilities—they were also influenced by the circumstances of their homes. Given the scarce financial conditions at their houses, for example, students often acted as extra hands to bring in additional sources of income/assisted in the work of their parents. There were also cases where post-school, students went for long hours to religious schools/madrassas. In the more extreme cases, abusive conditions at home made it difficult, for students to study after school-hours. To familiarize myself with these situations, and also to build trust within the community, I regularly visited the homes of my students after school, spoke to parents/guardians/mentors, and as far as possible attended the ceremonies/celebrations in the community.

So far, so laudable, we read about the young teacher who walks the extra mile. But there remain substantial questions about the sustainability of the approach and the flaws of the system:

> *For someone like me, therefore, with no family to support at home, I could concentrate my time completely on my classroom as I taught there. For teachers who had kids back home, for example, or families dependent on them for income, providing for every student in the classroom and also engaging with them beyond was simply not possible. It wasn't that they did not believe in a dignity-centered approach towards teaching or did not care for the students not doing well.*

The circumstances can make it very hard to pursue a dignity-sensitive approach in an institutional setting. A robust question remains, well articulated by this young teacher:

> *My question then is, how can a dignity-centered approach—one that takes into account each and every individual in a context and creates better outcomes for each of them—be sustained and employed throughout? More importantly, how can this be done without utterly exhausting the people who are executing it, or at the very least, adequately compensating them for it?*

Building and sustaining dignity-sensitive institutions is hard and requires intentionality. The French "Alzheimer village" Landais may be an example of both difficulty and intentionality (Renault 2022). A clear mission and people who believe in the mission are necessary, and this belief must be nurtured in a way similar to nurturing self-efficacy. Sustaining sensitivity to dignity may transcend the realm of institutional ethics and move us into the sphere of spirituality.

The Bethany Land Institute, introduced in chapter 8, is an example of an educational institution that is committed to institutionalizing integral human development. Emmanuel Katongole, its founder, mentions some of the challenges with institution-building.

> A great deal of BLI's efforts and resources have been spent on setting up BLI as an institution. This has involved, among other things: acquiring land, designing a campus, setting up structures, building dormitories and halls, incorporating the organization, hiring and training staff, setting up systems of management and accountability, running budgets, board meetings, fund raising, and filling financial returns. When we started, I did not realize that these efforts of institutionalization would come to take up so much time, and come to matter so significantly as we made various decisions. (Katongole 2022a, 175)

He connects the labor of institution-building in Africa with a wider issue of politics, naming the challenge in African contexts of "the social and political institutions within which decolonized Africans have lived and tried to survive" (Katongole 2011, 65). As mentioned in chapter 8, Katongole is aware of the "hardening effect" of institutionalizing. How can "tenderness" be preserved in an institutional setting? This is a spiritual question. Even though no organization is perfect and every institution has its flaws, we can point to examples of organizations that are good examples of institutionalizing integral human development.

Three Examples

As the example of BRAC has shown, an organization can be an inspiring and credible implementer of integral human development without making use of the concept or without being connected to the background tradition of the term. In this section, I briefly sketch three examples of organizations that can be considered IHD-implementing organizations: Jesuit Refugee Service (or JRS), Partners in Health, and Mary's Meals.

Jesuit Refugee Service

The *Jesuit Refugee Service* was founded in 1980, under the leadership of Father Pedro Arrupe. On November 14, 1980, Arrupe wrote a short letter about the challenge of refugees to all local superiors of the Jesuits. He talks about this personal shock witnessing the plight of thousands of boat refugees at Christmas 1979. He appealed to his fellow Jesuits to respond to this human tragedy and was encouraged by the response. He consulted with experts about the crisis and moved to a structural response by establishing the JRS. He followed a dignity-centered approach and the criteria of special attention to those most in need, the idea of the common good, and the principle of subsidiarity in identifying the niche that the Jesuits could fill.

The Jesuit Refugee Service works with an explicit commitment to accompaniment. The charter of the JRS states in section 9: the "Jesuit Refugee Service, therefore, is an international Catholic organisation whose mission is to accompany, serve and defend the rights of refugees and forcibly displaced people." Recognizing that a refugee is "so much more" than a refugee, the portfolio of JRS engagement includes emergency aid, health services, psychosocial support, pastoral services, education, income-generating activities, and peace-building efforts.

These activities are based on an accompaniment model. Accompaniment, in this context, includes active listening and spending time in being present to others. This model is linked to Ignatian spirituality, the roots of the Jesuit charism: "The first command for a JRS worker going to the field is: 'accompany and listen, listen, listen to the refugees.' The Jesuit spirituality is one of discernment that starts with listening" (Lopez 2013, 358). The Jesuit Refugee Service is an expression of the Jesuits' commitment to social justice (Cosacchi 2019, 663–65) and an example of a globally operating Jesuit agency (Hollenbach 2016, 180). The careful creation of an inner space for listening and "discernment of spirits" is a genuine part of the Jesuit charism.

Fr. Joe Hampson SJ and coauthors point out, "In accompaniment work, we move beyond a mere delivery of services through offering companionship, active listening and solidarity, focusing on individuals' personal needs and concerns." (Hampson et al. 2014). In this sense, a commitment to IHD is a commitment to a style of being with persons that cannot be exhausted, using a language of efficiency or efficacy. IHD could, here, mean walking the extra mile beyond the measurable, beyond the basic:

> To listen is to offer the refugee space and time to tell his or her story. Sometimes in the hurly-burly of flight and of coming to a refugee camp or of living in a hostile urban environment, it is the first opportunity of a human encounter where one person devotes their attention and empathy to the refugee. Ensuring that basic needs are met can be an overwhelming responsibility, and the chance to sit and listen to "clients" is simply not there. (Hampson 2010, 5)[1]

A former co-worker of the Jesuit Refugee Service reflects on his experience working with refugees in Ethiopia:

> *Accompaniment is how we build interpersonal relationships with people from all classes and from all walks of life particularly with the disadvantaged population. This notion dissolves the barriers created due to one's vulnerability. We often fail to recognize that vulnerable populations need "us" much more than material goods.*

I've reiterated Jesus's words throughout this book: "a person does not live on bread alone." Especially in situations of displacement, the challenge of finding a sense of belonging becomes existential. The Jesuit Refugee Service, through its threefold mission of accompaniment, service, and advocacy, seeks to encounter "the whole person." Organizational growth and professionalization have

---

[1] It is understood that not all work with refugees can follow a microapproach of personal listening; but IHD would encourage a sense of "these are persons," a sense of the fact that we are talking about real people with real stories (Hampson 2010, 5).

expanded the scope of JRS beyond refugees. Now, the Jesuit Refugee Service faces similar questions about faithfulness to roots and mission as BRAC. There is a debate about the "Jesuit" character of the Jesuit Refugee Service and the commitment to its original charism given its expansion (O'Neill 2022). Institutionalizing integral human development is, indeed, an ongoing challenge.

Partners in Health

Another organization based on a model of accompaniment is *Partners in Health*. In 1983, Paul Farmer and Ophelia Dahl started a community clinic in Cange, a village in rural Haiti, to provide health care to the local population. They wanted to "provide services to the destitute for free, and those services should meet the real needs of the place and of individual patients. So the first step was to find out exactly what the needs were" (Kidder 2003, 82). Listening became the first step, and it continued as the method all along. Four years later, the organization "Partners in Health" was launched.

Community health workers were trained to provide long-term care. Tracy Kidder reconstructs the origins of the organization as well as some of Paul Farmer's deepest beliefs, including his conviction that there is a connection between poverty and disease and that there cannot be real change without cost to oneself, without sacrifices (Kidder 2003). The commitment to the poorest of the poor was part of the organization's profile from the beginning. In an interview, Paul Farmer recounts how it began before he was a medical student: "I didn't have a well-thought-out plan—I was 23. We were idiots, right? But some understandings either came with us or came out of that year about how to do global health work. One thing we got right; we listened to people. We did surveys, we interviewed them. You learn a lot."[2] From the beginning, Partners in Health followed a community-based approach that has been a characteristic feature of the NGO, including in its treatment of HIV (Farmer 2001). Partnering with local institutions is recognized as necessary and beneficial in order to offer the kind of integrated approach the organization pursues (Kerry et al. 2014). In the treatment of tuberculosis in rural Haiti, for example, prevention and care activities are integrated, and supervised community-based care is offered to the patients. "Village health workers also serve as a vital link between village and clinic, and help attend to the pressing social problems that the majority of our patients face" (Walton et al. 2004, 152). Care has to be seen as a public good.

---

[2] Partners in Health, "Not Just One Person's Quest: An Oral History of Partners in Health," *Partners in Health* online, June 21, 2019.

The approach of Partners in Health is "integrated" in the sense that health care is seen in the wider context of accompaniment. Home visits are preferred to long transfers to a clinic. A community health worker gives support to a patient "not just giving him his pills but asking how he is feeling, finding out if he needs help with anything from child care to fees for education" (Farmer 2006, 7). The person and the context she lives in are taken into account, and empathy and deep listening emerge as institutionalized practices that shape the organization through its relational model of care and its commitment to personalized health care. Accompaniment is pursued as a humble and long-term mode of "assistance," "supporting the poor on the road toward well-being, prosperity, peace, and—indeed—aid independence. It begins with listening to and learning from one's intended beneficiaries, and working alongside them until they deem a task completed" (Kerry et al. 2014, 487). Listening comes with the humility to learn.

Steve Reifenberg and Elizabeth Hlabse, in a study on the work of Partners in Health (CES [Compañeros en Salud]) in Mexico, describe the approach of a community health worker, Gladys, to home visits. "Gladys brings hope. She breaks through the isolation that characterizes illness for many in this rural town.... Gladys spends much of her visits listening to her patients talk about their needs, concerns, daily troubles, and joys" (Reifenberg and Hlabse 2020, 139–40). In other words, she gains personal knowledge, knowledge by acquaintance, and second-person knowledge about the patient and through the interactions with the patient. This approach also challenges the medical profession: Reifenberg and Hlabse quote Hugo Flores, then-director of CES:

> We teach doctors to consider themselves in the situation of the patient, and help them to realize that blaming a patient for his or her lack of understanding is not an option. We teach our doctors that there are different ways people make sense of our world, our bodies, and the processes of disease, as well as the concept of healing.... We teach our doctors that in the Sierra we are the outsiders, and need to learn the language of our patients. (Reifenberg and Hlabse 2020, 142)

This patient-centered and community-based approach calls for reverse privileging and the letting go of privileges that come with societal position and education. This is also translated into structural design.

An accompaniment approach is seen and presented as an antidote to the standardization dynamics of institutions. As Paul Farmer observed,

> When patients began falling ill with drug-resistant strains of tuberculosis, WHO guidelines suggested they be treated with the same first-line drugs as non-resistant patients. Yet treating patients with the very drugs

to which their disease had developed resistance not only failed to help them; it enabled the worse strains to spread unchecked among patients' families and co-workers. This is the double-edged sword of routiniza-tion: Rationalized treatment protocols first helped health providers increase the effectiveness and reach of treatment but later prevented them from taking necessary steps to curb the spread of drug-resistant strains. Increases in bureaucratic efficiency can come at the price of decreased human flexibility. In other words, as institutions are rational-ized, and as platforms of accountability are strengthened, the potential for accompaniment can be threatened. (Farmer 2011)

Mary's Meals

A third example of how to institutionalize the idea of integral human develop-ment can be found in the Scottish NGO *Mary's Meals*, launched in 2003 by Magnus MacFarlane-Barrow. He developed an initiative of providing school meals, following an approach that tries to see the whole person and each person. The initiative started in Malawi with a simple vision: "for every child to receive a daily meal in their place of education" (MacFarlane-Barrow 2015, 142).[3] The faith-based organization reaches about two million children a day and connects material/biological needs with educational needs, working with local communi-ties and farmers.[4] Its impact story shows that there is indeed an ambition to reach "each child" and to serve a child in both material and nonmaterial dimensions.

---

[3] This is the founding story, as told by Magnus MacFarlane-Barrow: He was still working with another NGO that he had founded (Scottish Relief International) to respond to the sufferings of people in Bosnia; he visited Malawi and had a decisive encounter: "Father Gamba, a young friendly priest, then asked me if I would like to accompany him to the home of one of his parishioners, who was near death. Thus it was I came to meet that family whose picture remains on the wall above my desk: Emma surrounded by her six children, including fourteen-year-old Edward, who, when I asked him about his hopes in life, gave me an answer I will never forget. 'I would like to have enough food to eat and I would like to be able to go to school one day' had been his stark, shocking reply to my question" (MacFarlane-Barrow 2015, 137). Edward's statement reminded Magnus of a previous conversation with his friend Tony Smith who had found himself watching American Senator George McGovern's speech "in which he stated, with some passion, that if America decided to fund the provision of one daily meal in a place of education for every child in the world's poorest countries it would act like a 'Marshall Plan' that would lift the developing world out of poverty.... Tony said when he heard this speech he was inspired with the thought that if someone took the concept, gave it to Mary, the mother of Jesus, and called it Mary's Meals, then it would actually happen" (MacFarlane-Barrow 2015, 138).
[4] S. Milbank, "Mary's Meals Grows to Feed 1.8 Million Children." *The Tablet*, March 29, 2021.

They operate under the assumption that the initiative has to be owned by the local community. Mary's Meals works closely with local stakeholders. Its feeding programs are owned and run by community volunteers in the countries where the organization provides food. School-feeding committees—made up of parents, teachers, and volunteers—are crucial and one of the first things to be established in any new area receiving Mary's Meals. There are thousands of volunteers in Malawi who take turns preparing, cooking, and serving the daily meal in each school. There is a monitoring system in place with regular school visits. Additionally, there is a training component to the program that trains community volunteers. Wherever possible, Mary's Meals serves locally produced food. This supports the local community and its farmers as well as the wider economy.

Mary's Meals pursues a theory of change that connects the idea of involving donors and local communities in local education with the outcome of children gaining an education that would provide an escape route from poverty. They seek to achieve this outcome by making the classroom more inclusive, by strengthening community cohesion through children from different backgrounds eating together, by increasing community resilience through a social safety net provided by school feeding programs.[5]

The impact of Mary's Meals can be assessed by distinguishing short-term and long-term changes.[6] Short-term changes include reduced hunger; increased school enrollment; improved attendance, concentration, and learning; increased progression between grades; and improved health and well-being. Long-term changes include the encouragement of community support for education, support for smallholder farmers, and increasing government recognition of school feeding. Even though we could mention some limits, including a focus on recognized and institutionalized places of education and the intentional effort to align with the respective governments, the organization serves as a good example of integral human development in practice.

The three examples—and the list of candidates is long—illustrate that, while integral human development may be an idealistic concept, it is possible, and convincingly so, to build organizations based on a commitment to IHD. They have translated integral human development into institutional practices. Accompaniment, as mentioned above, has emerged as a key driver of an integral human development approach.

---

[5] Livingston James Group, "The Mary's Meals Theory of Change," January 17, 2020.

[6] Cf. some impact reports that can be found in Scottish Government International Development Programme End-Year Report, "Mary's Meals' Pre-school and Primary School Feeding Programme," 2021; Mary's Meals, "Mary's Meals 2021 Annual Impact Report" (Argyle, Scotland, 2022).

A Final Note on Accompaniment

Dean A. Shepherd, Vinit Parida, and Joakim Wincent have shown that four inter-related practices organize the exploitation of vulnerable individuals, including deceptive recruiting, entrapping through isolation, extinguishing alternatives by building barriers, and converting the exploited into exploiters (Shepherd et al. 2022). Counterpractices to these could be excellent candidates for dignity-sensitive institutions: show integrity in listening, bring people into relationality and build communities, stretch the imagination by opening a sense of possibilities, and convert the wounded into healers.

The practice of accompaniment expresses these practices. Accompaniment is a way of walking with someone. This is costly. In her award-winning novel *Go Went Gone*, briefly mentioned above, Berlin author Jenny Erpenbeck presents a story of accompaniment and integration. She describes the encounter of a retired university professor (Richard) with migrants. He must overcome ignorance and indifference and make an effort to build his life so that he has real points of contact with migrants. Ignorance, indifference, and safe lives are obstacles on the road to proper accompaniment.

The concern with accompaniment emerged in Latin American liberation theology as an expression of the attempt to reduce the prevailing elitism in academic approaches to social issues and to take the agency of poor people more seriously (Goizeuta 1995). Accompaniment is an integrated approach that, para-doxically, does not intend to integrate. Mireille Rosello (2016) has argued, in conversation with Rachid Boudjedra's 1975 novel *Topographie idéale*, that "integration" is a term that, more often than not, involves invisible violence, forcing migrants to reorient themselves. On the other hand, accompaniment opens new possibilities for mutuality, making accompaniment a process of mutual disorienting. There is a consoling and a disruptive moment of coming together in accompaniment. Accompaniment overcomes what Jill Stauffer (2015) has termed "ethical loneliness," a morally problematic lack of accompaniment that includes the experience of not being heard and not being seen. Kim Marie Lamberty (2012) has described accompaniment as a spirituality, in fact as the personal way to express solidarity.

Appropriate accompaniment is resource intensive and requires appropriate infrastructure. Georg Sporschill, for example, a Jesuit priest from the most western region of Austria, has been living and working in Eastern Europe since 1991. He has set up social projects for thousands of children from the streets and sewers of the Romanian capital and, since 2004, has dedicated himself to helping orphans and neglected children in Moldova. A few years ago, he returned to Romania to work with Roma families. He lives the accompaniment model, walking with the street children and the Roma families.

In the beginning, there was a house that developed its own gravitational pull. The house, symbolically speaking, at first provided simply a roof over the heads of those who needed one. Soon, it housed a farm, and then it became home to a craft bakery. In June 1992, the house was extended, and a farm was purchased: "We want our farm to be like a school teaching its pupils to express their feelings" (Sporschill 2006, 21). The infrastructure allowed for living together and for entrusting responsibilities to the children and the families. Accompaniment requires an infrastructure and a significant investment of time and personal energy. It cannot be reduced to a strategy, for doing so bears an immanent risk of instrumentalizing relationship-building. Again, the central virtue that emerges is the art of listening.

Accompaniment can provide mutual sources of recognition and support, creating relationships that stretch the imagination and offering possibilities for contributions and agency as ways to express the respect of human dignity in response to human needs. There are, however, clear ethical issues around accompaniment, including the question of "clear lines between *accompagné* and *accompagnant*," the question of autonomy, and the question of responsibility (Simondi and Perrenoud 2011). The first point refers to the illusion of clear-cut boundaries and categories, allowing for a sense of reciprocity. The second refers to the challenge of negotiating consideration of the other and the relationship as well as the respect for autonomy. The third point expresses the concern with responsibility levels that increase with increased trust and expectation levels. A special challenge for the concept of accompaniment is the status of reciprocity, avoiding the traps of infantilization, instrumentalization, and humiliation, discussed in the first part of this book.

One important aspect of accompaniment is its structural relevance. Accompaniment creates insights into structural needs and systemic gaps and is, in this sense, a source of policy-relevant knowledge. When you work with a patient closely, you develop the kind of "microtheory" presented in chapter 4. You will gain thick descriptions. Walking with a person or community, listening to a person or a community, may, however, take you into the wilderness of the unplanned and the unpredictable. Listening is the willingness to be taken to a place where you would not choose to go yourself. A young development worker from Bangladesh, for example, reflected on her experience about the realities of the Bangladeshi farmers with whom she worked:

Nearly all the farmers wanted to be able to maintain their current lifestyle because it was what brought them joy—this feeling of belonging through practicing local traditions around rice cultivation was what brought them a sense of belonging and happiness. Climate change was actively changing that but it brought forward a bigger problem of what to do with people who do not want to be included in the swell of "development" and growth-oriented social mobility. There are people who are content in their ways of lives and who are happy because they have a sense of place and pride in what they do—how do we accompany them and aid in their growth when their desires are so contrasting to our way of thinking regarding economic growth and mobility?

These are aspects that require discernment and call for a spiritual dimension. There may be a moment of "sacred shyness" in accompaniment. Pope Francis writes about "the 'art of accompaniment' which teaches us to remove our sandals before the sacred ground of the other (cf. Ex 3:5). The pace of this accompaniment must be steady and reassuring, reflecting our closeness and our compassionate gaze which also heals, liberates and encourages growth in the Christian life" (*Evangelii Gaudium* 169). This points us once again "beyond ethics," beyond development ethics, in the direction of the spiritual.

Epilogue

Beyond Development Ethics

In her fascinating book *On Looking*, Alexandra Horowitz describes the experience of doing the same walk around the block in New York City with different companions, each teaching her different ways of seeing and looking (Horowitz 2013). A geologist offers insights into the geological landscape of the city and the different rocks that can be found on the way. A sound designer helps her identify noises and sounds. A friend can tell stories about the typefaces. A biologist opens her eyes to the life of bugs in the city. A physician diagnoses people's illnesses by observing their gait in the street. Horowitz is accompanied by a blind person and experiences the walk in yet another way entirely. Horowitz is exposed to different ways of seeing the city, to different ways of inhabiting the experiential space, to different lenses to approach city life.

I suggest that integral human development is best appreciated as a lens, as a way of seeing. Or maybe, even more, as a form of life. One of the deep insights into the concept of human dignity comes from Swiss philosopher Peter Bieri, in *Human Dignity: A Way of Living* (2017). Bieri claims that our understanding of human dignity enables and constitutes a particular form of life, a particular way of experiencing the world. The "work" that the concept of human dignity can do affects our judgments and our perceptions. "Doing dignity" lays the foundation of a form of life. The same can be said about the dignity-centered approach of integral human development. The concept of human dignity changes our way of being in the world because it exercises an influence on the way we see and experience things. J. M. Coetzee, in his disturbing novel *Waiting for the Barbarians*, has the protagonist defend four prisoners who are about to be killed with a sledge hammer. "Not with that!" I shout.... You would not use a hammer on a beast.... Look at these men.... Men!"—and also "Look! We are the great miracle of creation!" (Coetzee 1981, 106). The idea of dignity shapes our perceptions and judgments; it also shapes our imagination, our sense of what is possible.

The background tradition of integral human development, the Christian Social Tradition, has contributed to a new way of seeing the person. In the year

191

368, there was a severe draught in Cappadocia, leading to a dramatic famine. It seems that the moral paradigm at the time was indifference, a sense of "them starving" and "us not being concerned." Basil of Caesarea, drawing from the Christian tradition, preached a sermon, "In time of famine and drought," and organized famine relief activities. He was motivated by a new way of seeing society as a community and the human person as a being with dignity (Holman 2001, 64–98). Peter Brown described this new way of seeing the community through a common good lens and the person through a dignity lens as "a revolution of social imagination," the values of dignity and solidarity translated into practices and institutions along with a new language to talk about community and justice (Brown 2002, 1). This revolution of the imagination was not so much based on insights into principles, let alone on abstract arguments or a process of reasoning. Rather, the revolution was based on a new way of seeing the world due to an encounter with the gospel.

Integral human development is a way of seeing the world and the person through a lens of dignity and the common good, the latter including nonhuman life and ecological relationships. The revolution of the social imagination described by Peter Brown was motivated by a simple step—the step from indifference to caring. We are, once again, faced with this challenge of indifference. The term "indifference" has become a cornerstone of Pope Francis's pontificate. His first sermon outside of Rome, in Lampedusa, on July 8, 2013, was dedicated to indifference vis-à-vis migrants. In his homily, Pope Francis talked about the globalization of indifference: "In this globalized world, we have fallen into globalized indifference. We have become used to the suffering of others: it doesn't affect me; it doesn't concern me; it's none of my business!" Pope Francis mentioned "indifference" several times in his encyclical *Laudato Si'* (14, 25, 52, 92, 115, 232), condemning a "nonchalant resignation" (14), and in his encyclical *Fratelli Tutti* (30, 57, 72, 73, 113, 199, 209, 224), talking about cool, comfortable, nervous, cruel, selfish indifference. In the concluding prayer of *Fratelli Tutti* Pope Francis even uses the phrase "the sin of indifference."

On October 16, 2017, on the occasion of the celebration of World Food Day, Pope Francis paid a visit to the Food and Agriculture Organization of the United Nations (FAO) Headquarters in Rome. "Death by starvation or the abandonment of one's own land is everyday news, which risks being met with indifference," he said to the major UN organization dedicated to ending hunger and providing food security globally. "We cannot resign ourselves to saying: 'someone else will take care of it,'" the pope continued. During his visit to the FAO, Pope Francis donated a marble sculpture that depicts the tragic death of Alan Kurdi (also known as Aylan), a three-year-old Syrian boy whose body washed up on the shore of Turkey in September 2015, after a small boat holding a dozen refugees had capsized. Next to Aylan, a childlike angel weeps over the boy's lifeless body. Pope Francis wanted the FAO experts to be aware of human realities. Integral Human Development is not compatible with indifference, for it is based on and expressed by structures of robust concern.

One of the big questions in ethics is how to motivate moral action, how to overcome indifference. The field of ethics, specifically of development ethics, is rich and important. The idea of integral human development can inspire a development ethics approach, as Lori Keleher has shown (Keleher 2017). Development ethics will deal with questions such as the following: What is a good life? What is a good society? What is a good institution? What is a good person? What is a good act? What do people think about ethics and how do they live? What does "good ethics" look like? All of these questions are relevant within the discourse context of international development. This constitutes specific tasks for development ethics.[1] Development as a planned endeavor must follow a particular direction and will ultimately have to ask the "good life" question (Gasper 2012, 120). Conceptions of the desirable and commitments to particular ways of understanding life quality will shape development efforts with their bottom line of "intending to improve people's lives." These questions will have to be asked, however, within societal and institutional frameworks that discuss issues such as distributive justice or good governance. On a national and societal level, development will move beyond the individual's "good life" questions and to broader and normative "ought-to" questions that impact the macrolevels of nations and the planet (Dower 2007; 2008). These normative questions need to have a foundation in people's values and their moral imagination. There cannot be proper institutions without proper agents, proper frameworks, and proper goals. In Adorno's timeless words, "Wrong life cannot be lived rightly" (Adorno 2005, 39).

Ethics can do a lot for us. It can offer a sense of general principles, fundamental imperatives, lists of virtues, a culture of moral argumentation, recommendations for positions, and disciplined reflection on moral issues. Ethics is particularly strong in the realm of human agency, where questions of options, choices, decisions, and the respective reasons and arguments are at the center of attention. Ethics, however, reaches limits when we are confronted

---

[1] David Crocker (2014), for instance, has suggested five different main tasks and foci: (1) inequality of power, (2) agency and empowerment, (3) democracy and development, (4) corruption, and (5) transitional justice. There may be new challenges due to climate change, which demand identifying climate change-related risks, negotiations of the global commons, new concepts of environment-sensitive well-being, and the dilemmas of a low-carbon future (St. Clair 2014).

with those dimensions of human life that cannot be managed, that transcend human control and human agency. This dimension "beyond human agency" is emphasized in the encyclical *Laudato Si'*.[2] *Laudato Si'* notes that "authentic development includes efforts to bring about an integral improvement in the quality of human life" (*Laudato Si'* 147). Categories like "improvement" and "quality of life" seem ethical in nature, and there are undeniable building blocks of an ethics of Integral Human Development in the encyclical. But a close reading of the text clearly shows that Integral Human Development is a theological and not an ethical concept. We find the strong warning that the absence of a sense of mystery is destructive: "When nature is viewed solely as a source of profit and gain, this has serious consequences for society" (*Laudato Si'* 82). The reference to "mystery" is not simply a reference to a category—it is the reference to an attitude toward life as a whole. And this attitude will move us "beyond development ethics."

The encyclical is consistently offering religious language and religious categories. In the 1930s, the German theologian Dietrich Bonhoeffer pursued a project of translating religious terms into nonreligious language; the encyclical seems to do the opposite. We see the project of translating nonreligious terms in religious language: "nature" becomes "creation" (*Laudato Si'* 76), "land" becomes "a gift from God" (*Laudato Si'* 146), "animals" become "creatures reflecting something of God" (*Laudato Si'* 221), human life becomes a journey "towards the sabbath of eternity" (*Laudato Si'* 243). This religious hermeneutics of the world is based on and gives us a sacramental view of the world, where "there is a mystical meaning to be found in a leaf, in a mountain trail, in a dewdrop, in a poor person's face" (*Laudato Si'* 233). Human life is seen as a gift (*Laudato Si'* 5), the roots of the environmental crisis are recognized as "ethical and spiritual" (*Laudato Si'* 9), and destructive and exploitative human behaviors are categorized as "sin" (*Laudato Si'* 66). The text introduces the language of "reconciliation" (*Laudato Si'* 66, 218), "conversion" (*Laudato Si'* 5, 216–21), and "repentance" (*Laudato Si'* 218). This is a language that expresses a perspective that is not prepared to leave the first word and the last word to this world.[3]

---

[2] The following paragraphs are based on Sedmak (2022).

[3] In fact, the encyclical points out, creation is harmed, according to an address by Pope Benedict XVI, "when we ourselves have the final word" (*Laudato Si'* 6). And here, one of the fundamental theological statements comes in: "We are not God" (*Laudato Si'* 67). Accepting that we are not God and accepting that the earth is not God is a theological statement that leads to the demythologizing of nature (*Laudato Si'* 78) and the resistance to a divinization of the earth (*Laudato Si'* 90). This is part of the idea that "the ultimate purpose of other creatures is not to be found in us" (*Laudato Si'* 83). We are not the source of the final word. The world is not able to offer a final word. Whatever we encounter is provisional, nonlasting.

Ultimately, the encyclical presents us with a vision of "development as depth." Development, as presented in *Laudato Si'*, is not primarily about progress and living standards; it is not even about maximizing freedoms and quality of life. In one passage, Pope Francis introduces the term "depth in life" (*Laudato Si'* 113), criticizing the superficiality created by the accumulation of constant novelties. This thought presents an alternative to a certain understanding of progress. In fact, the encyclical calls for a change of direction. Integral human development requires deep change (*Laudato Si'* 60). This change can be linked to a particular understanding of growth (moral growth, personal growth [*Laudato Si'* 127]). Such growth is anchored in deep commitments that may even motivate sacrifices. The text presents us with a vision of Integral Human Development that is explicit about the cost of "integrating," of accepting vulnerable beings, "however troublesome or inconvenient" (*Laudato Si'* 120). Here, we move into an area that transcends the language of "quality of life." We move into the sphere where a person is willing to see her quality of life reduced for the higher good of a commitment.

People are willing to make sacrifices on behalf of people they deeply care about and causes they consider important. These commitments add depth to life. Depth of life is the existential situation of a person who deeply cares about someone or something—this robust concern structures life and gives it weight and profoundness. When we read that "social love is the key to authentic development" (*Laudato Si'* 231), we can see the movement from individual freedoms to social commitments, from individual well-being to the common good, from quality of life to depth of life. It has been argued that there is a third dimension to human life, next to "the happy life" and "the good life," namely, "the meaningful life." Meaning, while connected to happiness and morality, is a distinctive dimension.[4]

The dimensions of meaning of life and depth of life move us "beyond ethics." There is a sense of the "mystery of the person" that cannot easily be translated into development ethics. The dignity of the human person is not defined by "functioning well" or by "visible achievements." In the language of *Laudato Si'*,

---

[4] Susan Wolf has offered the following language and the following examples to make this point: "The most obvious examples of what I have in mind occur when we act out of love for individuals about whom we deeply and especially care. When I visit my brother in the hospital, or help my friend move.... I act neither for egoistic reasons nor for moral ones. I do not believe that it is better for me that I spend a depressing hour in a drab, cramped room, seeing my brother irritable and in pain, that I risk back injury trying to get my friend's sofa safely down two flights of stairs.... Neither do I believe myself duty-bound to perform these acts, or fool myself into thinking that by doing them I do what will be best for the world. I act neither out of self-interest nor out of duty or any other sort of impersonal or impartial reason. Rather, I act out of love. (Wolf 2010, 4).

"We forget that the inalienable worth of a human being transcends his or her degree of development" (*Laudato Si'* 136).

French philosopher Simone Weil was asked by the Free French Resistance movement to write a text about rebuilding France (and Europe) after the war. In response to this request, Simone Weil chose to reflect not so much on structures and institutions but on the needs of the soul. The text, posthumously published under the title *L'Enracinement* (*The Need for Roots*), talks about the need to address the moral and spiritual *malaise* of the time, the need to respond to the dissolution of community by recognizing duties toward humanity. Simone Weil describes the challenge of uprootedness and the need to look beyond tangible structures: "Everyone knows that there are forms of cruelty which can injure a man's life without injuring his body. They are such as deprive him of a certain form of food necessary to the life of the soul" (Weil 1952, 6). Weil connected the challenge explicitly with the imagination, lamenting the plight of miners:

> Not only does nobody consider the moral well-being of the workmen, which would demand too great an effort of the imagination; but nobody even considers the possibility of not injuring them in the flesh. Otherwise one might perhaps have found something else for the mines than that appalling automatic drill worked by compressed air, which sends an uninterrupted series of shocks for eight hours through the body of the man manipulating it. (Weil 1952, 53)

Integral human development can be seen as an invitation to cultivate the imagination of what it means to be human. Integral human development is a lens through which to look at the world and see the human person. And this way of "seeing" becomes a form of life, expressed in embodied practices, in dignity practices. Behind these practices, we can find the big questions, the first question and the last question. "What is the purpose of our life in this world? Why are we here?" (*Laudato Si'* 160). And this question, articulated in the same passage of *Laudato Si'*, cannot be separated from the simple question "What kind of world do we want to leave to those who come after us, to children who are now growing up?"

BIBLIOGRAPHY

Abazi, Erida, and Sokol Dervishi. 2014. "Colour and Participative Process in Urban Requalification of Tirana." In *Proceedings of the 2nd ICAUD International Conference in Architecture and Urban Design*. Tirana, Albania: Epoka University.

Abdul Azeez, E. P., and P. Subramania Siva. 2019. "Graduation from Poverty and Deprivation: Reflections from an Intervention in the Graduation Model." *Social Indicators Research* 144 (3): 1135–50.

Abell, Peter, and Robin Jenkins. 1971. "Why Do Men Rebel? A Discussion of Ted Gurr's *Why Men Rebel*." *Race Class* 13:84–92.

Acemoglu, Daron, and James A. Robinson. 2012. *Why Nations Fail: The Origins of Power, Prosperity, and Poverty*. New York: Crown Business.

Adichie, Chimamanda Ngozi. 2009. "The Danger of a Single Story." *TED*. https://www.ted.com/talks/chimamanda_ngozi_adichie_the_danger_of_a_single_story.

Adkins, Arthur W. H., 1966. "Aristotle and the Best Kind of Tragedy." *Classical Quarterly* 16 (1): 78–102.

Adorno, Theodor W. 2005. *Minima Moralia: Reflections on a Damaged Life*. London: Verso.

Ahmed, Salehuddin, and Micaela French. 2006. "Scaling Up: The BRAC Experience." *BRAC University Journal* 3 (2): 35–40.

Ahmed, Zahir U., et al. 2015. "The BRAC Independence Movement: Accountability to Whom?" http://dx.doi.org/10.2139/ssrn.2680208.

———. 2022. "From Minnow to Mighty: A Hegemonic Analysis of Social Accountability in BRAC—The World's Largest Development NGO." *Critical Perspectives of Accounting*. https://doi.org/10.1016/j.cpa.2022.102503.

Aiken, S. Robert, and Colin H. Leigh. 2011. "In the Way of Development: Indigenous Land-Rights Issues in Malaysia." *Geographical Review* 101 (4): 471–96.

Akerlof, George A., and Rachel E. Kranton. 2000. "Economics and Identity." *Quarterly Journal of Economics* 115 (3): 715–53.

———. 2010. "Identity Economics." *Economists' Voice* 7 (2). https://doi.org/10.2202/1553-3832.1762.

Akula, Vikram. 2011. *A Fistful of Rice: My Unexpected Quest to End Poverty through Profitability*. Boston: Harvard Business Review Press.

Albahari, Maurizio. 2015. *Crimes of Peace: Mediterranean Migrations at the World's Deadliest Border*. Philadelphia: University of Pennsylvania Press.

_____. 2016. "After the Shipwreck: Mourning and Citizenship in the Mediterranean." *Social Research* 83 (2): 275–94.

Alexander, Peter. 2010. "Rebellion of the Poor: South Africa's Service Delivery Protests—A Preliminary Analysis." *Review of African Political Economy* 37 (123): 25–40.

Amann, Klaus. 1994. "Menschen, Mäuse und Fliegen: Eine wissenschaftssoziologische Analyse der Transformation von Organismen in epistemische Objekte." *Zeitschrift für Soziologie* 23 (1): 22–40.

Aminu-Kano, Muhtari, and Atallah FitzGibbon. 2014. *An Islamic Perspective on Human Development*. Birmingham: Islamic Relief Worldwide.

Anaehobi, Vitalis. 2021. "Lebret and the Birth of Development Ethics within Catholic Social Teaching." *Journal of Global Ethics* 17 (2): 127–45.

Anderson, Cameron, et al. 2020. "People with Disagreeable Personalities (Selfish, Combative, and Manipulative) Do Not Have an Advantage in Pursuing Power at Work." *Proceedings of the National Academy of Sciences* 117 (37): 22780–86.

Anderson, Elizabeth. 2012. "Epistemic Justice as a Virtue of Social Institutions." *Social Epistemology* 26 (2): 163–73.

Anderson, Hannah L. 2011. "That Settles It: The Debate and Consequences of the Homestead Act of 1862." *History Teacher* 45 (1): 117–37.

Annett, Anthony. 2016. "Human Flourishing, the Common Good, and Catholic Social Teaching." In *World Happiness Report 2016 Volume II*, ed. J. Sachs et al., 38–65. New York: Sustainable Development Solutions Network.

An'xian, Luo. 2014. "Human Dignity in Traditional Chinese Confucianism." In *The Cambridge Handbook of Human Dignity*, ed. M. Duwell et al., 177–81. Cambridge: Cambridge University Press.

Appleby, R. Scott. 1997. *Spokesmen for the Despised: Fundamentalist Leaders of the Middle East*. Chicago: University of Chicago Press.

_____. 2000. *The Ambivalence of the Sacred*. Chicago: University of Chicago Press.

Arbinger Institute. 2010. *Leadership and Self-Deception*. San Francisco: Berrett-Koehler.

Arendt, Hannah. 1998. *The Human Condition*. Chicago: University of Chicago Press.

Arluke, Arnold, and Jack Levin. 1984. "Another Stereotype: Old Age as a Second Childhood." *Aging* 346:7–11.

Arunotai, Narumon. 2017. 'Hopeless at Sea, Landless on Shore': Contextualising the Sea Nomads' Dilemma in Thailand. AAS Working Papers in Social Anthropology 31. Vienna: Austrian Academy of Sciences.

Ashraf, Hasan. 2017. "Beyond Building Safety: An Ethnographic Account of Health and Well-Being on the Bangladesh Garment Shop Floor." In *Unmaking the Global*

Sweatshop: Health and Safety of the World's Garment Workers, ed. R. Prentice and G. de Neve, 250–73. Philadelphia: University of Pennsylvania Press.

Astroulakis, Nikos. 2013. "Ethics and International Development: The Development Paradigm." *Journal of Economics and Business* 16 (1): 99–117.

Attané, Isabelle. 2009. "The Determinants of Discrimination against Daughters in China: Evidence from a Provincial-Level Analysis." *Population Studies* 63 (1): 87–102.

———. 2013. *The Demografic Masculinization of China: Hoping for a Son.* Wiesbaden: Springer.

Attané, Isabelle, Zhang Qunlin, Li Shuzhuo, Yang Xueyan, and C. Guilmoto. 2013. "Bachelorhood and Sexuality in a Context of Female Shortage: Evidence from a Survey in Rural Anhui, China." *China Quarterly* 215:703–26.

Audi, Robert. 2016. *Means, Ends, and Persons: The Meaning and Psychological Dimensions of Kant's Humanity Formula.* Oxford: Oxford University Press.

Autesserre, Séverine. 2014. *Peaceland: Conflict Resolution and the Everyday Politics of International Intervention.* New York: Cambridge University Press.

Avramidis, Christos, and Alexandros Minotakis. 2017. "Infantilizing the Refugees as a Means of Political Domination." *Belgrade Journal of Media and Communications* 6:51–66.

Azétsop, Jacquineau. 2019. *Integral Human Development. Challenges to Sustainability & Democracy.* Eugene, OR: Pickwick.

Badie, Bertrand. 2014. *Le temps des humiliés. Pathologie des relations internationals.* Paris: Odile Jacob.

Bailey, James. 2010. *Rethinking Poverty: Income, Assets, and the Catholic Social Justice Tradition.* Notre Dame, IN: University of Notre Dame Press.

Baillie, Lesley. 2009. "Patient Dignity in an Acute Hospital Setting: A Case Study." *International Journal of Nursing Studies* 46 (1): 23–37.

Baker, Pauline H., and Joyce E Leader. 2020. *From Hope to Horror: Diplomacy and the Making of the Rwanda Genocide.* Lincoln: University of Nebraska Press.

Bandura, Albert. 1997. *Self-efficacy: The Exercise of Control.* New York: W. H. Freeman.

Banerjee, A., and E. Duflo. 2011. *Poor Economics: A Radical Rethinking of the Way to Fight Global Poverty.* New York: Public Affairs.

Bangura, Zainab, Katherine Sierra, et al. 2019. *Committing to Change, Protecting People: Toward a More Accountable Oxfam.* Independent Commission on Sexual Misconduct, Accountability, & Culture Change.

Barder, Owen. 2009. What Is Poverty Reduction? CGD Working Paper 170. Washington, DC: Center for Global Development.

Barnhart, Joslyn. 2021. *The Consequences of Humiliation: Anger and Status in World Politics.* Ithaca, NY: Cornell University Press.

Bastagli, Francesca, et al. 2016. "Cash Transfers: What Does the Evidence Say? A Rigorous Review of Programme Impact and of the Role of Design and Implementation Features." London: Overseas Development Institute.

Becker, Gary S. 1957. *The Economics of Discrimination*. Chicago: University of Chicago Press.

Belk, Russell. 1988. "Possessions and the Extended Self." *Journal of Consumer Research* 15 (2): 139–68.

Bergbom, I., M. Pettersson, and E. Mattsson. 2017. "Patient Clothing—Practical Solution or Means of Imposing Anonymity?" *Journal of Hospital & Medical Management* 3 (22): 1–6.

Berlekamp, Elwyn. 2012. "Small Science: Radical Innovation." *Science* 338 (6109): 882.

Bevans, Stephen. 2002. *Models of Contextual Theologies*. Maryknoll, NY: Orbis Books.

Bhandari, Medani P. 2017. "Role of Nongovernmental Organization in Bangladesh. Are They Challenging the Government Power? A Case Study from Bangladesh Rural Advancement Committee (BRAC)." *SocioEconomic Challenges* 1 (4): 6–22.

Bhargava, R. 2013. "Overcoming the Epistemic Injustice of Colonialism." *Global Policy* 4 (4): 413–17.

Bieri, Peter. 2017. *Human Dignity: A Way of Living*. Cambridge: Polity.

Bok, Francis, with Edward Tivnan. 2003. *Escape from Slavery: The True Story of My Ten Years in Captivity—And My Journey to Freedom in America*. New York: St Martin's Press.

Bolten, Catherine. 2018. "Productive Work and Subjected Labor: Children's Pursuits and Child Rights in Northern Sierra Leone." *Journal of Human Rights* 17 (2): 199–214.

———. 2020. "Being 'for Others.' Human Rights, Personhood and Dignity in Sierra Leone." In *The Practice of Human Development and Dignity*, ed. P. Carozza and C. Sedmak, 261–78. Notre Dame, IN: University of Notre Dame Press.

Bommer, Christian, et al. 2022. "Home Bias in Humanitarian Aid: The Role of Regional Favoritism in the Allocation of International Disaster Relief." *Journal of Public Economics* 207:104604.

Bone, Christopher, et al. 2011. "Assessing the Impacts of Local Knowledge and Technology on Climate Change Vulnerability in Remote Communities." *International Journal of Environmental Research and Public Health* 8:733–61.

Borgman, Christine L. 2015. *Big Data, Little Data, No Data: Scholarship in a Networked World*. Cambridge, MA: MIT Press.

Bossi, A. 2012. "Economy and Humanism." *Estudos Avançados* 26 (75): 249–66.

Braarvig, Jens. 2014. "Hinduism: The Universal Self in a Class Society." In *The Cambridge Handbook of Human Dignity*, ed. M. Duwell et al., 163–69. Cambridge: Cambridge University Press.

Brall, C., et al. 2019. "Ethics, Health Policy-making and the Economic Crisis: A Qualitative Interview Study with European Policy-makers." *International Journal for Equity in Health* 18:art. 144.

Braun, Adam. 2014. *The Promise of a Pencil: How an Ordinary Person Can Create Extraordinary Change*. New York: Scribner.

Breyer, Sarah J. 2016. "Using the Organization of American States to End the Abuse of Restaveks." *Columbia Human Rights Law Review* 48 (1): 147–97.

Briggs, John. 1999. "The Use of Indigenous Knowledge in Development: Problems and Challenges." *Progress in Development Studies* 5 (2): 99–114.

Brock, Karen, et al. 2002. Poverty Knowledge and Policy Processes. IDS Research Report 53. Brighton: Institute for Development Studies.

Brown, Peter. 2002. *Poverty and Leadership in the Later Roman Empire.* Hanover, NH: University Press of New England.

Búzás, Zoltán I. 2021. *Evading International Norms: Race and Rights in the Shadow of Legality.* Philadelphia: University of Pennsylvania Press.

Cabrera, Luis. 2021. "Ambedkar on the Haughty Face of Dignity." *Politics and Religion* 14:83–105.

Campbell, Andrea L. 2012. "Policy Makes Mass Politics." *Annual Review of Political Science* 15 (1): 333–51.

Carel, H., and G. Györffy. 2014. "Seen but Not Heard: Children and Epistemic Injustice." *The Lancet* 384 (9950): 1256–57.

Catholic Bishops Conference of South Africa. 2012. *Catholic Church Vision for Land Reform in South Africa.* Pretoria: Justice and Peace Department.

Cernea, Michael M., and Hari Mohan Mathur, eds. 2008. *Can Compensation Prevent Impoverishment?: Reforming Resettlement through Investments and Benefit-Sharing.* New Delhi: Oxford University Press.

Chambers, Robert. 1997. *Whose Reality Counts?* London: Intermediate Technology Publications.

———. 2001. "The World Development Report: Concepts, Content and a Chapter 12." *Journal of International Development* 13 (3): 299–306.

———. 2013. *Rural Development: Putting the Last First.* New York: Routledge.

Chen, Toby, et al. 2020. "Occidentalisation of Beauty Standards: Eurocentrism in Asia." *International Socioeconomics Laboratory* 1 (2): 1–11.

Childress, Sarah. 2007. "A Young Tinkerer Builds a Windmill, Electrifying a Nation: Mr. Kamkwamba's Creation Spurs Hope in Malawi." *Wall Street Journal*, December 12.

Chimni, Bhupinder. 2008. "The Sen Conception of Development and Contemporary International Law Discourse: Some Parallels." *Law and Development Review* 1 (1): 1–22.

Chochinov, Harvey M., et al. 2005. "Dignity Therapy: A Novel Psychotherapeutic Intervention for Patients near the End of Life." *Journal of Clinical Oncology* 23 (24): 5520–25.

Christian, Alvin. 2015. "Microfinance as a Determinant of Domestic Violence in Bangladesh: Who Is at Risk?" Ph.D. diss. City University of New York.

Clausen, Fabian, and Amir Attaran. 2011. "The Chad-Cameroon Pipeline Project—Assessing the World Bank's Failed Experiment to Direct Oil Revenues towards the Poor (2011)." *Law and Development Review* 4 (1): 30–65.

Cleaver, F. 1999. "Paradoxes of Participation: Questioning Participatory Approaches to Development." *Journal of International Development* 11:597–612.

Coetzee, John M. 1981. *Waiting for the Barbarians*. New York: Penguin.

Cohen, Gerald A. 1993. "Equality of What? On Welfare, Goods, and Capabilities." In *The Quality of Life*, ed. M. Nussbaum and A. Sen. New York: Oxford University Press.

_____. 2008. *Rescuing Justice and Equality*. Cambridge, MA: Harvard University Press.

Cole, H. R. 1990. "Towards a Biblical Theology of Land and Environment." *Melanesian Journal of Theology* 6 (2): 42–51.

Collins, Eamon, with Mick McGovern. 1997. *Killing Rage*. London: Granta Books.

Conte, Verónica. 2016. "Tirana: Colour and Art on the Way to Utopia." In *Utopia(s)— Worlds and Frontiers of the Imaginary*, ed. M. Rosário Monteiro, M. Ming Kong, and M. João Pereira Neto, 247–50. London: CRC Press.

Cooper, Elizabeth. 2021. "What's Law Got to Do With It? Dignity and Menstruation." *Columbia Journal of Gender and Law* 41 (1): 39–52.

Coppola, Andrea, et al. 2014. *Big Data in Action for Development*. Washington, DC: World Bank.

Corburn, Jason. 2003. "Bringing Local Knowledge into Environmental Decision Making. Improving Urban Planning for Communities at Risk." *Journal of Planning Education and Research* 22:420–33.

Córdova, Abby, and Helen Kras. 2022. "State Action to Prevent Violence against Women: The Effect of Women's Police Stations on Men's Attitudes toward Gender-Based Violence." *Journal of Politics* 84 (1): 1–17.

Cornut, Jérémie. 2015. "To Be a Diplomat Abroad: Diplomatic Practice at Embassies." *Cooperation and Conflict* 50 (3): 385–401.

Cornwall, Andrea, and Mamoru Fujita. 2007. "The Politics of Representing 'The Poor.'" In *The Power of Labelling: How People Are Categorized and Why It Matters*, ed. J. Moncrieffe and R. Eyben. New York: Routledge.

_____. 2012. "Ventriloquising 'the Poor'? Of Voices, Choices and the Politics of 'Participatory' Knowledge Production." *Third World Quarterly* 33 (9): 1751–65.

Corradi Fiumara, Gemma. 1990. *The Other Side of Language: A Philosophy of Listening*. London: Routledge.

Cosacchi, Daniel. 2019. "Jesuits and Social Justice." *Journal of Jesuit Studies* 6:651–75.

Cosmao, Vincent, and Louis-Joseph Lebret, OP. 1970. "From Social Action to the Struggle for Development." *New Blackfriars* 51 (597): 62–68.

Council of Europe. 2020. *Strategic Action Plan for Roma and Traveller Inclusion*. Strasbourg: Council of Europe.

Crépon, Bruno, et al. 2013. "Do Labor Market Policies Have Displacement Effects? Evidence from a Clustered Randomized Experiment." *Quarterly Journal of Economics* 128 (2): 531–80.

Crins, Rieki. 2004. "Religion and Gender Values in a Changing World." In *The Spider and the Piglet: Proceedings of the First International Seminar on Bhutan*

Studies, ed. Karma Ura and Sonam Kinga, 581–98. Thimphu: Centre for Bhutan Studies.

Crocker, David. 2014. "Development and Global Ethics: Five Foci for the Future." *Journal of Global Ethics* 10 (3): 245–53.

Crost, Benjamin, et al. 2014. "Aid under Fire: Development Projects and Civil Conflict." *American Economic Review* 104 (6): 1833–56.

Cunningham, Philip A. 2013. "A Catholic Theology of the Land?: The State of the Question." *Studies in Jewish-Christian Relations* 8:1–15.

Damir-Geilsdorf, Sabine. 2016. "Contract Labour and Debt Bondage in the Arab Gulf States. Policies and Practices within the Kafala System." In *Bonded Labour: Global and Comparative Perspectives (18th–21st Century)*, ed. Sabine Damir-Geilsdorf et al, 163–90. Bielefeld, Germany: Transcript Verlag.

Darwall, Stephen. 2006. *The Second-Person Standpoint: Morality, Respect, and Accountability*. Cambridge, MA: Harvard University Press.

Davis, Benjamin, et al. 2022. "Do Not Transform Food Systems on the Backs of the Rural Poor." *Food Security* 14:729–40.

Davis, Kevin E., and Michael J. Trebilcock. 2008. The Relationship between Law and Development: Optimists versus Skeptics. Public Law & Legal Theory Research Paper Series Working Paper 08-14. Law & Economics Research Paper Series Working Paper 08-24. New York: New York University School of Law.

de Jesus, Carolina Maria. (1960) 2003. *Child of the Dark: the Diary of Carolina Maria de Jesus*. London: Penguin Books.

Dekker, Sidney. 2007. "Discontinuity and Disaster: Gaps and the Negotiation of Culpability in Medication Delivery." *Journal of Law, Medicine and Ethics* 35 (3): 463–70.

de la Pena de Berrazueta, Lucia Vidal. 2019. *Despite Haiti Abolishing Slavery, Why Is the Restavek System Still in Place?* MA thesis, Columbia University, Graduate School of Art & Sciences.

Deneulin, Séverine. 2018. Integral Human Development through the Lens of Sen's Capability Approach and the Life of a Faith Community at the Latin American Urban Margins. Working Paper 427. Kellogg Institute for International Studies.

———. 2021. *Human Development and the Catholic Social Tradition: Towards an Integral Ecology*. Milton, UK: Routledge.

Dennen, Xenia. 2017. "'And I Will Tell the Best People in All the Earth.' Faith and Resilience in the Gulag." In *The Dangerous God: Christianity and the Soviet Experiment*, ed. D. Erdozain, 170–86. Ithaca, NY: Cornell University Press.

Desierto, Diane, and Ilaria Schnyder von Wartensee. 2021. "The Right to Development, Integral Human Development, and Integral Ecology in the Amazon." *International Journal of Human Rights* 25 (9): 1525–42.

De Torre, Joseph M. 2001. "Maritain's 'Integral Humanism' and Catholic Social Teaching." In *Reassessing the Liberal State: Reading Maritain's Man and the State*, ed. T. Fuller, and J. P. Hittinger, 202–08. Washington, DC: Catholic University of America Press.

Devereux, Stephen. 2001. "Sen's Entitlement Approach: Critiques and Counter-critiques." *Oxford Development Studies* 29 (3): 245–63.

Diallo, Amadou, and Denis Thuillier. 2005. "The Success of International Development Projects, Trust and Communication: An African Perspective." *International Journal of Project Management* 23 (3): 237–52.

Diamond, Jared. 2005. *Collapse: How Societies Choose to Fail or Survive.* New York: Penguin.

Diekens, Julia. 2007. *Local Knowledge for Disaster Preparedness: A Literature Review.* Kathmandu, Nepal: International Center for Integral Mountain Development.

Dikötter, F. 2010. *Mao's Great Famine: The History of China's Most Devastating Catastrophe, 1958–62.* London: Bloomsbury.

Diop, Cheikh Tidiane. 2006. *L'Afrique en Attente?* Paris: L'Harmattan.

Dobko, Taras. 2022. "The Trauma of 'Homo Sovieticus.'" In *The Trauma of Communism*, ed. C. Sedmak and J. McAdams, 249–63. Lviv: Ukrainian Catholic University Press.

Dotson, Kristie. 2011. "Tracking Epistemic Violence, Tracking Practices of Silencing." *Hypatia: A Journal of Feminist Philosophy* 26 (2): 236–57.

_____. 2012. "A Cautionary Tale: On Limiting Epistemic Oppression." *Frontiers* 33 (1): 24–47.

Dovring, Folke. 1962. "European Reactions to the Homestead Act." *Journal of Economic History* 22 (4): 461–72.

Dower, Nigel. 2007. *World Ethics: The New Agenda.* 2nd ed. Edinburgh: Edinburgh University Press.

_____. 2008. "The Nature and Scope of Development Ethics." *Journal of Global Ethics* 4 (3): 183–93.

Downs, Jim. 2012. *Sick from Freedom: African-American Illness and Suffering during the Civil War and Reconstruction.* New York: Oxford University Press.

Dragoş, Manea, and Mihaela Precup. 2020. "Infantilizing the Refugee: On the Mobilization of Empathy in Kate Evans' *Threads from the Refugee Crisis*." *a/b: Auto/Biography Studies* 35 (2): 481–87.

Dübgen, Franziska. 2012. "Africa Humiliated? Misrecognition in Development Aid." *Res Publica* 18 (1): 65–77.

Dworkin, Ronald. 2011. *Justice for Hedgehogs.* Cambridge, MA: Harvard University Press.

Ebenstein, Avraham. 2008. "The 'Missing Girls' of China and the Unintended Consequences of the One Child Policy." *Journal of Human Resources* 45 (1): 87–115.

Edgar, Stacey. 2011. *Global Girlfriends: How One Mom Made It Her Business to Help Women in Poverty Worldwide.* New York: St. Martin's Press.

Edlund, Lena, et al. 2007. Sex Ratios and Crime: Evidence from China's One-Child Policy. IZA Discussion Paper 3214. Bonn, Germany: Institute for the Study of Labor.

_____. 2013. "Sex Ratios and Crime: Evidence from China." *Review of Economics and Statistics* 95 (5): 1520–34.

Edmondson, Amy C. 2011. "Strategies for Learning from Failure." *Harvard Business Review* 89 (4).

Efron, Sara Efrat. 2008. "Moral Education between Hope and Hopelessness: The Legacy of Janusz Korczak." *Curriculum Inquiry* 38 (1): 39–62.

Elledge, Annie M., and Caroline Faria. 2020. "'I Want to. . . . Let My Country Shine': Nationalism, Development, and the Geographies of Beauty." *Society and Space* 38 (5): 829–48.

Emirbayer, Mustafa, and Ann Mische. 1998. "What Is Agency?" *American Journal of Sociology* 103 (4): 962–1023.

Enns, Charis, and Adam Sneyd. 2020. "More-Than-Human Infrastructural Violence and Infrastructural Justice: A Case Study of the Chad-Cameroon Pipeline Project." *Annals of the American Association of Geographers* 111 (2): 481–97.

Erpenbeck, Jenny. 2017. *Go, Went, Gone.* New York: New Directions Publishing.

Evans, Robert. 2022. "SAGE Advice and Political Decision-Making: 'Following the Science' in Times of Epistemic Uncertainty." *Social Studies of Science* 52 (1): 53–78.

Farmer, Paul. 2001. "Community-Based Approaches to HIV Treatment in Resource-Poor Settings." *The Lancet* 358 (929): 404–409.

_____. 2006. *Accompaniment: The Missing Piece of the Funding Puzzle.* Washigton, DC: Grantmakers in Health.

_____. 2011. "Partners in Help: Assisting the Poor over the Long Term." *Foreign Affairs*, July 29.

Farmer, Paul, and Gustavo Gutiérrez. 2013. *In the Company of the Poor: Conversations between Dr. Paul Farmer and Father Gustavo Gutiérrez.* Edited by Michael Griffin and Jennie Weiss Block. Maryknoll, NY: Orbis Books.

Fattah, Khaled, and Karin M. Fierke. 2009. "A Clash of Emotions: The Politics of Humiliation and Political Violence in the Middle East." *European Journal of International Relations* 15 (1): 67–93.

Fleurbaey, Marc. 2009. "Beyond GDP: The Quest for a Measure of Social Welfare." *Journal of Economic Literature* 47 (4): 1029–75.

Fleurbaey, Marc, and Didier Blanchet. 2013. *Beyond GDP: Measuring Welfare and Assessing Sustainability.* New York: Oxford University Press.

Foner, Eric. 1982. "Reconstruction Revisited." *Reviews in American History* 10 (4): 82–100.

Fong, Mei. 2016. *One Child: The Story of China's Most Radical Experiment.* Boston: Houghton Mifflin Harcourt.

Foucault, Michel. 2010. *The Birth of Biopolitics.* New York: Picador.

Frayne, Michael. 2005. *A Very Private Life*. London: Faber and Faber.

Frevert, Ute. 2020. *The Politics of Humiliation: A Modern History*. Oxford: Oxford University Press.

Fricker, Miranda. 1999. "Epistemic Oppression and Epistemic Privilege." *Canadian Journal of Philosophy* 25 (Suppl): 191–210.

_____. 2007. *Epistemic Injustice Power and the Ethics of Knowing*. Oxford: Oxford University Press.

_____. 2012. "Silence and Institutional Prejudice." In *Out from the Shadows: Analytical Feminist Contributions to Traditional Philosophy*, ed. Sharon Crasnow and Anita Superson. Oxford: Oxford University Press.

Fromm, Erich. 1976. *To Have or to Be?* New York: Harper & Row.

Gamazon, Eric. 2012. "Small Science: High Stakes." *Science* 338 (6109): 883.

Garreau, Lydie, and Louis-Joseph Lebret. 2011. *Précurseur de Vatican II: Dans la Dynamique Sociale de l'Eglise, auprès des Marins-pêcheurs Bretons—Et dans le Développement Économique Mondial*. Paris: L'Harmattan.

Gasper, Des. 2012. "Development Ethics—Why? What? How? A Formulation of the Field." *Journal of Global Ethics* 8 (1): 117–35.

Gasper, Des, and Lori Keleher. 2021. "Investigating L.-J. Lebret as a Pioneer of Human Development Thinking and Global Development Ethics. *Journal of Global Ethics* 17 (2): 115–26.

Gasper, Des, and Irene van Staveren. 2003. "Development as Freedom—And as What Else?" *Feminist Economics* 9 (2–3): 137–61.

Gates, Paul W. 1996. *The Jeffersonian Dream: Studies in the History of American Land Policy and Development*. Ed. Allan G. Bogue and Margaret B. Bogue. Albuquerque: University of New Mexico Press.

Geertz, Clifford. 1993. *The Interpretation of Cultures*. New York: Fontana Press.

Genova, Lisa. 2019. *Still Alice*. New York: Gallery Books.

Gentile, V. 2013. "'Epistemic Injustice' and the 'Right Not to Be Poor'. Bringing Recognition into the Debate on Global Justice." *Global Policy* 4 (4): 425–27.

Gianfreda, Fausto. 2019. "The Anthropological Basis of Integral Human Development." In *Integral Human Development: Challenges to Sustainability & Democracy*, ed. J. Azétsop, 32–49. Eugene, OR: Pickwick.

Gibson-Graham, J. K. 2014. "Rethinking the Economy with Thick Description and Weak Theory." *Current Anthropology* 55 (9): 147–53.

Giri, Birendra. 2009. "The Bonded Labour System in Nepal: Perspectives of Haliya and Kamaiya Child Workers." *Journal of Asian and African Studies* 44 (6): 599–623.

Glendon, Mary Ann. 2001. *A World Made New: Eleanor Roosevelt and the Universal Declaration of Human Rights*. New York: Random House.

_____. 2013. "The Influence of Catholic Social Doctrine on Human Rights." *Journal of Catholic Social Thought* 10 (1): 69–84.

Glover, Jonathan. 2001. *Humanity: A Moral History of the 20th Century*. New Haven, CT: Yale University Press.

Goerg, Odile. 2012. "Between Infantilization and Colonial Repression. Film Censorship in French West Africa, 'Great Children,' and Youth Protection." *Cahiers d'Études Africaines* 205 (1): 165–98.

Goffman, Erving. 1959. *The Presentation of Self in Everyday Life*. New York: Doubleday.

Goh, Esther C. L. 2006. "Raising the Precious Single Child in Urban China—An Intergenerational Joint Mission between Parents and Grandparents." *Journal of Intergenerational Relationships* 4:7–28.

Goizueta, Roberto. 1995. *Caminemos con Jesús: Toward a Hispanic/Latino Theology of Accompaniment*. Maryknoll, NY: Orbis Books.

Goodman, Nelson. 1978. *Ways of Worldmaking*. Indianapolis, IN: Hackett.

———. 1991. "On Capturing Cities." *The Journal of Aesthetic Education* 25 (1): 5-9.

Gorjestani, N. 2000. Indigenous Knowledge for Development. UNCTAD Conference Paper. Geneva: UNCTAD.

Goulet, Denis. 1976. "On the Ethics of Development Planning." *Studies in Comparative International Development* 11 (1): 25–43.

———. 1995. *Development Ethics: A Guide to Theory and Practice*. London: Zed Books.

———. 1996. A New Discipline: Development Ethics. Working Paper 231. Notre Dame, IN: Kellogg Institute for International Studies.

Grosz, Stephen. 2013. *The Examined Life: How We Lose and Find Ourselves*. London: Chatto & Windus.

Gurr, Ted Robert. 2011. *Why Men Rebel*. Boulder, CO: Paradigm.

Gutiérrez, Gustavo. 1993. "Option for the Poor," In *Mysterium Liberationis*, ed. I. Ellacuría and J. Sobrino, 235–50. Maryknoll, NY: Orbis Books.

Halpern, J., and H. M. Weinstein. 2004. "Rehumanizing the Other: Empathy and Reconciliation." *Human Rights Quarterly* 26 (3): 561–83.

Hampson, Joe. 2010. "JRS-Accompaniment: A New Way of Being Present?" *Grace & Truth: A Journal of Catholic Reflection of Southern Africa* 27 (2): 15–28.

Hampson, Joe, et al. 2014. "The Value of Accompaniment." *Forced Migration Review* 48 (November).

Harrison, Elizabeth. 2013. "Beyond the Looking Glass? 'Aidland' Reconsidered." *Critique of Anthropology* 33 (3): 263–79.

Havel, Václav. 1993. *Summer Meditations*. London: Vintage.

Heidt, Mari Rapela. 2017. "Development, Nations, and 'The Signs of the Times': The Historical Context of *Populorum Progressio*." *Journal of Moral Theology* 6 (1): 1–20.

Hellsten, Sirrku K. 2019. "Corruption. Concepts, Costs, Causes and Challenges." In *Routledge Handbook of Development Ethics*, ed. Jay Drydyk and Lori Keleher, 353–66. Abingdon, UK: Routledge.

Herzog, Benno. 2018. "Invisibilization and Silencing as Ethical and Sociological Challenge." *Social Epistemology: A Journal of Knowledge, Culture and Policy* 32 (1): 13–23.

Himes, Kenneth. 2017. "Catholic Social Teaching on Building a Just Society: The Need for a Ceiling and a Floor." *Religions* 8 (49).

Hoffman, Lisa, and Brian Coffey. 2008. "Dignity and Indignation: How People Experiencing Homelessness View Services and Providers." *Social Science Journal* 45:207–22.

Hoffmann, Nimi, and Thaddeus Metz. 2017. "What Can the Capabilities Approach Learn from an Ubuntu Ethic? A Relational Approach to Development Theory." *World Development* 97:153–64.

Hoffnagle, Warren. 1970. "The Southern Homestead Act: Its Origins and Operations." *The Historian* 32 (4): 612–29.

Hollenbach, David. 2002. *The Common Good and Christian Ethics*. Cambridge: Cambridge University Press.

_____. 2016. "The Jesuits and the 'More Universal Good': At Vatican II and Today." In *Jesuits and Globalization*, ed. T. Banchoff and J. Casanova, 169–87. Washington, DC: Georgetown University Press.

Holman, Susan. 2001. *The Hungry Are Dying: Beggars and Bishops in Roman Cappadocia*. Oxford: Oxford University Press.

Honig, Dan. 2018. *Navigation by Judgment: Why and When Top-Down Management of Foreign Aid Doesn't Work*. Oxford: Oxford University Press.

Honneth, Axel. 2001. "Invisibility: On the Epistemology of 'Recognition.'" *Proceedings of the Aristotelian Society*, Supplementary Volume 75 (1): 111–26.

Horowitz, Alexandra. 2013. *On Looking: A Walker's Guide to the Art of Observation*. New York: Scribner.

Hossain, Naomi, and Anasuya Sengupta. 2009. Thinking Big, Going Global: The Challenge of BRAC's Global Expansion. IDS Working Paper Series 339. Brighton: Institute for Development Studies.

Howden, David, and Yang Zhou. 2014. "China's One-Child-Policy: Some Unintended Consequences." *Economic Affairs* 34 (3): 353–69.

Hulme, David. 2003. Thinking "Small" and the Understanding of Poverty: Maymana and Mofizul's Story. CPRC Working Paper 22. Manchester: Chronic Poverty Research Center.

Hulme, David, and Karen Moore. 2010. "Thinking Small, and Thinking Big about Poverty: Maymana and Mofizul's Story Updated." *Bangladesh Development Studies* 33 (3): 69–96.

Husuma, Tonje Lossius, et al. 2019. "'A Plea for Recognition': Users' Experience of Humiliation during Mental Health Care." *International Journal of Law and Psychiatry* 62:148–53.

Hutchings, Kimberly. 2019. "Decolonizing Global Ethics: Thinking with the Pluriverse." *Ethics & International Affairs* 33 (2): 115–25.

Hutchinson, Emma. 2014. "A Global Politics of Pity? Disaster Imagery and the Emotional Construction of Solidarity after the 2004 Asian Tsunami." *International Political Sociology* 8:1–19.

ID Insight, Dignity and Cash. 2022. "GiveDirectly's Unconditional Cash Transfers in Kiryandongo Refugee Settlement." ID Insight Report. San Francisco: ID Insight.

Ignatieff, Michael. 2017a. "Human Rights, Global Ethics, and the Ordinary Virtues." *Ethics & International Affairs* 31 (1): 3–16.

———. 2017b. *The Ordinary Virtues: Moral Order in a Divided World*. Cambridge, MA: Harvard University Press.

Ika, Lavagnon A. 2012. "Project Management for Development in Africa: Why Projects Are Failing and What Can Be Done about It." *Project Management Journal* 43 (4): 27–41.

Ika, Lavagnon A., and Jennifer Donnelly. 2017. "Success Conditions for International Development Capacity Building Projects." *International Journal of Project Management* 35:44–63.

Ikediashi, Dubem I., Stephen O. Ogunlana, and Abdulaziz Alotaibi. 2014. "Analysis of Project Failure Factors for Infrastructure Projects in Saudi Arabia: A Multivariate Approach." *Journal of Construction in Developing Countries* 19 (1): 35–52.

Independent Commission on Sexual Misconduct, Accountability, and Culture Change. 2019. *Committing to Change, Protecting People: Toward a More Accountable Oxfam.*

Intrator, Jessica. 2011. "From Squatter to Settler: Applying the Lessons of Nineteenth Century U.S. Public Land Policy to Twenty-first Century Land Struggles in Brazil." *Ecology Law Quarterly* 38 (179): 179–232.

Irby, Decoteau, et al., eds. 2022. *Dignity-Affirming Education; Cultivating the Somebodiness of Students and Educators*. New York: Teachers College Press.

Iyer, Lakshmi. 2010. "Direct versus Indirect Colonial Rule in India: Long-Term Consequences." *Review of Economics and Statistics* November 92 (4): 693–713.

Izenberg, Dafna. 2007. "We Pay Cash for Good Behavior." *Maclean's* 120 (49–50): 37.

James, Aaron. 2012. *Assholes: A Theory*. New York: Doubleday.

———. 2016. "On the Philosophical Interest and Surprising Significance of the Asshole." *Harvard Review of Philosophy* 23:41–52.

Jaros, Kyle. 2019. *China's Urban Champion: The Politics of Spatial Development*. Princeton, NJ: Princeton University Press.

Jensen Newby, Tina Maria. 2010. Unintended Effects of Development Aid—A Brief Overview. DIIS Working Paper 06. Copenhagen: Danish Institute for International Studies.

Jiao, S., et al. 1986. "Comparative Study of Behavioral Qualities of Only Children and Sibling Children." *Child Development* 57:357–61.

Jisheng, Yang. 2012. *Tombstone*. London: Allen Lane.

Jonker, Kim. 2009. "In the Black with BRAC." *Stanford Innovation Review* (Winter).

Juran, Luke, et al. 2019. "Purity, Pollution, and Space: Barriers to Latrine Adoption in Post-disaster India." *Environmental Management* 64:456–69.

Kämpchen, Martin. 2011. *Leben ohne Armut: Wie Hilfe wirklich helfen kann—meine Erfahrungen in Indien*. Freiburg, Germany: Herder.

Kamali, Mohammad Hashim. 2002. *The Dignity of Man: An Islamic Perspective*. Cambridge: Islamic Texts Society.

Kamkwamba, William, and Bryan Mealer. 2010. *The Boy Who Harnessed the Wind*. New York: William Morrow.

Kant, Immanuel. 1785. *Grundlegung der Metaphysik der Sitten*. Riga: JF Hartknoch.

_____. 1996. *Practical Philosophy*. Trans. and ed. M. Gregor. Cambridge: Cambridge University Press.

Kara, Siddarth. 2018. *Modern Slavery: A Global Perspective*. New York: Columbia University Press.

Katongole, Emmanuel. 2011. *The Sacrifice of Africa, A Political Theology for Africa*. Grand Rapids, MI: Eerdmans.

_____. 2013. *Stories of Bethany: On the Faces of the Church in Africa*. Nairobi: Pauline Publishers.

_____. 2022a. "Mission as Integral Ecology: Doing Theology at Bethany." *Mission Studies* 39:163–85.

_____. 2022b. *Who Are My People? Love, Violence, and Christianity in Sub-Saharan Africa*. Notre Dame, IN: University of Notre Dame Press.

Kaufman, Peter, et al. 2011. "Human Dignity Violated: A Negative Approach—Introduction." In *Humiliation, Degradation, Dehumanization: Human Dignity Violated*, ed. P. Kaufmann et al., 1–6. Dordrecht: Springer.

Kaziga, Ruth, et al. 2021. "Beauty Is Skin Deep; The Self-Perception of Adolescents and Young Women in Construction of Body Image within the Ankole Society." *International Journal of Environmental Research and Public Health* 18 (15): 7840.

Keleher, Lori. 2017. "Toward an Integral Human Development Ethics." *Veritas: Revista de Filosofía y Teología* 37:19–34.

_____. 2018. "Integral Human Development." In *Routledge Handbook of Development Ethics*, ed. J. Drydyk and L. Keleher, 29–34. New York: Routledge.

Khaji, Ali, et al. 2019. "Ethical Considerations for Living in Temporary Shelters (i.e., Camps) Following a Natural Disaster." *Archives of Bone and Joint Surgery* 7 (5): 445–52.

Kim, Mikyung, et al. 2021. "Problems and Implications of Shelter Planning Focusing on Habitability: A Case Study of a Temporary Disaster Shelter after the Pohang Earthquake in South Korea." *International Journal of Environmental Research and Public Health* 18 (6): 2868.

Kirby, Emma J. 2016. *The Optician of Lampedusa*. London: Allen Lane.

Kerry, Vanessa, et al. 2014. "From Aid to Accompaniment: Rules of the Road for Development Assistance." In *The Handbook of Global Health Policy*, ed. G. Brown et al., 483–504. Oxford: Wiley.

Kerstein, Samuel. 2009. "Treating Others Merely as Means." *Utilitas* 21 (2): 163–80.

Khiok-Khng, Yeo, and Gene L. Green, eds. 2021. *Theologies of Land: Contested Land, Spatial Justice, and Identity*. Eugene, OR: Cascade Books.

Kidder, Tracy. 2003. *Mountains beyond Mountains*. New York: Random House.

Klooster, D. J. 2002. "Toward Adaptive Community Forest Management: Integrating Local Forest Knowledge with Scientific Forestry." *Economic Geography* 78 (1): 43–70.

Knorr Cetina, Karin. 1999. *Epistemic Cultures.* Cambridge, MA: Harvard University Press.

Koch, Dirk-Jan, et al. 2021. "Assessing International Development Cooperation: Becoming Intentional about Unintended Effects." *Sustainability* 13:1–26.

Kohn, Nina A. 2009. "Outliving Civil Rights." *Washington University Law Review* 86 (5): 1053–115.

Kopf, Martina. 2019. "Encountering Development in East African Fiction." *Journal of Commonwealth Literature* 54 (3): 334–51.

Korthals, Michiel. 2012. "Two Evils in Food Country: Hunger and Lack of Representation." In *The Philosophy of Food*, ed. D. M. Kaplan, 103–21. Berkeley: University of California Press.

Kowalski, Julia. 2022. "Language Beyond Labeling: Toward a Language Ideologies Analysis of Anti-Violence Interventions." *Violence against Women* 1–21.

Králová, Kateřina. 2017. "The "Holocausts" in Greece: Victim Competition in the Context of Postwar Compensation for Nazi Persecution." *Holocaust Studies* 23 (1–2): 149–75.

Kristiansen, Lisbet, et al. 2010. "Left Alone—Swedish Nurses' and Mental Health Workers' Experiences of Being Care Providers in a Social Psychiatric Dwelling Context in the Post-Health-Care-Restructuring Era: A Focus-Group Interview Study." *Scandinavian Journal of Caring Sciences* 24:427–35.

Krumer-Nevo, M. 2010. "Critical Poverty Knowledge: Contesting Othering and Social Distancing." *Current Sociology* 58 (5): 693–714.

Kuch, Hannes. 2011. "The Rituality of Humiliation: Exploring Symbolic Vulnerability." In *Humiliation, Degradation, Dehumanization: Human Dignity Violated*, ed. P. Kaufmann et al., 37–56. Dordrecht: Springer.

Kuhle, Helene, et al. 2017. "Leaving No One Behind: Graduation for Refugees." *Policy in Focus* 14 (2): 62–66.

Lai, Hor Yan. 2014. "Childhood Poverty and Psychological Health of Youths in Hong Kong: Mentoring as a Social Capital Intervention." *Arts & Sciences Electronic Theses and Dissertations*. St. Louis: Washington University in St. Louis.

Lamberty, Kim M. 2012. "Toward a Spirituality of Accompaniment in Solidarity Partnerships." *Missiology: An International Review* 40 (2): 181–93.

Lansing, Stephen J. 2009. *Priests and Programmers: Technologies of Power in the Engineered Landscape of Bali.* Princeton, NJ: Princeton University Press.

Lanza, Michael L. 1990. *Agrarianism and Reconstruction Politics: The Southern Homestead Act.* Baton Rouge: Louisiana State University.

La Piana, David. 2010. "The Nonprofit Paradox." *Stanford Social Innovation Review* (Summer): 22–24.

Latour, Bruno, and Steve Woolgar. 1986. *Laboratory Life: The Construction of Scientific Facts.* Princeton, NJ: Princeton University Press.

Lavigne, Jean-Claude, and Hugues Puel. 2007. "For a Human-Centred Economy: Louis Joseph Lebret (1897–1966)." In *Preaching Justice. Dominican Contributions to Social Ethics in the Twentieth Century,* ed. Francesco Compagnoni and Helen Alford. Dublin: Dominican Publications.

Lazare, A. 1987. "Shame and Humiliation in the Medical Encounter." *Archives of Internal Medicine* 147:1653–58.

Leape, Lucian L., et al. 2012. "Perspective: A Culture of Respect, Part 1: The Nature and Causes of Disrespectful Behavior by Physicians." *Academic Medicine* 87 (7): 845–52.

Lebret, Louis-Joseph. 1958. "Le Gigantesque Effort à Entreprendre." *Présence Africaine: Nouvelle Série* 21:42–47.

———. 1961. *Dynamique Concrète du Développement.* Paris: Economie et Humanisme, Les Editions Ouvrierès.

Lederach, John Paul. 2005. *The Moral Imagination.* Oxford: Oxford University Press.

Levi, Primo. 1959. *If This Is a Man.* New York: Orion Press.

Li, Yong. 2019. "Virtues and Human Dignity: Confucianism and the Foundation of Human Rights." *International Philosophical Quarterly* 59 (2): 175–92.

Libecap, Gary D., and Zeynep K. Hansen. 2002. "'Rain Follows the Plow' and Dryfarming Doctrine: The Climate Information Problem and Homestead Failure in the Upper Great Plains 1890–1925." *Journal of Economic History* 62 (1): 86–120.

Locatelli, Giorgio, et al. 2017. "Corruption in Public Projects and Megaprojects: There Is an Elephant in the Room!" *International Journal of Project Management* 35 (3): 252–68.

Lopez, Elias. 2013. "Ready to Become 'Collateral Damage': A Jesuit Refugee Service Experience." *Journal of Catholic Social Thought* 10 (2): 353–60.

Lukes, Steven. 1995. *The Curious Enlightenment of Professor Caritat.* London: Verso.

Maathai, Wangari. 2007. *Unbowed: A Memoir.* New York: Anchor Books.

MacFarlane-Barrow, Magnus. 2015. *The Shed That Fed a Million Children: The Mary's Meals Story.* London: William Collins.

Mackenzie, Catriona, et al. 2014. "Introduction." In *Vulnerability,* ed. C. Mackenzie et al., 1–32. Oxford: Oxford University Press.

MacMillan, Scott. 2022. *Hope over Fate: Fazle Hasan Abed and the Science of Ending Global Poverty.* Lanham, MD: Rowman & Littlefield.

Mahlmann, Matthias. 2012. "Human Dignity and Autonomy in Modern Constitutional Orders." In *The Oxford Companion of Comparative Constitutional Law,* ed. Michael Rosenfeld and András Sajo, 370–96. Oxford: Oxford University Press.

Mahood, Linda. 2009. *Feminism and Voluntary Action: Eglantyne Jebb and Save the Children.* New York: Palgrave.

Mahmood, Saba. 2012. *Politics of Piety: The Islamic Revival and the Feminist Subject.* Princeton, NJ: Princeton University Press.

Malavisi, Anna. 2019. "Epistemic Injustice znd Distortion in Development Theory znd Practice." In *Routledge Handbook of Development Ethics*, ed. J. Drydyk and L. Keleher, 41–51. London: Routledge.

Manchanda, Rita. 2004. "Gender Conflict and Displacement: Contesting 'Infantilisation' of Forced Migrant Women." *Economic and Political Weekly* 39 (37): 4179–86.

Mandela, Nelson. 1998. "Address by President Nelson Mandela at 53rd United Nations General Assembly, New York—United States." September 21, 1998.

Mankell, Henning. 2005. *I Die, But My Memory Lives On.* New York: Free Press.

Manomano, Tatenda, and Mulwayini Mundau. 2017. "Preserving Human Dignity: Promises and Pitfalls—A South African Perspective." *International Social Work* 60 (6): 1358–69.

Marcuse, Herbert. 2002. *One-Dimensional Man: Studies in the Ideology of Advanced Industrial Society.* New York: Routledge.

Margalit, Avishai. 1996. *The Decent Society.* Cambridge, MA: Harvard University Press.

Maróth, Miklós. 2014. "Human Dignity in the Islamic World." In *The Cambridge Handbook of Human Dignity*, ed. M. Duwell et al., 155–62. Cambridge: Cambridge University Press.

Martins, Nuno. 2021. "Vitor Eixeira, Lebret's Christian-inspired Societal Project and Integral Human Development." *Journal of Global Ethics* 17 (2): 167–84.

Masaki, Katsu. 2022. "Exploring the 'Partial Connections' between Growth and Degrowth Debates: Bhutan's Policy of Gross National Happiness." *Journal of Interdisciplinary Economics* 34 (1): 86–103.

Matta, Nadim F., and Ronald N. Ashkenas. 2003. "Why Good Projects Fail Anyway." *Harvard Business Review*, September.

Matthews, Stephen. 2002. "Review: *Voices of the Poor Vol. I: Can Anyone Hear Us?* by Deepa Narayan: *Voices of the Poor Vol. II: Crying Out for Change* by Deepa Narayan and Robert Chambers." *Community Development Journal* 37 (2): 200–202.

Max-Neef, Manfred. 1991. *Human Scale Development: Conception, Application and Further Reflections.* New York: Apex Press.

McCann, M. 2014. "The Unbearable Lightness of Being of Rights: On Sociolegal Inquiry in the Global Era." *Law and Society Review* 48:245–74.

McConkey, J. 2004. "Knowledge and Acknowledgement: 'Epistemic Injustice' as a Problem of Recognition." *Politics* 24 (3): 198–205.

McDowell, Christopher, ed. 1996. *Understanding Impoverishment: The Consequences of Development-Induced Displacement.* Oxford: Berghahn Books.

Mckay, Ashley, et al. 2018. "Western Beauty Pressures and Their Impact on Young University Women." *International Journal of Gender and Women's Studies* 6 (2): 1–11.

McKenzie, Donald. 1999. *Bibliography and the Sociology of Texts*. Cambridge: Cambridge University Press.

Mead, Margaret. 1962. "The Underdeveloped and the Overdeveloped." *Foreign Affairs* 41 (1): 78–89.

Medina, José. 2011. "Toward a Foucaultian Epistemology of Resistance: Counter-Memory, Epistemic Friction, and *Guerrilla* Pluralism." *Foucault Studies* 12:9–35.

Meier, Christian. 2005. *From Athens to Auschwitz: The Uses of History*. Cambridge, MA: Harvard University Press.

Merton, Robert K. 1968. "The Matthew Effect in Science." *Science New Series* 159 (3810): 56–63.

Mettler, Suzanne. 2019. "Making What Government Does Apparent to Citizens: Policy Feedback Effects, Their Limitations, and How They Might Be Facilitated." *Annals of the American Academy of Political and Social Science* 685 (1): 30–46.

Miller, Daniel. 2009. *The Comfort of Things*. Cambridge: Polity.

Mintz, Alex, and Carly Wayne. 2016. "The Polythink Syndrome and Elite Group Decision-Making." *Advances in Political Psychology* 37 (1): 3–21.

Mishra, Pradeep Kumar. 2016. "Managing International Development Projects: Case Studies of Implementation of Large-Scale Projects in India." *International Journal of Rural Management* 12 (1): 4–26.

Mohammed, Amina. 2015. "I Foresee a World without Poverty." *Africa Renewal* 29 (3): 6–7.

Moore, C., et al. 2003. "Medical Errors Related to Discontinuity of Care from an Inpatient to an Outpatient Setting." *Journal of General Internal Medicine* 18 (8): 646–51.

Morsink, Johannes. 1999. *The Universal Declaration of Human Rights*. Philadelphia: University of Pennsylvania Press.

———. 2017. *The Universal Declaration and the Challenge of Religion*. Columbia: University of Missouri Press.

———. 2022. *Article by Article: The Universal Declaration of Human Rights for a New Generation*. Philadelphia: University of Pennsylvania Press.

Mortenson, Greg, with David Oliver Relin. 2007. *Three Cups of Tea*. London: Penguin.

Mosel, Irina, and Kerrie Holloway. 2019. Dignity and Humanitarian Action in Displacement: Humanitarian Policy Group Report. London: Overseas Development Institute.

Moss, Todd J., et al. 2006. An Aid-Institutions Paradox? A Review Essay on Aid Dependency and State Building in Sub-Saharan Africa. CGD Working Paper 74. Washington, DC: Center for Global Development.

Mosse, David, ed. 2011. *Adventures in Aidland: The Anthropology of Professionals in International Development*. New York: Berghahn Books.

Moyn, Samuel. 2010. *The Last Utopia: Human Rights in History*. Cambridge, MA: Belknap Press.

_____. 2014. "A Powerless Companion: Human Rights in the Age of Neoliberalism." *Law and Contemporary Problems* 77 (4): 147–69.

_____. 2015. *Christian Human Rights.* Philadelphia: University of Pennsylvania Press.

_____. 2018. *Not Enough: Human Rights in an Unequal World.* Cambridge, MA: Belknap Press.

Mulley, Clare. 2009. *The Woman Who Saved the Children: A Biography of Eglantyne Jebb, Founder of Save the Children.* Oxford: Oneworld Publications.

Murphy, Laura. 2014. *Survivors of Slavery: Modern-Day Slave Narratives.* New York: Columbia University Press.

Murray, Amy Jo, et al. 2022. "Everyday Dehumanization: Negative Contact, Humiliation, and the Lived Experience of Being Treated as 'Less than Human.'" *British Journal of Social Psychology* 61 (3): 1050–66.

Murray, Duncan, and Bianca Price. 2011. "The Globalization of Beauty—Aspiration or Threat? A Comparison of the Effect of Western Beauty Types on Asian and Western Females' Attitudes and Purchase Intentions." *International Journal of Business Research* 11 (2): 146–55.

Mutua, Makau. 2008. "Human Rights in Africa: The Limited Promise of Liberalism." *African Studies Review* 51 (5): 17–39.

Muurlink, O., and S. A. Macht. 2020. "Managing (Out) Corruption in NGOs: A Case Study from the Bangladesh Delta." *Journal of Management & Organization* 26:1014–29.

Nagel, Thomas. 1986. *The View from Nowhere.* Oxford: Oxford University Press.

Narayan, Deepa, et al. 2000. *Voices of the Poor: Can Anyone Hear Us?* New York: Oxford University Press for the World Bank.

Neuhäuser, Christian. 2011. "Humiliation: The Collective Dimension." In *Humiliation, Degradation, Dehumanization: Human Dignity Violated,* ed. P. Kaufmann et al., 21–36. Dordrecht, the Netherlands: Springer.

Ni, Peimin. 2014. "Seek and You Will Find It; Let Go and You Will Lose It: Exploring a Confucian Approach to Human Dignity." *Dao: A Journal of Comparative Philosophy* 13 (2): 173–98.

Nicholson, C. Phifer. 2021. "Made Known in the Breaking of the Bread: Accompaniment and the Practice of Medicine." *Linacre Quarterly* 88 (3): 281–90.

Norris, Lucy. 2012. "Economies of Moral Fibre? Recycling Charity Clothing into Emergency Aid Blankets." *Journal of Material Culture* 17 (4): 389–404.

Novogratz, Jacqueline. 2009. *The Blue Sweater: Bridging the Gap between Rich and Poor in an Interconnected World.* New York: Rodale.

Nussbaum, Martha. 2003. "Capabilities as Fundamental Entitlement: Sen and Social Justice." *Feminist Economics* 9 (2–3): 33–59.

_____. 2013. *Creating Capabilities: The Human Development Approach.* Cambridge, MA: Harvard University Press.

_____. 2016. *Not for Profit: Why Democracy Needs the Humanities.* Princeton, NJ: Princeton University Press.

Okere, A., and K. Okezie Okeyika. 2016. "Nigeria's Conditional Grants Scheme in the Light of the Sustainable Development Goals (SDGs): Lessons and Policy Options in a Post-2015 Era." *International Journal of Innovative Research and Development* 5 (9): 174–85.

Omer, Atalia. 2013. *When Peace Is Not Enough: How the Israeli Peace Camp Thinks about Religion, Nationalism, and Justice.* Chicago: University of Chicago Press.

O'Neill, Onora. 2022. *A Question of Trust.* Cambridge: Cambridge University Press.

———. 2004. "Accountability, Trust and Informed Consent in Medical Practice and Research. *Clinical Medicine* 4 (3): 269–76.

O'Neill, William R. 2002. *The "Jesuit" in Jesuit Refugee Service.* Washington, DC: Jesuit Conference of Canada and the United States.

Onyebuchi, Livie. 2000. "Aid to Africa and Human Dignity." *The Furrow* 51 (7–8): 413–20.

Ostrom, Elinor. 1998. *Coping with Tragedies of the Commons: Workshop in Political Theory and Policy Analysis.* Bloomington: Indiana University Press.

Oubre, Claude F. 1976. "'Forty Acres and a Mule': Lousiana and the Southern Homestead Act." *Louisiana History: The Journal of the Louisiana Historical Association* 17 (2): 143–57.

Oz, Amos. 1999. *The Story Begins: Essays on Literature.* New York: Hartcourt Brace.

Page, Benjamin I., et al. 2013. "Democracy and the Policy Preferences of Wealthy Americans." *Perspectives on Politics* 11 (1): 51–73.

Pallikkathayil, Japa. 2010. "Deriving Morality from Politics: Rethinking the Formula of Humanity." *Ethics* 121 (1): 116–47.

Peel, John David. 1978. "Olaju: A Yorba Concept of Development." *Journal of Development Studies* 14 (2): 139–65.

Pellicer, Miquel, et al. 2019. "Perceptions of Inevitability and Demand for Redistribution: Evidence from a Survey Experiment." *Journal of Economic Behavior and Organization* 159:274–88.

Perrin, Paul. 2022. *Integral Human Evaluation: Concept Note.* Notre Dame, IN: Pulte Institute.

Pfeffer, Jeffrey. 2016. "Why the Assholes Are Winning: Money Trumps All." *Journal of Management Studies* 53 (4): 663–69.

Pfeil, Margaret R. 2018. "Fifty Years after *Populorum Progressio*: Understanding Integral Human Development in Light of Integral Ecology." *Journal of Catholic Social Thought* 15 (1): 5–17.

Pharo, Lars Kirkhusmo. 2014. "The Concepts of Human Dignity in Moral Philosophies of Indigenous Peoples of the Americas." In *The Cambridge Handbook of Human Dignity*, ed. M. Duwell et al., 147–154. Cambridge: Cambridge University Press.

Pirjevec, Anja. 2021. *The Shelter and Sustainability Overview.* Geneva: UNHCR.

Pohlhaus Jr., Gaile. 2012. "Relational Knowing and Epistemic Injustice: Toward a Theory of Willful Hermeneutical Ignorance." *Hypatia: A Journal of Feminist Philosophy* 27 (4): 715–35.

Pommaret, Françoise. 1999. "Traditional Values, New Trends." In *Bhutan: A Fortress at the Edge of Time? Selected Papers of the Bhutan Seminar 1998*, 13–26. Vienna: VIDC-Austrian Development Cooperation.

Pope, Stephen. 2019. "Integral Human Development: From Paternalism to Accompaniment." *Theological Studies* 80 (1): 123–47.

Popper, Karl. 1971. *The Open Society and Its Enemies*, vol. 1. Princeton, NJ: Princeton University Press.

Pritchett, Lant, Michael Woolcock, and Matt Andrews. 2010. Capability Traps? The Mechanisms of Persistent Implementation Failure. Working Paper 234. Washington, DC: Center for Global Development.

Pyo, Sunyoung. 2023. "Does an Increased Share of Black Police Officers Decrease Racial Discrimination in Law Enforcement?" *Urban Affairs Review* 59 (2): 534–79.

Rabelo, Veronica C., and Ramaswami Mahalingamb. 2019. "'They Really Don't Want to See Us': How Cleaners Experience Invisible 'Dirty' Work." *Journal of Vocational Behavior* 113:103–14.

Radchenko, Sergey. 2020. "'Nothing but Humiliation for Russia': Moscow and NATO's Eastern Enlargement, 1993–1995." *Journal of Strategic Studies* 43 (6–7): 769–815.

Rademacher, Anne, and Raj Patel. 2002. "Retelling Worlds of Poverty." In *Knowing Poverty: Critical Reflections on Participatory Research and Policy*, ed. K. Brock, R. McGee, 166–88. London: Earthscan Publications.

Rahner, Karl. 1961. "Current Problems in Christology." In *Theological Investigations I*, trans. Cornelius Ernst, 149–214. London: Darton, Longman and Todd.

———. 1973. "The Peace of God and the Peace of the World." In *Theological Investigations X*, trans. David Burke, 371–88. London: Darton, Longman and Todd.

———. 1974. "The Sin of Adam." In *Theological Investigations XI*, trans. David Burke, 247–62. London: Darton, Longman and Todd.

Rana, Nisha, et al. 2019. "Implementing Delayed Umbilical Cord Clamping in Nepal—Delivery Care Staff's Perceptions and Attitudes towards Changes in Practice." *PLOS ONE* 14 (6): e0218031.

Rawls, John. 1999. *A Theory of Justice, Revised Edition*. Cambridge, MA: Harvard University Press.

Rawson, David. 2018. *Prelude to Genocide: Arusha, Rwanda, and the Failure of Diplomacy*. Athens: Ohio University Press.

Reid, Atka, and Hana Schofield. 2011. *Goodbye Sarajevo: A True Story of Courage, Love and Survival*. London: Bloomsbury.

Reifenberg, Steve, and Elizabeth Hlabse. 2020. "Dignity in Accompaniment: Integrated Healthcare in the Sierra Madres." In *The Practice of Development and Dignity*, ed. P. Carozza and C. Sedmak. Notre Dame, IN: University of Notre Dame Press.

Renault, Marion. 2022. "A French Village's Radical Vision of a Good Life with Alzheimer's." *New Yorker*, November 23.

Reus-Smit, Christian. 2019. "Being a Realist about Human Rights." In *The Limits of Human Rights*, ed. Bardo Fassbender and Knut Traisbach, 121–36. Oxford: Oxford University Press.

Reyes, Emma. 2017. *The Book of Emma Reyes*. New York: Penguin.

Rigney, David. 2010. *The Matthew Effect: How Advantage Begets Further Advantage*. New York: Columbia University Press.

Riley, Charlotte Lydia. 2020. "Powerful Men, Failing Upwards: The Aid Industry and the 'Me Too' Movement." *Journal of Humanitarian Affairs* 2 (3): 49–55.

Robeyns, Ingrid. 2017. *Wellbeing, Freedom and Social Justice: The Capability Approach Re-Examined*. Cambridge: Open Books.

Romero, Óscar. 1993. *A Shepherd's Diary*. Translated by Irene B. Hodgson. Cincinnati: St. Anthony Messenger Press.

Rosello, Mireille. 2016. "Disorientation and Accompaniment: Paris, the Metro and the Migrant." *Culture, Theory and Critique* 57 (1): 77–91.

Rosenblum, Nancy L. 2016. *Good Neighbors: The Democracy of Everyday Life in America*. Princeton, NJ: Princeton University Press.

Roszak, Theodore. 1969. *The Making of a Counter Culture: Reflections on the Technocratic Society and Its Youthful Opposition*. Garden City, NJ: Doubleday.

Russell, Bertrand. 2009. "Knowledge by Acquaintance and Knowledge by Description." In *The Basic Writings of Bertrand Russell*, ed. R. Egner and L. Denonn, 191–98. London: Routledge.

Ryle, Gilbert. 1971. *The Thinking of Thoughts: Collected Papers II*. London: Hutchinson.

Sachedina, Abdulaziz. 2009. *Islam and the Challenge of Human Rights*. Oxford: Oxford University Press.

Salari, Sonia Miner. 2005. "Infantilization as Elder Mistreatment: Evidence from Five Adult Day Centers." *Journal of Elder Abuse & Neglect* 17 (4): 53–91.

Salari, Sonia Miner, and Melinda Rich. 2001. "Social and Environmental Infantilization of Aged Persons: Observations in Two Adult Day Care Centers." *International Journal of Aging and Human Development* 52 (2): 115–34.

Sandel, Michael J. 2020. *The Tyranny of Merit: What's Become of the Common Good?* New York: Farrar, Straus and Giroux.

Sarfaty, Galit. 2009. "Why Culture Matters in International Institutions: The Marginality of Human Rights at the World Bank." *American Journal of International Law* 103:647–83.

———. 2021. "Toward an Anthropology of International Law." In *International Law as Behavior*, ed. H. G. Cohen and T. Meyer, 128–57. Cambridge: Cambridge University Press.

Saurette, Paul. 2006. "You Dissin Me? Humiliation and Post 9/11 Global Politics." *Review of International Studies* 32 (3): 495–522.

Scheepers, Ella, and Ishtar Lakhani. 2020. "Caution! Feminists at Work: Building Organisations from the Inside Out." *Gender & Development* 28 (1): 117–33.

Schervish, Paul. 2016. "The Moral Biography of Wealth: Philosophical Reflections on the Foundation of Philanthropy." *Nonprofit and Voluntary Sector Quarterly* 35 (3), https://doi.org/10.1177/0899764006288287.

Schicho, Walter. 2007a. "What Did Mr. Wolfensohn Mean (Intend), When He Spoke of (about) Poverty?" In *Perspectives in Poverty Alleviation*, ed. Clemens Sedmak and Thomas Böhler, 265–80. Münster, Germany: LIT.

———. 2007b. "Power and Poverty: Stichproben." *Wiener Zeitschrift für kritische Afrikastudien* 13: 7–29.

Schimmel, Noam. 2009. "The Abuse of 'Development' and Its Consequences for Indigenous People: A Case Study of Botswana's Bushman Community." *Development* 52:514–18.

Schirch, Lisa. 2005. *Ritual and Symbol in Peacebuilding*. Bloomfield, CT: Kumarian Press.

Schmidt, Jante, et al. 2020. "The Dignity Circle: How to Promote Dignity in Social Work Practice and Policy?" *European Journal of Social Work* 23 (6): 945–57.

Schroeder, Kent. 2018. *Politics of Gross National Happiness: Governance and Development in Bhutan*. Cham, Switzerland: Palgrave Macmillan.

Schweiger, Gottfried. 2016. "Epistemic Injustice and Powerlessness in the Context of Global Justice: An Argument for 'Thick' and 'Small' Knowledge." *Wagadu* 104–15.

Schweiger, Gottfried, and Gunter Graf. 2015. *A Philosophical Examination of Social Justice and Child Poverty*. Basingstoke, UK: Palgrave Macmillan.

Scrimgeour, Jean. 2012. *Silky Promises, Torn Realities: Failed Expectations in Post-Apartheid South Africa*. MA thesis, King's College London.

Scudder, Thayer. 2006. *The Future of Large Dams: Dealing with Social, Environmental, Institutional and Political Costs*. London: Earthscan.

Sedmak, Clemens. 2017. "The Soul of Development." *Journal for Moral Theology* 6 (1): 21–38.

———. 2018. "Bien Común y Vulnerabilidad." *Metafísica y Persona* 20:157–72.

———. 2022. "Development as Depth: Towards a Theology of Integral Human Development." In *Catholic Peacebuilding and Mining: Integral Peace, Development, and Ecology*, ed. C. A. Montevecchio and G. F. Powers, 155–68. London: Routledge.

Sedmak, Clemens, et al. 2021. *Subsidiarität: Tragendes Prinzip menschlichen Zusammenleben*. Regensburg, Germany: Friedrich Pustet.

Seedhouse, David, and Ann Gallagher. 2002. "Undignifying Institutions." *Journal of Medical Ethics* 28:368–72.

Sellers-García, Sylvia. 2016. "The Biography of a Colonial Document: Creation, Mobility, Preservation, Politics, Research." In *Latin American History Oxford Research Encyclopedia*. Oxford: Oxford University Press.

Sen, Amartya. 1988. "The Concept of Development." In *Handbook of Development Economics*, vol. 1, ed. H. Chenery and T. N. Srinivasan, 9–26. Amsterdam: Elsevier Science Publishers.

_____. 1999. *Development as Freedom*. New York: Oxford University Press.

_____. 2006. *Identity and Violence: The Illusion of Destiny*. New York: W. W. Norton.

_____. 2009. *The Idea of Justice*. Cambridge, MA: Belknap Press of Harvard University Press.

Sevilla-Liu, Anton. 2022. "Buddhist Philosophical Approaches to Human Dignity." In *Human Dignity in Asia*, ed. J. Chia-Shin Hsu, 269–84. Cambridge: Cambridge University Press.

Shannon, Fred A. 1936. "The Homestead Act and the Labor Surplus." *American Historical Review* 41 (4): 637–51

Sharman, Zena, et al. 2008. "'We Only Own the Hours': Discontinuity of Care in the British Columbia Home Support System." *Canadian Journal on Aging* 27 (1): 89–99.

Shea, Elise. 2022. *No Dignity in the Dark: Perceptions of Aid in Burkina Faso*. Vienna: Ground Truth Solutions Report.

Shepherd, Dean A., et al. 2022. "Organizing the Exploitation of Vulnerable People: A Qualitative Assessment of Human Trafficking." *Journal of Management* 48 (8): 2421–57.

Sherraden, Michael. 1991. *Assets and the Poor: A New American Welfare Policy*. Armonk, NY: Sharp.

Siddiquee, Noree A., and Gofram M. Faroqi. 2009. "Holding the Giants to Account? Constraints on NGO Accountability in Bangladesh." *Asian Journal of Political Science* 17 (3): 243–64.

Sierakowski, Robert J. 2019. *Sandinistas: A Moral History*. Notre Dame, IN: University of Notre Dame Press.

Siminovitch, Lou. 2012. "Small Science: Big Science Will Prevail." *Science* 338 (6109): 882–83.

Simondi, É., and B. Perrenoud. 2011. "Savoirs et Éthique dans l'Accompagnement." *Recherche et Formation* 66:79–92.

Sixsmith, Judith. 1986. "The Meaning of Home: An Exploratory Study of Environmental Experience." *Journal of Environmental Psychology* 6: 281–98.

Skidelsky, E., and R. Skidelsky. 2012. *How Much Is Enough?* New York: Other Press.

Smart, Roderick Ninian. 1958. "Negative Utilitarianism." *Mind* 67 (268): 542–43.

Snyder, C. R. 2002. "Hope Theory: Rainbows in the Mind." *Psychological Inquiry* 13 (4): 249–75.

Sobrino, Jon. 2004. *Where Is God? Earthquake, Terrorism, Barbarity and Hope*. Maryknoll, NY: Orbis Books.

Sperber, Dan, et al. 2010. "Epistemic Vigilance." *Mind & Language* 25 (4): 359–93.

Spiegelberg Mira L. 2020. *Statelessness: A Modern History*. Cambridge, MA: Harvard University Press.

Spivak, Gayatri. 1988. "Can the Subaltern Speak?" In *Marxism and the Interpretation of Culture*, ed. C. Nelson and L. Grossberg, 271–314. London: Macmillan.

Bibliography

221

Sporschill, George. 2006. *Die zweite Meile: Ein Leben mit Hoffnungskindern*. Vienna: Athesia.
Stauffer, Jill. 2015. *Ethical Loneliness: The Injustice of Not Being Heard*. New York: Columbia University Press.
St. Clair, Asuncion Lera. 2014. "The Four Tasks of Development Ethics at Times of a Changing Climate." *Journal of Global Ethics* 10 (3): 283–91.
Stevenson, Caral. 2014. "A Qualitative Exploration of Relations and Interactions between People Who Are Homeless and Use Drugs and Staff in Homeless Hostel Accommodation." *Journal of Substance Use* 19 (1–2): 134–40.
Stiglitz, Joseph. 2021. "Globalization in the Aftermath of the Pandemic and Trump." *Journal of Policy Modeling* 43:794–804.
Stout, Harry S. 2006. *Upon the Altar of the Nation: A Moral History of the American Civil War*. New York: Viking.
Strother, Emma. 2013. "El Sistema: On Music and Social Justice." *Washington Report on the Hemisphere* 33 (9): 1–3.
Struckmann, Christine. 2018. "A Postcolonial Feminist Critique of the 2030 Agenda for Sustainable Development: A South African Application." *Agenda* 32 (1): 12–24.
Studer, Nina S. 2021. "The Infantilization of the Colonized: Medical and Psychiatric Descriptions of Drinking Habits in the Colonial Maghreb." I: *Re-Configurations: Contextualising Transformation Processes and Lasting Crises in the Middle East and North Africa*, ed. Ouaissa et al., 135–52. Wiesbaden, Germany: Springer VS.
Stutzer, Alois, and Bruno Frey. 2012. Recent Developments in the Economics of Happiness: A Selective Overview. IZA Discussion Paper 7078. Bonn, Germany: Institute for the Study of Labor.
Subramni, Supriya. 2018. "The Moral Significance of Capturing Micro-Inequities in Hospital Settings." *Social Science & Medicine* July 2018 (209): 136–144.
Sultana, Farhana. 2011. "Suffering *for* Water, Suffering *from* Water: Emotional Geographies of Resource Access, Control and Conflict." *Geoforum* 42 (2): 163–72.
Sutton, Robert I. 2007. *The No Asshole Rule: Building a Civilized Workplace and Surviving One That Isn't*. New York: Warner Business Books.
Sunderland, Judith, and Benjamin Ward. 2012. *"The Root of Humiliation": Abusive Identity Checks in France*. New York: Human Rights Watch.
Sweet, Rachel. 2021. "Concealing Conflict Markets: How Rebels and Firms Use State Institutions to Launder Wartime Trade." *International Organization* 75:1109–32.
Taylor, Charles. 1989. *Sources of the Self: The Making of the Modern Identity*. Cambridge: Cambridge University Press.
Thomas, Catherine C., et al. 2020. "Toward a Science of Delivering Aid with Dignity: Experimental Evidence and Local Forecasts from Kenya." *Proceedings of the National Academy of Sciences* 117 (27), https://doi.org/10.1073/pnas.1917046117.

Thompson, Randal, and Edin Ibrahimefendic. 2017. "The Cellist of Sarajevo: Courage and Defiance through Music as Inspirations for Social Change." In *Grassroots Leadership and the Arts for Social Change*, ed. Susan J. Erenrich and Jon S. Wergin, 3–28. Bingley, UK: Emerald.

Traoré, Aminata. 2009. *L'Afrique Humilie'*. Paris: Hachette.

Truth and Reconciliation Commission of South Africa. 1998. *Report*, vol. 1. Johannesburg: TRC.

Tsosie, Rebecca. 2012. "Indigenous Peoples and Epistemic Justice: Science, Ethics, and Human Rights." *Washington Law Review* 87:1133–201.

Twomey, Gerald S. 2006. "Pope John Paul II and the 'Preferential Option for the Poor.'" *Catholic Legal Studies* 45 (2): 321–68.

Ulrich, Roger S. 1984. "View through a Window May Influence Recovery from Surgery." *Science, New Series* 224 (4647): 420–21.

Valentin, Karen, and Lotte Meinert. 2009. "The Adult North and the Young South: Reflections on the Civilizing Mission of Children's Rights." *Anthropology Today* 25 (3): 23–28.

Villegas, Paloma. 2015. "Moments of Humiliation, Intimidation and Implied 'Illegality': Encounters with Immigration Officials at the Border and the Performance of Sovereignty." *Journal of Ethnic and Migration Studies* 41 (14): 2357–75.

Vis, Barbara. 2019. "Heuristics and Political Elites' Judgment and Decision-Making." *Political Studies Review* 17 (1): 41–52.

Volet, Annie Kibongani, et al. 2022. "Vaccine Hesitancy among Religious Groups: Reasons Underlying This Phenomenon and Communication Strategies to Rebuild Trust." *Frontiers in Public Health* 10:824560.

Waardenburg, Jacques. 2002. *Islam: Historical, Social and Political Perspectives*. Berlin: De Gruyter.

Walton, David, et al. 2004. "Integrated HIV Prevention and Care Strengthens Primary Health Care: Lessons from Rural Haiti." *Journal of Public Health Policy* 25 (2): 137–58.

Wan, C., et al. 1994. "A Comparative Study of Certain Differences in Individuality and Sex-Based Differences between 5- and 7-Year-Old Only Children and Non Only Children." *Acta Psychologic Sinica* 16:383–91.

Wang, Zheng. 2012. *Never Forget National Humiliation: Historical Memory in Chinese Politics and Foreign Relations*. New York: Columbia University Press.

Warburton, Hilary, and Adrienne Martin. 1999. "Local People's Knowledge in Natural Resources Research." In *Socio-economic Methodologies for Natural Resources Research*. Chatham, UK: Natural Resources Institute.

Ware, Vicki-Ann, and Kim Dunphy. 2020. "How Do Arts Programmes Contribute in International Development? A Systematic Review of Outcomes and Associated Processes." *Progress in Development Studies* 20 (2): 140–62.

Warren, D. M., and B. Rajasekaran. 1993. "Putting Local Knowledge to Good Use." *International Agricultural Development* 13 (4): 8–10.

Weil, Simone. 1952. *The Need for Roots: Prelude to a Declaration of Duties towards Mankind*. London: Routledge & Kegan Paul.

Werkheiser, Ian. 2014. "Asking for Reasons as a Weapon: Epistemic Justification and the Loss of Knowledge." *Journal of Cognition and Neuroethics* 2 (1): 173–90.

White, Kimberly. 2018. *The Shift: How Seeing People as People Changes Everything*. Oakland, CA: Berrett-Koehler.

Widenhorn, Saskia. 2014. "Towards Epistemic Justice with Indigenous Peoples' Knowledge? Exploring The Potentials of the Convention on Biological Diversity and the Philosophy of Buen Vivir." *Development* 56 (3): 378–86.

Wilbanks, John T., and Thomas J. Wilbanks. 2010. "Science, Open Communication and Sustainable Development." *Sustainability* 2:993–1015.

Williams, Bernard. 2001. "From Freedom to Liberty: The Construction of a Political Value." *Philosophy and Public Affairs* 30 (1): 3–26.

Williams, Cate. 2018. "Brueggemann, the Land and the Forest: A Forest Church Perspective on the Theology of the Land." *Practical Theology* 11 (5): 462–76.

Williams Shanks, Trina R. 2003. "Asset-Building Policy as a Response to Wealth Inequality: Drawing Implications from the Homestead Act." St. Louis, MO: Center for Social Development, Washington University.

———. 2005a. "The Homestead Act: A Major Asset-Building Policy in American History." In *Inclusion in the American Dream: Assets, Poverty, and Public Policy*, ed. Michael Sherraden. New York: Oxford University Press.

———. 2005b. The Homestead Act of the Nineteenth Century and Its Influence on Rural Lands. CSD Working Papers. St. Louis, MO: Center for Social Development, Washington University.

Williams, Kristina, and Kay Devine. 2005. "In Focus/Leadership Styles: If It's *Lagom*, This Must Be Sweden." *Leadership in Action* 25 (3): 19–20.

Wittgenstein, Ludwig. 1967. *Philosophical Investigations*. Oxford: Blackwell.

———. 2007. *Zettel*. Berkeley: University of California Press.

Wolf, Susan R. 2010. *Meaning in Life and Why It Matters*. Princeton, NJ: Princeton University Press.

Wolff, Jonathan, and Avner De-Shalit. 2007. *Disadvantage*. Oxford: Oxford University Press.

Wong, David B. 2017. "Reflection Dignity in Confucian and Buddhist Thought." In *Dignity: A History*, ed. R. Debes, 67–72. Oxford: Oxford University Press.

World Health Organization. 2015. *Postnatal Care for Mothers and Newborns*. Washington, DC: WHO Department of Maternal, Newborn, Child and Adolescent Health.

Wright, Gemma, et al. 2015. "Social Assistance and Dignity: South African Women's Experiences of the Child Support Grant." *Development Southern Africa* 32 (4): 443–57.

Wydick, Bruce, et al. 2020. "Hope and Human Dignity." In *The Practice of Human Development and Dignity*, ed. P. Carozza and C. Sedmak, 139–59. Notre Dame, IN: University of Notre Dame Press.

Wylie, Jeanie. 1989. *Poletown: A Community Betrayed*. Urbana: University of Illinois Press.

Yang, B., et al. 1995. "Only Children and Children without Siblings in the People's Republic of China: Levels of Fear, Anxiety and Depression." *Child Development* 66:1301–11.

Yunus, Muhammad. 2007. *Creating a World without Poverty: Social Business and the Future of Capitalism*. New York: Public Affairs.

Yunusa, B. Yusuf, and D. Hulme. 2019. Service Delivery Reform in Nigeria: The Rise and Fall of the Conditional Grant Scheme to Local Government Areas (CGS to LGAs). ESID Working Paper 114. Manchester, UK: Effective States and Inclusive Development Research Centre.

Zerubavel, Eviatar. 1979. "The Temporal Organization of Continuity: The Case of Medical and Nursing Coverage." *Human Organization* 38:78–83.

Ziai, Aram. 2011. Some Reflections on the Concept of "Development." ZEF Working Paper Series 81. Bonn, Germany: University of Bonn, Center for Development Research.

_____. 2015. *Development Discourse and Global History: From Colonialism to the Sustainable Development Goals*. London: Routledge.

INDEX

Abed, Fazle Hasan, 43, 173, 174–76
Abreu, José Antonio, 33
accompaniment, 47, 108, 189
    BRAC program, accompaniment
        process in, 71, 174
    in IHD framework, 46, 68, 186
    Jesuit Refugee Service's commitment
        to, 181–83
    Partners in Health model, 183–85
    Sporschill as living the accompaniment
        model, 187–88
accountability, 17, 29, 98, 100, 107, 109,
    175–77, 180, 185
Acemoglu, Daron, 178
Adorno, Theodor, 193
Adventures in Aidland (Mosse), 162
Africa, 5, 21, 23, 44, 92
    Chad-Cameroon Pipeline project, 106
    institution-building in, 181
    land concerns, 125, 126
agency, 8, 11, 42, 44, 67, 68, 93, 119,
    155, 182, 188, 193
    development agents, commitment to,
        94–95
    in dignity work, 18, 75, 101
    enslavement, agency in response to, 43
    epistemic agency, 50, 111
    foreign aid and issues with agency,
        99–100
    in IHD framework, 137, 156, 158
    infantilization and perceived lack of
        agency, 12, 15
    Laudato Si' on dimension beyond
        human agency, 194

    laws as setting limits to agency, 145
    in liberation theology, 187
    Mandela on failed agency, 159
    in moral biographies, 118
    policy makers and, 9, 133, 139, *164*
    poverty conditions and, 154, 158
    principle of subsidiarity and, 75–76,
        100
    research failing to recognize agency, 50
Aiken, Robert, 139
Akerlof, George, 39
Akula, Vikram, 88–89, 91, 114
Alzheimer village, 180
Ambedkar, B. R., 28
Ambrose, Saint, 160
American Civil War, 118, 154
American Homestead Act, 141–44
Anderson, Hannah, 142
Annett, Anthony, xv
Annus Iam Plenus letter, 87
apartheid, 20–21
Appleby, Scott, 31
Apthorpe, Raymond, 162
Aquinas, Thomas, 116
Arendt, Hannah, 115
Aristotle, 56–57, 85, 155
Arrupe, Pedro, 181
Ashraf, Hasan, xxvi
assets, 43, 71, 105, 106, 135
    asset independence, 114–15
    asset vulnerability, 62, 63, 64, 68
    Homestead Act and asset building,
        141–44